DBT, CBT

— AND —

ACT

WORKBOOK

3 IN 1

ULTIMATE GUIDE TO BEHAVIOR THERAPY AND
ACCEPTANCE AND COMMITMENT SKILLS FOR ANXIETY,
DEPRESSION, AND SELF-ESTEEM

ANNA NIERLING

CONTENTS

DBT WORKBOOK

CONTENTS

CBT WORKBOOK

CONTENTS

ACT WORKBOOK

DBT

WORKBOOK

—— FOR ——

ADULTS

How to Use Dialectical Behavior Therapy Skills for Easy
Anxiety Management, Relationship Success, Emotion
Regulation, and Trauma Recovery

ANNA NIERLING

Discovering Your Path to Inner Peace with Dialectical Behavior Therapy

Welcome to a place of healing, support, and personal well-being.

I get it- starting on the path to feeling better can feel pretty overwhelming. I'm here to offer you guidance with care and understanding.

As we go through this workbook together, we'll take things one step at a time. My main goal is to assist you in feeling better as well as equip you with the tools and support you need to handle life's challenges. I also aim to nurture a sense of peace and well-being throughout your journey.

I know that seeking help can sometimes feel awkward, uncomfortable, and even scary, but please know that you're not alone in this. I'm here to create a safe and comforting space where you can explore your emotions, deal with tricky situations, and ultimately find the healing you absolutely deserve.

I understand that life can sometimes feel like an endless exhausting loop, with emotions that seem to have a mind of their own. Perhaps you've faced moments when your thoughts race uncontrollably, your emotions overwhelm you, and your relationships feel like a tangled web of confusion. Trust me, I've been there too.

Let me share my own story with you. My journey into the world of mental health disorders began with learning about my mom. Initially diagnosed with Bipolar Disorder, her true diagnosis turned out to be Borderline Personality Disorder.

I wasn't even 8 years old when I began to realize that my mother was different. On one particular day, she took me and my older brother to the local park to play. It should have been a day of laughter and fun, but it took an unexpected turn.

"Why are there so many people here?" she wondered aloud.

"We should have come earlier," she grumbled

"Can you see them staring at us?" she anxiously asked.

"You know what? I want to go home now," she pressed.

It wasn't the first time I had witnessed my mother's mood swings, but this time was different. I started noticing that the other mothers weren't as emotionally unpredictable as mine. It was the beginning of my travels into understanding BPD without even knowing what it was yet.

Describing BPD, psychologist Marsha Linehan aptly wrote, "People with BPD are like people with third-degree burns over 90% of their bodies. Lacking emotional skin, they feel agony at the slightest touch or movement" (Goodreads, n.d.).

For those diagnosed with BPD, the world around them often feels overwhelming. Noises can become unbearable, intimacy can feel suffocating, and people can be emotionally exhausting. BPD sufferers may even believe that their own personalities are too much, fearing that their emotional volatility makes them hard to love. My mother would shower us with passionate love one moment, only to withdraw and become emotionally distant the next.

My mother's initial diagnosis was Bipolar Disorder Type 2. The symptoms were misunderstood, and she fell into the 40% of patients who meet BPD criteria but are initially misdiagnosed with Bipolar Disorder (Ruggero et al., 2010). It's easy to see why, as the symptoms often overlap and both can include mood swings, impulsive behaviors, and suicidal thoughts. However, BPD's unique aspects, such as shame, fear of abandonment, and chronic feelings of emptiness, couldn't be properly addressed by bipolar disorder treatment.

It wasn't until I turned 20 that my mother received the correct diagnosis. I could sense her relief when a doctor told her that she wasn't crazy and that her condition wasn't something to be ashamed of. "We are all complicated," the doctor said, "and you can learn to live with your complexities."

Decades have passed since my mother began accepting her BPD diagnosis and embracing those complexities. Growing up with the highs and lows of being raised by a mentally ill mother inspired me to pursue a degree in psychology and dedicate my life to supporting, helping and understanding the uniqueness of the mind.

What is my hope for you? By the time you've finished this workbook, you'll have a toolbox filled with powerful skills to:

- **Regulate your emotions.** Say 'goodbye' to feeling overwhelmed by anger, sadness, or anxiety. You'll learn how to manage and control your emotions effectively.
- **Improve your relationships.** Say 'hello' to healthier interactions with your loved ones. DBT will equip you with the tools to communicate and connect more effectively.

- ⊙ **Boost your mental resilience.** Say 'farewell' to the constant barrage of negative thoughts. You'll develop the ability to calm your mind and find peace within yourself.
- ⊙ **Enhance your quality of life.** Say 'yes' to living a life that aligns with your values, free from the constraints of impulsive behaviors and emotional chaos.

Why DBT Is Meaningful to Me

You might be wondering, "*Why should I trust this author?*" Well, you're absolutely right to ask. Here's the scoop: I'm not just an armchair expert on DBT. I've dedicated my life to understanding and applying these principles because of my personal experiences growing up with a mom with BPD, as well as my academic background in psychology. I've seen DBT work wonders both in my life and in my mom's, and in the lives of countless others. So, consider me your friendly guide on this journey.

How to Use This Self-Directed Workbook

Now, you might be aware that traditional DBT therapy involves various modes of treatment, including group skills training, individual therapy, phone skills coaching, and therapist consultation teams. While these modes are invaluable, this workbook is designed for the self-directed learner.

But here's the good news: DBT skills and exercises are incredibly useful on their own, even without the full complement of treatment modes. Think of this workbook as your personal DBT coach, always at your side, ready to assist you.

Before we dive into the practical exercises and transformative knowledge, let's make sure we're on the same page about what DBT is all about:

- **Marsha Linehan and the balance between acceptance and change.** DBT was developed by Marsha Linehan, a pioneer in the field of psychology. Her approach strikes a delicate balance between accepting where you are right now and empowering you to make positive changes in your life (Emeritus, 2019).

- **DBT as an adaptation of CBT.** DBT is an adaptation of Cognitive Behavioral Therapy (CBT), tailored specifically to address emotional dysregulation, self-destructive behaviors, and interpersonal challenges.

- **The four core principles.** DBT rests on four foundational principles: Mindfulness, Distress Tolerance, Emotion Regulation, and Interpersonal Effectiveness. These principles are your compass for navigating the challenges of life.

As we journey through this workbook, you'll become intimately familiar with these core principles and how to apply them in your daily life.

I want to thank you for trusting me enough to pick up this book. Now, I would like to encourage you to turn that page...because you are worthy, I see you, and I am here every step of the way.

In today's rush, we all think too much—seek too much—want too much—and forget about the joy of just being.

— ECKHART TOLLE

CHAPTER 1

Week One — Strengthening DBT with Present Moment Awareness

Welcome to the initial week of our DBT expedition. Did you know that research has demonstrated the remarkable effectiveness of DBT in enhancing emotional regulation and interpersonal skills? But before we immerse ourselves in this transformative therapy, let me divulge a bit of my personal journey.

Growing up, my life was anything but ordinary. You see, when I was a young girl starting fifth grade, I began to notice even more things that set my mom apart from the other moms. What do I mean by that?

My friends would invite me over to their houses without a second thought. But for me, it was different. I always had that voice in my head asking, *"I wonder what version of my mom we'll be walking in to meet today."* Would she be mad, loving, angry, or paranoid? Would she yell at me about something for 20 minutes in front of my friends?

You see, up until I started noticing how other mothers treated their kids, I thought this was normal. My mom was amazing, loving, caring, and supportive...until she wasn't. That's where the issue was. I had no control over when that switch flipped.

As I grew into a teenager and young adult, I had to learn how to cope, and I didn't always make the best choices. My mom's impulsive decisions became more frequent. She'd rush out of our home and tell us she was 'never coming back' and not to follow her. Her risky behaviors escalated, like drinking excessively and then getting behind the wheel. She became fixated on prescription drugs, convinced she would find the magic cocktail to quiet the storm in her head. This led to more erratic behavior, like regularly keeping me awake on a school night to 'help with my homework' until 3am, or to tell my brother to please take care of me because she would die soon.

I grew up in a home that never felt safe, even though it was theoretically full of love. My mom told my brother and I all the time how much she loved us but then would turn on us because we 'hurt her' and 'don't actually love her.' I also struggled as I grew older because my mom couldn't bear to be alone. I always felt guilty leaving her. I never had sleepovers or went to summer camp because 'we are a family. Why should you leave?' When I finally did leave and found my own place after college, I felt unable to navigate regular day-to-day life. Every small event made me believe that doom was lurking around the corner. I vaguely knew this was the result of growing up with a mom who was different but I didn't know what to do about it. My mom hadn't yet started using DBT and I didn't know about it either.

It was during this challenging period that I accidentally stumbled upon a powerful tool: mindfulness. It was life-saving for me. Mindfulness helped me interrupt those negative thought loops, bring myself back to the present moment, and acknowledge that the past was the past and that I had control over my future. Mindfulness is a huge part of DBT, but I wouldn't discover that until later.

When my mom's behavior reflected on me, I would take some time and space for myself. I'd find a quiet place and remind myself that her actions were not a reflection of who I was. I could empathize with her, but I no longer had to live through it myself.

What is Mindfulness?

You might have encountered the term 'mindfulness' tossed around, but what does it truly entail? We hear it all over social media, but trust me, it is not just another trendy catchphrase. Mindfulness revolves around being completely in the present moment. It's about observing your thoughts, emotions, sensations, and the surrounding world without passing judgment. What does this mean? It means digging in deep to your thoughts and emotions, even those tough ones, and practicing grace and kindness towards yourself. The goal is not to sit in your 'stuff' just to end up with that negative loop of thoughts judging every action you've ever taken in this lifetime. When we are mindful of ourselves, we often find the reasoning behind why we do what we do. That is the key to freedom. Our freedom. Our happiness. Our calm.

I want you to imagine yourself behind the wheel of your car and, suddenly, you realize you can't recall the past few miles of your journey. We've all done it! Were those lights green? Did I run a stop sign? You were on autopilot.

Now, ask yourself the last time you found yourself in a conversation, but your mind had wandered far away, only half-engaged. It could have been your boss giving further instruction, or your spouse telling you about their day. Regardless, this experience can leave us in a vulnerable position of lying when being asked, "Did you just hear what I said?" It can be embarrassing.

Being inattentive can lead to feelings of disorientation, anxiety, and frustration when reality doesn't align with our expectations. Fortunately, mindfulness can allow you to regain mastery over your thoughts and emotions.

WORKBOOK EXERCISE: A 'Mindless' Skill

Now, let's get hands-on. Mindfulness is a skill, akin to any other, that needs to be honed through practice. Many of us find ourselves frequently operating on autopilot, a state of *mindlessness*. Consider these commonplace scenarios and respond below them with a personal scenario of your own.

You find yourself driving or traveling (even just walking) and you don't recall the experience or the routes taken. In the space below, describe your most recent experience of this in detail. Where were you going? What time of day was it? Do you know what had you distracted? Were you alone on your travels?

_____

_____

_____

_____

_____

In the midst of a conversation, you suddenly realize you're clueless about the subject at hand. In the space below, describe the most recent, or the most embarrassing, time this happened. Who were you speaking with? Was the topic of conversation important? Did the person notice you were not engaged, and if so, how did you explain it?

_____

_____

_____

_____

_____

While reading, you abruptly discover that your thoughts have wandered, leaving you oblivious to the content you just read. In the space below, describe the most recent time this occurred. Was the content you were reading important? Was it for work or school? Does this happen often, leaving you frustrated?

_____

_____

_____

_____

The list goes on. These instances may appear benign, but for individuals grappling with overwhelming emotions, the inability to stay present can have profound repercussions on their lives.

The Power of Mindfulness: What Skills

Imagine yourself as the security guard at the entrance of a concert, carefully watching the crowd entering and leaving. Now, think of these people as your thoughts. You're not stopping each thought; you're simply observing as it enters. This is the essence of observing—sensing and experiencing without putting labels or descriptions on anything you witness.

In the beginning, it might feel a bit tricky. Our minds have a habit of talking non-stop, commenting on everything. But with practice, you can gradually quiet that mental chatter.

The real challenge of observing is to embrace the moment without passing judgment, without labeling your thoughts as good or bad, pleasant or unpleasant. It's like gazing at clouds drifting across the sky: You lie on the grass and peacefully watch them go by. No need to label them; just let them float along.

WORKBOOK EXERCISE: Let It Be

Find a quiet space, close your eyes, and observe your breath for a few minutes. Don't label it as good or bad, too fast, or too slow. Your job is to just relax and breathe. After a time that is comfortable for you, I would like you to reflect in the space below about how you felt in that moment. Be honest. Were you able to focus without distraction? Did your mind wander easily?

_____

_____

_____

_____

WORKBOOK EXERCISE: Observation of the Senses

I would like you to go wash some dishes. This is less about doing a chore and more about observing the act. Pay attention to the temperature of the water and silky suds as they flow over your hands. Focus on each dish as you hold it. The texture of a glass, a fork. In the space below, I want you to reflect on how this experience made you feel. Was it calming, relaxing, soothing?

_____

_____

_____

_____

_____

Quieting our minds and practicing observation can be hard, especially when we're dealing with thoughts that make us uncomfortable. Our natural instinct is to react quickly and get rid of these thoughts as soon as possible. But here's the beauty of observing: it helps us understand that thoughts, feelings, and sensations are like passing clouds—they come and go, never staying for too long. This practice can actually dial down the intensity of our emotions.

DBT has a term for this: having a "Teflon Mind." It's like experiences, feelings, and thoughts enter your mind and gently slip away, just like a fried egg sliding off a non-stick frying pan.

Now, sometimes when we observe, it might stir up painful emotions. That's entirely normal. Think of it as a form of exposure therapy for your mind. Gradually, as you keep observing these thoughts and emotions coming and going, you'll find yourself less entangled in their grip. It's a journey toward emotional freedom.

Describing

The next skill in mindfulness is describing. It's about putting words to what you observe, without judgment. Imagine you're washing dishes, and you say to yourself, "*The water is murky. The soap feels slimy in my hands. The dish is heavy.*" You're simply labeling the experience without prejudice.

WORKBOOK EXERCISE: Daily Journal

I want to encourage you to keep a journal for three days, noting what you do and feel without judgment. For example, you go for a walk and notice the fluffy clouds, a child riding a bike, the sound of birds, and so forth.

DAY 1

_____

_____

_____

_____

_____

DAY 2

_____

_____

_____

_____

_____

DAY 3

_____

_____

_____

_____

_____

Participate

Participating is diving wholeheartedly into an activity and being fully present. It's like dancing skillfully, one with the music and with your partner. This skill helps you step back from your thoughts and realize you're okay in this moment.

WORKBOOK EXERCISE: Mindfully Participating

Start by choosing something you do often, like folding the laundry or walking your dog. This time, I want you to try and pay full attention while doing this task. Below, I want you to comment on how it felt different this time. Did you notice anything new?

_____

_____

_____

_____

_____

_____

_____

_____

_____

_____

_____

_____

Practical Exercises

EXERCISE 1: Without Judgement

Take a moment to contemplate a recent situation where you passed judgment on yourself or others. It could be an event, a person's actions, or even a personal decision. Take a moment to reflect on this situation and record your judgments in the space provided below.

_____

_____

_____

_____

_____

_____

Now, let's shift our perspective. Take the situation you wrote down above and try to look at it without any judgment at all. Imagine viewing it from a neutral and objective standpoint, like an observer rather than a judge.

In this section, try to describe the situation in a way that focuses on facts, actions, and observable details without incorporating any personal opinions or criticisms.

_____

_____

_____

_____

_____

EXERCISE 2: One-Mindfully

Select a straightforward task, such as washing dishes.

Rather than juggling multiple tasks or allowing your mind to wander, devote your complete focus to the task at hand. Feel the water's temperature, the texture of the dishes. Feel the bubbles and the rhythm of your movements. In the space below, I would like you to write about how this task felt different this time in comparison to previous times.

_____

_____

_____

_____

_____

EXERCISE 3: Effectively

In the space below, reflect on a situation where you reacted impulsively or ineffectively due to overwhelming emotions. For example, maybe you had a fight with your spouse the night before, yet you blew up at a coworker because those emotions boiled over.

_____

_____

_____

_____

_____

_____

Think about how the application of mindfulness could have empowered you to respond more effectively in that circumstance. Below, I want you to write how you would have handled that exact situation if you would have taken a moment to pause, and then been mindful.

_____

_____

_____

Remember, mindfulness is a skill that flourishes with practice. Commence with small steps, and, over time, you'll perceive its positive influence on your emotional well-being.

The Power of Mindfulness: The 'How' Skills

Let's explore the concept of 'one-mindfully' which is all about doing one thing at a time. It might sound simple, but in our modern, multitasking world, it's a skill worth mastering.

Imagine this: you're about to read a book. Instead of multitasking by scrolling your phone or watching TV simultaneously, you dive into that book wholeheartedly. Or when you're at work, you give it your all, without getting lost in making to-do lists or worrying about that upcoming dentist appointment. And when you're having a chat with a friend, you're fully present, not distracted by writing an email or preparing dinner.

I'll confess, I've been guilty of being 'that' friend, the one who's always distracted by scrolling on my phone while on a call. But let's talk about why it's essential to try and be focused on one thing at a time. We owe it to ourselves to give our full attention to what we're doing. We need to feel whole and undivided when we engage in these activities.

Mindfulness is all about the quality of awareness we bring to our actions and experiences, about being fully here and now. It's the practice of focusing on the present, on the task at hand, without being pulled in different directions by past memories, future worries, negative emotions, or anxieties. Let's not be too hard on ourselves; this skill can be tough to learn. It takes practice, patience, and a willingness to embrace it.

If you're struggling to concentrate on a single task, try letting go of distractions as they come. And if they persist, let them go again. Rinse and repeat! Concentrate your mind on the task in front of you. If you catch yourself doing multiple things at once, pause and choose only one to focus on. With time, this will become a habit.

For example, when I notice myself mindlessly scrolling while talking to a friend on the phone, I place my phone down. It's my small step towards improving, and yes, I admit, I still catch myself scrolling 50% of the time. But remember, we're all works in progress, and that's perfectly okay.

WORKBOOK EXERCISE: Train Your Mind to Be Present

Take a moment to reflect on your daily routines. Jot down instances when you notice yourself multitasking. Do you find yourself scrolling through your phone while having conversations with others? Perhaps you catch yourself eating while drafting work emails?

_____

_____

_____

_____

_____

If you ever find yourself multitasking, remember what we discussed earlier about letting go of distractions and giving your full attention to what you're doing. Here's a space below for you to jot down what distracted you and how you tried to stay focused. It can be enlightening to become more aware of these moments and to figure out what strategies are working best for you.

_____

_____

_____

_____

_____

Non-Judgmentally: Free Yourself from Criticism

Let's talk about judgments, something we're all familiar with. We tend to judge, whether it's others or ourselves, almost constantly. But here's the thing: judgment can create a hostile and negative environment, leading to emotions like shame, sadness, and guilt. So, what's the alternative? It's about taking a nonjudgmental stance, a way to explore those same old thoughts in your mind or observations in your environment, but from a different perspective.

Here's an example of what a nonjudgmental stance looks like: Sadness is like any other emotion, it isn't good or bad. Just because I'm experiencing the symptoms of sadness doesn't make me a bad person. Experiencing this emotion isn't a matter of being good or bad; it just is. It is normal and expected to feel sad.

WORKBOOK EXERCISE: Embrace Non-Judgmental Thinking

Let's try something the next time you're doing a regular chore, like folding laundry. While folding those clothes, practice observing and describing, in detail, what you're doing.

Here's what I'd like you to do: when you catch your mind starting to make a judgment, jot it down in the space below. Don't get tangled up in the judgment itself or worry that you've made one. Just recognize that your mind is passing judgment and then gently let it go. It can be as simple as, "Laundry is boring."

_____

_____

_____

_____

_____

_____

_____

_____

_____

_____

Let's explore practicing mindfulness in situations that stir up strong emotions. It could be dealing with a difficult family member, a challenging coworker, or even a stranger at the grocery store.

Here's what I suggest: Pay close attention to your judgments, but don't let them overwhelm you. Treat your judgments like the tone of someone's voice–simply notice them without getting caught up in them. See if this approach helps you avoid impulsive reactions and stay calm.

In the space below, jot down the situation you faced, how mindfulness helped you in that moment, and how you might have reacted differently in the past.

_____

_____

_____

_____

_____

_____

_____

Key Takeaways for Week 1

- ⊙ Mindfulness entails immersing oneself fully in the present moment without judgment.
- ⊙ Inattentiveness can lead to anxiety and frustration.
- ⊙ The 'how' and 'what' skills of mindfulness.
- ⊙ The practice of mindfulness can enhance emotional regulation, distinguish judgmental thoughts, and facilitate wiser decision-making.
- ⊙ Embark on the exercises provided to initiate the development of your mindfulness skills.

"

Feelings come and go like clouds in a windy sky. Conscious breathing is my anchor.

— THICH NHAT HANH

CHAPTER 2

Week Two — Finding Balance and Mindfulness

In this chapter, we're going to explore the three states of mind. I would like to really focus on the "wise mind," a state of being that can be incredibly helpful when dealing with difficult emotions and challenging situations. But before we get into all that, let me give you a quick overview of all we'll be covering in this chapter:

- ⊙ We'll explore the concept of the wise mind and its three states: emotion mind, reasonable mind, and wise mind.
- ⊙ I'll share a bit more about my own experiences growing up with my mom and her BPD traits and how mindfulness helped me cope then and now.
- ⊙ We'll dive into various wise mind exercises, from concentrative mindfulness to generative mindfulness, and everything in between.

Let's get started!

Three States of Mind

Join me in the world of mindfulness and the intriguing concept of the three states of mind. As someone who can relate to the challenges you might be facing, I'm genuinely excited to share what I've learned with you.

Emotion Mind

Think of this as the time when your feelings are in the driver's seat. We've all been there, right? Those moments when you're super angry, frustrated, or profoundly sad. In emotion mind, emotions are in charge, and logical thinking kind of takes a break. We'll talk more about what's good and not-so-good about this state in a bit.

Reasonable Mind

This is when your brain goes all logical and factual. You might know folks who are super into data and facts; they're hanging out in reasonable mind. Guess what? We all have this state too. It's like having Google in your noggin, and you can switch between emotion mind and reasonable mind.

Now, here's the cool part. DBT has its eyes on something called wise mind. It's like finding that perfect balance, the best of both worlds. It's like mixing emotion mind and reasonable mind, with a sprinkle of intuition. DBT really likes intuition—it's like your gut feeling or just knowing something without needing loads of proof.

But let's dig deeper into these states:

- ⊙ **Emotion Mind:** When emotions are in control, it's like a rollercoaster. We've all had our ups and downs with this. You may react quickly in situations where you feel fear or anger. It is possible you may want to lash out or hurt who hurt you. You could find yourself acting impulsively or on urges.
- ⊙ **Reasonable Mind:** This is the logical, data-driven side. Some people live here most of the time, and it can be good and bad. You can feel cut off from your emotions in this space, often feeling numb. If you act out, you will often give excuses for this

behavior. In those difficult situations, you will shut off that emotional part of your brain that wants to acknowledge what is happening and end up in denial. If your emotions try to well up, you will try to minimize them.

- **Wise Mind:** This is the fantastic mix. It's having this deep sense of knowing. Ever look back and think, "When did I make a decision that just felt right?" That's wise mind at work. It's like having your very own unique compass. You will have that keen ability to think both logically and emotionally at the same time. The other great thing is the ability to see things from not only your own perspective. You will see situations from all points of view.

Remember, wise mind is personal. Nobody else can peek into your wise mind, and it's not something you can always explain with loads of facts and numbers. It's about trusting that deep sense of knowing inside you.

Key points to keep in mind:

- We've got three states of mind: wise mind, emotion mind, and reasonable mind.
- Wise mind is the goal in DBT, and it's all about following your intuition.
- Your wise mind is like your secret superpower; it belongs to you.

My Mom and Mindfulness

Growing up, I always knew my mom loved me. But she was on her own emotional rollercoaster, and I was often riding it with her. She could go from showering me with love and affection to seeing me as the most selfish person on Earth in a matter of minutes. Her outbursts of anger were frequent, and she often talked about feeling empty and even threatened suicide quite a few times. She had this constant fear that I didn't love her enough. She had this constant fear that nobody loved her at all.

One mindfulness technique I unintentionally adapted was what I called "Mom Pause." Whenever things got intense, I would sometimes take a deep breath, close my eyes for a moment, and then start again, more calmly. It was as if I was briefly tapping into my wise mind without even realizing it. This pause allowed me to step back from my overwhelming emotions—most that I couldn't name at that age—and think more rationally, at least for a moment. It was my way of coping with the turmoil inside my mom.

I learned that even in the toughest situations, finding moments of mindfulness can make a significant difference in your emotional well-being.

Wise Mind Exercises

Now, let's explore some practical wise mind exercises that can help you find that inner balance.

The Stone and The Blue Lake

Close your eyes and picture yourself beside a crystal-clear, serene lake on a beautiful, sunlit day. The air is fresh, carrying a gentle breeze that softly caresses your cheek. Now, imagine transforming into a tiny, feather-light flake of stone. You're as flat as a pancake and weightless. Someone has tossed you onto the lake's surface, and you begin a slow, tranquil drift through the calm, azure waters until you gracefully settle on the soft, sandy lakebed. Pay careful attention to your senses. What sights greet you as you descend? What sensations do you experience? Are you spiraling gently as you descend? As you nestle into the comforting sand below, take a moment to savor that sensation. Feel the lake's tranquility wash over you, and embrace the inner calm and quiet. Now, take a deep breath, visualizing your ascent towards the surface, drawing closer and closer to the warming sun, feeling yourself grow lighter and lighter. What emotions or sensations emerge within you during this journey? Use the space below to jot down your responses. Engaging mindfully with your surroundings can be a grounding and centering experience.

_____

_____

_____

_____

_____

_____

_____

Box Breathing

1. **Find a comfortable position.** Sit or lie down in a comfortable position. You can close your eyes if it helps you concentrate.
2. **Inhale (count of four).** Begin by taking a slow, deep breath in through your nose, counting to four as you inhale. Imagine filling your lungs from the bottom to the top, allowing your abdomen to rise.
3. **Hold (count of four).** Once you've inhaled fully, hold your breath for a count of four. During this pause, focus on the stillness and the sensation of holding your breath.
4. **Exhale (count of four).** Slowly release your breath through your mouth, counting to four as you exhale. Empty your lungs completely, feeling the tension leave your body.

5. **Pause (count of four).** After exhaling, maintain a count of four before taking your next breath. This moment of stillness allows you to prepare for the next cycle.

6. **Repeat.** Continue this rhythmic cycle of inhaling for four counts, holding for four counts, exhaling for four counts, and pausing for four counts. Repeat for several cycles, or as long as you like.

Make sure your breaths are slow and controlled. The goal is to calm your nervous system, so avoid rushed or shallow breathing.

Box breathing can be done virtually anywhere and is particularly useful in moments of stress, anxiety, or when you need to regain focus and composure. Like any relaxation technique, box breathing becomes more effective with practice. Consider incorporating it into your daily routine or during stressful situations.

Pay close attention to your breath throughout the process. Use the space below to write down what you notice about the sensation of air entering and leaving your body. Maintain an equal count for each phase of the breath (four counts for inhale, hold, exhale, and pause). This balance is a key aspect of box breathing.

_____

_____

_____

_____

_____

_____

_____

5-7-8 Breathing

1. Sit or lie down in a comfortable position. You can close your eyes if you prefer, but it's not necessary.

2. Take a deep breath in through your nose, allowing your abdomen to expand as you fill your lungs. Exhale slowly and completely through your mouth, letting go of any tension or stress with each breath. This is a preparatory breath.

3. Close your mouth and inhale quietly through your nose to the count of five. Imagine drawing in calm, positive energy as you breathe in. Focus on the sensation of the air entering your nostrils and filling your lungs.

4. After your inhalation, hold your breath for a count of seven. During this pause, try to remain still and relaxed. This holding phase allows your body to absorb the oxygen.

5. Slowly exhale through your mouth, counting to eight as you release the breath. Imagine expelling any tension, stress, or negativity from your body with each breath out. Focus on the sensation of your breath leaving your body.

6. This completes one cycle of 5-7-8 breathing. Begin again by inhaling through your nose to the count of five, holding for seven counts, and exhaling through your mouth for eight counts. Continue this cycle for four full breaths.

7. To experience the full benefits of 5-7-8 breathing, practice it for several cycles (four breaths in each cycle) or as long as you like. You can gradually increase the number of cycles as you become more comfortable with the technique.

Keep your body relaxed throughout the exercise, especially your shoulders and neck. Be sure to pay close attention to your breath and the counting. Let go of distracting thoughts.

The 5-7-8 breathing exercise is a valuable tool for promoting relaxation and reducing anxiety. By controlling your breath and engaging in this practice, you can create a sense of calm and balance in your life. Jot down how you felt before beginning this exercise and how you felt after. Did you notice tension decreasing? Do you feel more relaxed?

_____

_____

_____

_____

_____

_____

Asking Wise Mind a Question

When you encounter a situation where you're feeling stuck or uncertain, seek out a peaceful and quiet space. Take a deep breath in and within your mind, posing the question, "What would my wise mind do or say?" As you exhale, be attentive and receptive, listening for the answer. It's crucial to emphasize that this is a moment for active listening, not attempting to provide the answer yourself. Go through this process a few times. If you don't receive a clear response, don't worry; you can try again later.

Concentrative Mindfulness (Meditation)

Imagine it's a quiet evening, and you're sitting comfortably in your favorite spot at home. You decide to try concentrative mindfulness meditation. This technique involves directing your full attention to a single point of focus, like a flickering candle or a gentle stream. It's like zooming in on a single frame in the movie of your mind.

Here's how you can practice it (Compitus, 2020):

1. **Select your point of focus.** Begin by choosing your 'anchor'. It could be a flickering candle, a flowing stream, or anything that captures your interest and can hold your attention. Your anchor is your entry point into the present moment.

2. **Find a comfortable space.** Be sure to find a comfortable place to sit. You can use a cushion, chair, or simply sit on the floor. Ensure you're in a quiet place where you won't be easily distracted.

3. **Gently close your eyes (optional).** Closing your eyes can help reduce visual distractions, but it's not necessary. If you prefer to keep your eyes open, that's perfectly fine too.

4. **Begin observing.** Now, start observing your chosen focal point. If it's a candle, watch the flame dance and flicker. If it's a stream, observe the movement of the water, the ripples, and reflections. Let your attention rest there.

5. **Focus your thoughts.** You can expect your mind to wander, and that's okay; it's what minds tend to do. When you notice your thoughts drifting away, gently and without judgment, bring your attention back to your chosen point of focus. It's like guiding a wandering puppy back to its spot.

6. **Breathe naturally.** While you observe your focal point, let your breathing be natural. There's no need to control it. Your breath can serve as a gentle reminder of the present moment.

7. **Be patient and persistent.** Concentrative mindfulness takes practice. Your mind might resist staying focused at first, but that's normal. Be patient with yourself. Each time you bring your attention back, it's a small victory.

8. **Set a timer.** If you're new to meditation, you can start with just a few minutes and gradually increase the duration as you become more comfortable with the practice.

Generative Mindfulness (Loving Kindness)

I want you to picture yourself in your happy place. Maybe it is a sandy beach hearing the waves crash on the shore. Maybe it is in your pajamas nestled in your cozy bed. It's now time to go down a path of warmth and compassion. This is the essence of loving-kindness meditation, a practice that allows you to send out well-wishes and love to someone special in your life.

Here's how you can practice it (Compitus, 2020):

1. **Find a peaceful place.** Begin by finding a quiet and comfortable place to sit or lie down. Ensure you won't be disturbed during your meditation.

2. **Close your eyes (optional).** You can choose to close your eyes to minimize distractions, but it's perfectly fine to keep them open if you prefer.

3. **Take a few deep breaths.** Start with a few deep, calming breaths to center yourself. Feel the sensation of each breath as you inhale and exhale.

4. **Visualize someone you love.** Bring to mind someone you care deeply about. It could be a family member, friend, or even a beloved pet. Picture their face, imagine their presence in the room with you. This person could even be you!

5. **Offer loving-kindness.** As you focus on this person, silently repeat well-wishes for their well-being. You might say something like, "May they be safe, may they feel loved, may they be at peace." These phrases convey your genuine desires for their happiness and tranquility.

6. **Feel the emotions.** As you continue to send these wishes, try to genuinely connect with the feelings of love and care you have for this person. Let those emotions fill your heart.

7. **Extend the wishes.** After some time, you can expand your well-wishes. Start by including yourself: "May I be safe, may I feel loved, may I be at peace." Then, gradually extend these wishes to others, such as friends, acquaintances, and even those you may have conflicts with. The goal is to cultivate feelings of kindness and compassion for all beings.

8. **Breathe mindfully.** Throughout the meditation, maintain your focus on your breath. Let it flow naturally and use it as an anchor to the present moment.

9. **Set a timer.** You can choose to set a timer for your meditation session. Start with a manageable duration, such as 5 or 10 minutes, and gradually increase it as you become more comfortable with the practice.

Receptive Mindfulness

You're sitting comfortably in a serene park, and your eyes are gently open. In this practice, you're going to engage all your senses to truly experience the world as it unfolds around you.

Here's how you can practice it (Compitus, 2020):

1. **Choose your spot.** Find a quiet place to sit comfortably. It could be a chair, a cushion on the floor, or even a cozy spot in nature.

2. **Keep your eyes open.** Unlike many meditation practices, in receptive mindfulness, you keep your eyes open. This allows you to take in the world around you.

3. **Start with your breath.** Begin by taking a few slow, deep breaths. Let the rhythm of your breath settle you into the present moment.

4. **Use your senses.** Now, start to use your five senses:

- o **Sight:** Look around you, paying attention to even the tiniest details. Notice the colors, shapes, and textures of objects. See the play of light and shadow.
- o **Hearing:** Listen to the sounds around you, both near and far. Be aware of the subtle sounds you might not typically notice, like distant birdsong or the rustling of leaves.
- o **Smell:** Take a few deep breaths and notice any scents in the air. It might be the earthy aroma of the ground or the subtle fragrance of flowers.
- o **Taste:** If you have a drink or a small snack with you, take a moment to savor it mindfully. Pay attention to the taste and texture as you eat or drink slowly.
- o **Touch:** Feel the sensation of your body in contact with the chair or the ground. Run your fingers over different textures nearby, like the fabric of your clothing or the bark of a tree if you're outside.

5. **Stay present.** As you engage your senses, stay present and avoid getting lost in thought. If your mind starts to wander, gently bring your attention back to what you're sensing in the moment.

6. **Take your time.** There's no rush in receptive mindfulness. Let each sense exploration be a slow, deliberate process. Savor each moment as it unfolds.

7. **Appreciate the experience.** As you immerse yourself in the world around you, take a moment to appreciate the beauty and wonder of the present moment.

In this chapter, we've taken a closer look at something pretty cool: finding balance through mindfulness. We talked about those three states of mind: emotion mind, reasonable mind, and that special wise mind.

You've figured out that balance isn't about picking one mind over the others; it's about blending them all together like a perfect recipe. It's about trusting your inner wisdom and that gut feeling you have.

In our next chapter, we're going to tackle something important—distress tolerance: what it is, how it focuses on acceptance, along with some actual, helpful tips and strategies for practicing it.

Remember, finding balance through mindfulness isn't just a goal; it's a way of living. And with each step we take, we're getting closer to being the best version of ourselves.

Stay kind to yourself, and let's keep moving forward together.

Key Takeaways for Week 2

- ⊙ Wise mind is the balance between emotion mind and reasonable mind.
- ⊙ Mindfulness can help you pause and find your wise mind, even in challenging situations.
- ⊙ Wise mind exercises include breathing techniques, asking wise mind for guidance, and various forms of mindfulness meditation.

Out of suffering have emerged the strongest souls; the most massive characters are seared with scars.

— KHALIL GIBRAN

CHAPTER 3

Week Three — Distress Tolerance

In this chapter, we're diving deep into the world of Distress Tolerance. As someone who not only grew up with a mom who had a tough time managing her emotions, but who's struggled with anxiety and panic myself, I get it. Life can throw some seriously challenging situations our way, and sometimes, it feels like we're drowning in a sea of emotions. But don't worry; I'm here to guide you through it.

What is Distress Tolerance?

Growing up as the child of a mother with BPD, my childhood was a unique journey, to say the least. It was a rollercoaster of emotions and unpredictability. The one thing I never really learned to do was regulate my own emotions because most of my energy went into helping my mom deal with hers. It was an exhausting and often overwhelming experience.

Fast forward to when I was living on my own as an adult, and that's when the panic and anxiety reared its ugly head. All those years of focusing on my mom's emotions left me ill-equipped to manage mine. I found myself in a sea of emotions without a lifeboat. I had no coping skills, and I desperately needed to change that.

It was a pivotal moment when I realized that I needed help with coping. Accepting that fact was the first step on my journey toward healing. This is actually when I found my mom's Martha Linehan book of DBT exercises, the DBT Skills Training Handouts and Worksheets book. My mom hadn't filled out more than the first few pages, and wouldn't do so until later when she switched therapists. When I started reading through the dense book and I discovered distress tolerance skills, I can honestly say they changed my life. I saw a psychodynamic therapist for years after that, and talked about my past, which was helpful. Yet the DBT skills I learned have been even more helpful for me overall.

Now, let's dive into the concept of distress tolerance. Imagine it as that lifeboat you never knew you needed until you found yourself in the midst of a stormy sea of emotions. Distress tolerance is your ability to navigate and survive emotional distress without making things worse. It's your emotional survival toolkit, something I wish I had in my earlier years.

From a scientific standpoint, distress tolerance is closely linked to the limbic system, the part of your brain responsible for emotions. If you have low distress tolerance, you might easily become overwhelmed by stress and resort to unhealthy coping mechanisms (Compitus, 2020). Trust me, I've been there.

This is where DBT steps in to provide a lifeline. It helps us build healthier ways to cope with life's challenges. And guess what? It's working.

It's been working for my mom, who still has her rough days, but she's improved tremendously. Each day, I see her using her newfound DBT techniques to soothe her emotions. DBT has also worked for me – I have more confidence in my capacity to handle strong negative emotions and work through any kind of craziness that life throws my way. And that, my friend, is a monumental victory.

Distress Tolerance and Acceptance

Distress tolerance and acceptance go hand in hand, forming the foundation of emotional resilience and effective coping. These concepts are akin to the warm embrace of a friend when life feels overwhelming. So, let's look deeper into the power of acceptance and how it relates to distress tolerance.

Much like the practice of mindfulness, distress tolerance places a significant emphasis on embracing and acknowledging our current reality, warts and all. It serves as the initial stepping stone in our road to managing emotional distress effectively.

Picture this scenario: You're stuck in the middle of an endless traffic jam. Honking horns, frustration in the air, and there's not a thing you can do to change the situation. This is precisely where the magic of acceptance comes into play. Mindfulness and distress tolerance equip you with the strength to accept that traffic jam without letting frustration consume you.

Acceptance isn't about surrendering to life's difficulties; it's about acknowledging that some circumstances are beyond our control. It's the art of letting go of resistance and surrendering to what is. In essence, acceptance is the key that unlocks your ability to stay calm when life hurls unexpected curveballs your way.

Acceptance isn't a passive act; it's an active choice. It empowers you to face life's challenges head-on, armed with a sense of serenity. When you accept the reality of a situation, you free up mental and emotional space to respond thoughtfully rather than react impulsively.

In my own journey, acceptance was a hard-earned lesson. I spent much of my life trying to fix, control, or change my mother's emotions, only to realize that I couldn't. It was only when I accepted this reality that I could shift my focus to managing my own emotions and well-being.

Acceptance allows us to stop the futile battle against the inevitable and channel our energy toward what truly matters: our emotional well-being and growth. It's a cornerstone of distress tolerance, offering us the strength and resilience to weather life's storms while maintaining our inner peace.

So remember, acceptance isn't a defeat; it's a triumph of self-compassion. It's the path that leads you to a place of greater emotional strength and the ability to navigate life's challenges with grace and resilience.

TIPP Skills: Your Fast-Acting Rescue

Alright, let's get into those practical skills that can help you feel in control again! TIPP skills are your go-to tools when you need a quick emotional rescue. They work lightning fast, usually within seconds to minutes, to calm your emotional storm. You can do them anywhere—at work, school, in bed—without any side effects or cost. Let's break them down:

- **Temperature:** Ever tried splashing cold water on your face or holding ice cubes in your hands? Cold water gives your system a shock, instantly lowering emotional arousal. It's like hitting the emotional reset button. I always keep ice packs in my freezer for emergencies! If I feel I am having a rather difficult day I will grab an ice pack and occasionally put it on my face the back of my neck or hold it in my hands. This can literally remind me to cool down and can stop panic or anger in their tracks.

- **Intense Exercise:** When your heart rate goes up during intense exercise, adrenaline floods your system, giving you that euphoric feeling. It's hard to feel distressed when you're elated.

I swear by this one; even doing jumping jacks in a bathroom stall can work wonders if you're not at home and are desperate to calm down. Try counting the jumping jacks—even in your head—to add that distraction component.

- ⊙ **Paced Breathing:** Slow, controlled breathing through your nose (count to two; hold your breath; count to three; exhale through your mouth; count to five) can help you regain control. It's like taking charge of your body's panic button.

- ⊙ **Paired Muscle Relaxation (PMR):** Tense and relax muscle pairs while breathing in and out. PMR teaches you to calm your body, to then calm your mind. It's an excellent practice for mindfulness and self-awareness.

Once you have completed the exercise, take some time to reflect on any thoughts, feelings, or emotions that may have come up during it. Did you find any of these were helpful? Will you keep some in your toolbox? If yes, why?

_____

_____

_____

_____

_____

_____

_____

Five Senses Exercise

Use this exercise as a simple, versatile way to practice mindfulness throughout the day. Aim to be fully present in the moment, especially when formal mindfulness practices like meditation aren't feasible. This exercise helps you become attuned to your five senses.

- **Sight:** Without thinking much at all, what are the first five things you can see?
  - o Look around and focus on five things you wouldn't typically pay attention to, such as a shadow or a small crack in the concrete.
- **Taste:** Focus on one thing you can taste right now.
  - o It could be taking a sip of your coffee, savoring a piece of chocolate, or simply noticing the taste in your mouth.
- **Touch:** Bring your awareness to four things you can feel.
  - o Pay attention to the texture of your clothing, the sensation of the breeze on your skin, or the smooth surface of a table under your hands.
- **Smell:** Tune your senses to two things you can smell.
  - o Delve into scents you might usually overlook, whether they're pleasant or unpleasant. Maybe it's the scent of pine trees in the breeze or the aroma of a nearby cafe.
- **Hearing:** Tune in to three things you can hear.
  - o Listen to the sounds of your surroundings. Whether it's a bird singing, the hum of a refrigerator, or faint traffic noises nearby, be present and take it all in.

This exercise is a quick and effective way to anchor yourself in the present moment and promote mindfulness, even during the busiest of days. Once you have had a chance to try this one out, reflect below how it worked for you. What about after practicing it a few times? Will you add this one to your toolbox?

_____

_____

_____

_____

_____

_____

_____

_____

STOP Method

The STOP method is a simple and effective technique that can be used to manage and navigate through intense emotional situations. It's designed to help you gain better control over your emotions and make more thoughtful and rational decisions. Let's break down each step of the STOP method:

1. **Stop:** The first step involves recognizing when you are experiencing strong emotions, such as anger, frustration, anxiety, or even excitement. Instead of immediately reacting to these emotions, you pause and intentionally stop whatever you are doing or about to do. This pause is crucial because it interrupts the automatic response that often accompanies strong emotions.

2. **Take a Step Back:** Once you've paused, the next step is to mentally and emotionally distance yourself from the situation. This can be done by taking a literal step back physically or by

creating mental space. By doing so, you give yourself a moment to detach from the immediate intensity of the emotions and gain a broader perspective.

3. **Observe:** With some emotional distance established, the next step is to observe your thoughts, feelings, and bodily sensations without judgment. This means being aware of what is happening within you without trying to change or suppress your emotions. It's about accepting that you have these feelings and acknowledging them without criticism.

4. **Proceed Mindfully:** After you've observed your emotions and gained a better understanding of them, you can proceed with a more mindful and intentional response. This step involves making a conscious choice about how you want to react to the situation based on your observations and your values. Instead of reacting impulsively, you respond with greater awareness and control.

Here are some key benefits of using the STOP method:

- **Emotional Regulation:** It helps you regulate your emotions by preventing impulsive reactions and giving you the space to decide how you want to respond.
- **Conflict Resolution:** It can be particularly useful in conflict situations, allowing you to approach conflicts with a calmer and more rational mindset.
- **Better Decision-making:** By taking a step back and observing your emotions, you're more likely to make decisions that align with your long-term goals and values rather than short-term emotional impulses.

- ◯ **Stress Reduction:** The method can reduce stress by preventing the buildup of negative emotions and helping you manage them more effectively.
- ◯ **Improved Communication:** It can enhance communication by allowing you to respond thoughtfully and empathetically in conversations, rather than reacting defensively or emotionally.

Cope Ahead Strategy

This strategy is used to help you prepare for and manage challenging situations effectively. It involves anticipating difficult situations, identifying potential emotional and behavioral reactions, and developing coping strategies in advance to reduce distress and improve problem-solving abilities. Here's a step-by-step guide and a workbook exercise to help you practice this strategy:

Step 1: Identify a challenging situation. Think of a specific situation or event that you anticipate will be challenging for you in the near future. It could be a social event, a work-related issue, or a personal situation. In the space below, write down a brief description of the situation, including when and where it will occur.

Example: Upcoming job interview next week.

_____

_____

_____

_____

_____

_____

_____

Step 2: List potential emotional reactions. Consider how you might feel in this challenging situation. List the emotions you anticipate experiencing. Be honest with yourself about your emotional responses.

Example: anxiety, nervousness, self-doubt

_____

_____

_____

_____

_____

_____

_____

_____

Step 3: Identify unhelpful behaviors. Think about how you tend to react when you experience these emotions. Are there any unhelpful behaviors or responses you usually engage in? Write them down.

Example: avoiding preparation, negative self-talk, procrastination

_____

_____

_____

_____

_____

_____

_____

_____

Step 4: Challenge negative thoughts. If you have identified any negative thoughts or beliefs related to the situation, challenge them with more rational and balanced thinking. Write down the negative thought and then counter it with a more realistic and positive perspective.

Example: Negative Thought: "I'm going to fail the interview." **Balanced Thought:** "I've prepared well, and I have the skills required for the job."

_____

_____

_____

_____

Step 5: Develop coping strategies. Now, brainstorm and write down specific coping strategies you can use to manage your emotions and behaviors in the challenging situation. Focus on strategies that will help you stay calm and effective. Give some of the ones offered here a try and see what sticks.

Example: Prepare thoroughly by researching the company and practicing interview questions. Practice deep breathing exercises to manage anxiety. Use positive affirmations to boost confidence.

_____

_____

_____

_____

_____

_____

Step 6: Rehearse coping strategies. Imagine yourself in the challenging situation. Mentally rehearse using the coping strategies you've identified. Visualize yourself handling the situation calmly and effectively. This mental rehearsal can help you build confidence in your ability to cope. Write down which tools you felt were most effective and why.

_____

_____

_____

_____

_____

_____

_____

Step 7: Create an action plan. Outline a step-by-step action plan for how you will implement your coping strategies when the challenging situation arises. Include specific details and timelines.

Example:

Two Days Prior to Interview	Night Before Interview	Morning of Interview
What did you find helpful in the research?	Practice deep breathing exercises.	Repeat positive affirmations.

Step 8: Monitor and evaluate. After the challenging situation has passed, take some time to reflect on how well your coping strategies worked. Write down what worked or if they helped you manage your emotions and behaviors effectively. If not, consider what adjustments you can make for future situations.

_____

_____

_____

_____

_____

_____

_____

Step 9: Practice and adapt. Continue practicing the cope ahead strategy with different challenging situations in your life. As you gain experience, you can adapt and refine your coping strategies to suit your needs better.

Remember that the cope ahead strategy takes practice, and it may not eliminate all distress in challenging situations, but it can significantly improve your ability to manage them. Over time, you'll become more skilled at anticipating and responding to difficult circumstances in a healthier and more constructive manner.

Crisis Survival Skills – ACCEPTS

ACCEPTS is another powerful tool in your distress tolerance toolbox. The skills help you manage distress by encouraging you to engage in healthy activities, seek support, reframe thoughts, and more. Let me walk you through how they work:

- ⊙ **Activities:** Distract yourself with a walk or a hobby.
- ⊙ **Contribute:** Talk to someone you trust about your feelings.
- ⊙ **Comparisons:** Remember past successes in managing anxiety.
- ⊙ **Emotions:** Allow yourself to feel without judgment.
- ⊙ **Pushing Away:** Shift your focus to a pleasant memory.
- ⊙ **Thoughts:** Use positive self-talk to counter negative thoughts.
- ⊙ **Sensations:** Practice deep breathing to relax.

These skills can be a game-changer in managing distress, helping you avoid impulsive or harmful behaviors.

Surviving a Crisis with IMPROVE

Another valuable technique is IMPROVE, an acronym that represents a set of strategies to help individuals navigate through crises. IMPROVE stands for:

- ⊙ **Imagery:** This strategy involves using your imagination to create calming mental images. When facing a crisis, you can close your eyes and visualize a peaceful place or scenario. This can help reduce anxiety and provide a temporary escape from the stress of the situation.
- ⊙ **Meaning:** Finding meaning in a crisis can be a powerful coping mechanism. This involves trying to understand the significance of the crisis in your life and how it might contribute to personal growth or a deeper understanding of yourself. It can provide a sense of purpose and resilience during difficult times.
- ⊙ **Prayer:** For individuals who are religious or spiritual, prayer can be a source of comfort and guidance during a crisis. Engaging in prayer can help you feel connected to something greater than yourself and provide emotional support.

- **Relaxation:** Relaxation techniques, such as deep breathing exercises, progressive muscle relaxation, or meditation, can help calm your body and mind during a crisis. These techniques can reduce stress and promote a sense of relaxation and well-being.

- **One Thing in the Moment:** Sometimes, focusing on just one thing in the present moment can be helpful. This strategy encourages you to concentrate your attention on a single task or activity, diverting your mind from the crisis and providing a brief respite from overwhelming emotions.

- **Vacation:** While it may not always be possible to take a physical vacation during a crisis, this strategy suggests mentally 'escaping' from the crisis by temporarily shifting your thoughts to a place or activity that brings you joy or relaxation. It's a way to provide yourself with a mental break.

- **Encouragement:** Self-encouragement is about being kind and supportive to yourself during difficult times. It involves using positive self-talk and self-compassion to boost your self-esteem and resilience. Remind yourself that you have the strength to get through the crisis.

These strategies collectively serve as a lifeline during times of crisis, enabling individuals to regain a sense of control and discover moments of tranquility amid the chaos.

By incorporating these elements into your coping toolkit, you can enhance your ability to cope with and ultimately overcome challenging situations. Each component of the IMPROVE technique provides a unique approach to managing distress, making it a versatile and adaptable resource for navigating life's crises.

Building a Distress Tolerance Kit

Building a distress tolerance kit is a valuable self-help strategy for managing emotional distress. Think of it as your personal emergency toolkit, filled with items that can provide comfort and help ground you when you're feeling overwhelmed. In the following steps, we'll provide a checklist and guidance to assist you in assembling your very own kit.

Understand the Purpose

Before you start gathering items for your kit, it's important to understand its purpose. This kit is meant to provide emotional support and help you cope in those really tough times. The items you choose should have a calming or soothing effect, and they can serve as reminders of self-care and resilience.

Create a Checklist

To help you get organized, make a checklist of items you can consider including in your kit. Keep in mind that your kit should be personalized to your preferences and needs, so feel free to add or modify items as you see fit.

Gather Your Items

Using the list as a guide, gather the items you've selected for your kit. These items can vary widely, depending on what brings you comfort and helps you manage distress. Examples might include:

- Stress-relief toys (e.g., stress balls, fidget spinners)
- Inspirational quotes or affirmations
- A comforting book or journal
- Photos of loved ones or happy memories
- A scented candle or essential oils

- A playlist of calming music or guided meditations
- Tea bags or your favorite snacks
- A soft blanket or plush toy
- Mindfulness exercises or prompts

Assemble Your Kit

Find a container or bag to store your distress tolerance items in. It can be a box, a pouch, a backpack, or anything that suits your preference and allows for easy access when needed. Organize the items neatly inside the container.

Personalize Your Kit

Add a personal touch to your kit by including a note or letter to yourself. Write encouraging words, self-compassionate reminders, or instructions on how to use the items effectively. This can serve as a source of motivation and comfort during tough times.

Keep It Accessible

Place your kit in a location where you can easily access it when you're feeling overwhelmed or distressed. Whether it's at home, in your car, or at your workplace, having it nearby is essential for its effectiveness.

Use It Mindfully

When you find yourself in a distressing situation, open your kit and use its contents mindfully. Engage with the items to help calm your emotions and regain your emotional balance. Remember that this kit is a tool for self-care and resilience.

Building a Distress Tolerance Kit is a proactive step toward managing emotional distress effectively. By assembling a kit tailored to your preferences, you can better equip yourself to navigate tough times and provide yourself with much-needed comfort and support.

That's a lot to take in, I know, but remember, this journey is about building skills that will empower you to manage life's challenges with grace and resilience. You're not alone on this path, my friend. Let's continue together.

Key Takeaways for Week 3

- Distress tolerance is your ability to manage and survive emotional distress.
- Acceptance is the first step in distress tolerance.
- TIPP Skills (Temperature, Intense Exercise, Paced Breathing, Paired Muscle Relaxation) provide fast-acting relief from distress.
- The STOP method and Cope Ahead strategy help you respond to distress effectively.
- ACCEPTS and IMPROVE techniques offer valuable distress tolerance tools.
- Build a Distress Tolerance Kit to support yourself during tough times.

We're making progress, and you're doing amazing. As we wrap up this chapter on distress tolerance, remember that life is not a smooth road and we should anticipate many "under construction" signs along our way. By cultivating the skills and strategies we've explored here, you are building a strong foundation for navigating the detours of life with resilience and grace. Now, as we venture into the next chapter on radical acceptance, you'll discover how letting go of resistance and embracing reality can be a powerful complement to your distress tolerance toolkit.

66

There is something wonderfully bold and liberating about saying 'yes' to our entire imperfect and messy life

— ANONYMOUS

CHAPTER 4

Week 4— Radical Acceptance

I grew up with an emotionally unstable mother. My childhood lacked the normalcy and innocence most kids experience. While I knew she loved me, she relied on me to meet her emotional needs. I became her rock, her continual source of stability. Over time, her BPD diagnosis forced us into a challenging, codependent relationship, with deeply ingrained habits that took me years to break free from. I often felt like I was walking on eggshells, constantly navigating the unpredictable terrain of her emotions. She needed my constant validation to feel worthy because she grappled with chronic emptiness and a lack of trust in her own judgment.

DBT changed not only my mother for the better, but our relationship in the long-run. A huge part of that was exploring radical acceptance.

Understanding Radical Acceptance

Imagine a cozy scene where you're enveloped in the comforting embrace of a cherished grandmother. There's a feeling of warmth, security, and unconditional love. Radical acceptance is like that hug. It's a tender, nurturing embrace for your soul, a moment where you allow yourself to be cared for without judgment. It's a pivotal pillar of DBT, deeply rooted in the teachings of Buddhism.

The wisdom of Carl Rogers resonates here: He believed that acceptance is the first step toward change. Just as a seed must first be accepted into the soil before it can grow into a mighty tree, you too must accept your reality before you can nurture the growth and transformation that you seek (Main, 2022).

Radical acceptance isn't about putting on a façade, pretending that everything is fine, or forcing yourself to agree with the pain in your life. It's not about denying your feelings or bottling them up. They are your feelings, they are your emotions and you are entitled to them. They are a part of who you are. Instead, it's something much deeper and more profound.

Radical acceptance is the art of acknowledging the reality of your situation without allowing yourself to be engulfed by the dark storm cloud of suffering that often accompanies it. It's recognizing that storms happen, but you have the power to choose whether you stand drenched in the rain or seek shelter. It is asking yourself if you are worthy of that umbrella. Then, asking yourself if you are worthy of that rainbow.

Here's the crux of it: suffering doesn't always stem from the pain itself; it often arises from our attachment to that pain. Think about a situation where you're confronted with something beyond your control—perhaps the loss of a loved one or your job. In those moments, grief, sadness, and disappointment are natural and valid emotions. But clinging tightly to these emotions and resisting acceptance inadvertently prolongs our suffering. It's like standing under that metaphorical storm cloud for years, soaked to the skin without an umbrella.

Radical acceptance isn't about saying, "I'm okay with this pain." It's about freeing ourselves from the chains of suffering. It's the courageous choice to step out from under that storm cloud, even when you're knee-deep in rain. It's about understanding that you deserve sunshine, even when the sky seems perpetually gray.

In essence, Radical Acceptance is a profound act of self-compassion. It's choosing hope by accepting things as they are, even when they appear impossibly tough. It's not merely choosing an umbrella; it's about realizing that you are worthy of basking in the warmth of the sun. It's a radical shift from enduring suffering to embracing life with open arms, even in the face of adversity.

Recognizing the Signs of Non-Acceptance

Before we dive into practical exercises, let's become detectives of our own behavior and emotions. Here are some signs that you might be resisting acceptance:

Thought patterns:

- "I can't deal with this."
- "This is not fair."
- "Things shouldn't be like this."
- "Why is this is happening?"

Emotions and reactions:

- Blaming yourself for everything bad that happens.
- Feeling stuck and powerless.
- Wishing things were different but feeling helpless.
- Holding onto anger and resorting to unhealthy coping mechanisms.

Relationship patterns:

- Constantly nagging your loved ones, hoping they'll change.
- Frequent disappointment in others' choices.
- Holding onto grudges and harboring resentments.

Do any of these patterns sound familiar? It's okay if they do; we've all been there. Recognizing them is the first step towards embracing radical acceptance.

The Roots of Radical Acceptance: DBT

Enter Marsha Linehan, a brilliant psychologist who introduced DBT in 1993 (Cuncic, 2021). This therapy was initially designed to assist individuals with Borderline Personality Disorder, often characterized by intense emotions. DBT teaches us that while we can't alter the facts of a situation, we have the power to change how we perceive and respond to them.

We discussed earlier how DBT emphasizes a delicate balance between our emotional and logical minds, creating what Linehan refers to as the "wise mind," that place where we can make thoughtful decisions, removing the overwhelming emotions that often cloud our judgment. Acceptance, in this context, means taking reality as it is so we can move forward.

Now, you might be wondering why it's so challenging to accept things as they are. Well, rest assured, this is normal for many of us. We grapple with this, fearing that acceptance equals agreement or condoning the pain. Others dodge acceptance to avoid the inevitable discomfort it brings.

Remember, these feelings are entirely okay, but they're not insurmountable. Change is possible, but it requires practice and dedication. You need to want it.

The problem with resisting acceptance is that in our attempt to avoid pain, we inadvertently block out joy and happiness. Avoiding our emotions can lead to anxiety, depression, addiction, and a host of other mental health concerns. Instead, embracing calm acceptance allows us to process our emotions and take steps forward. Remember, you deserve the sunshine.

Practicing Radical Acceptance Exercise

Welcome to a hands-on exercise designed to help you enhance your ability to practice radical acceptance. Just like any skill, it becomes more refined with practice. Take a moment to reflect on each question or prompt and jot down your thoughts or feelings after considering them.

Identify Triggers: Pay close attention to situations or thoughts that trigger resistance within you. What tends to make it difficult for you to accept certain things in life? Write down your triggers.

_____

_____

_____

_____

_____

Embrace the Unchangeable: Remind yourself that in this very moment, the reality you're facing cannot be changed. Reflect on a specific situation in your life where this applies, and write it down.

_____

_____

_____

_____

_____

Recognize Lack of Control: Acknowledge that there are causes and circumstances contributing to your current reality that are entirely outside of your control. What are some factors in your life that you have no control over? Note them down.

_____

_____

_____

_____

_____

Actions of Acceptance: Envision what actions you would take if you had already accepted the situation. How would you behave differently? Write down these actions.

_____

_____

_____

_____

_____

Imagination Exercise: Close your eyes and imagine what life would be like if you fully accepted the situation you've been resisting. Describe this scenario in detail, noting how it feels.

_____

_____

_____

_____

_____

Emotional Exploration: Utilize relaxation strategies, mindfulness practices, or journaling to delve into your emotions regarding a challenging situation. What emotions arise when you think about it? Write them down.

_____

_____

_____

_____

_____

Physical Sensations: Pay attention to how your emotions manifest in your body. Is there any tightness, pain, or restriction? Describe any physical sensations you notice.

_____

_____

_____

_____

_____

Life's Worth: Consider that life can still hold value and meaning even when you're experiencing pain or difficulty. Write down ways in which your life remains meaningful despite challenges.

_____

_____

_____

_____

_____

Commitment to Acceptance: Make a firm commitment to yourself that you will practice acceptance when resistance arises in the future. What strategies will you employ to ensure you stay committed?

_____

_____

_____

_____

_____

By engaging with these steps, you'll gradually shift your focus away from dwelling on how things "could have been" and instead learn to embrace the present moment.

Empowering Statements for Radical Acceptance Exercise

Here are eleven empowering statements that can serve as your go-to tools when you find it challenging to accept certain situations and move forward. Keep these statements handy, so you can easily access them in the moments when you're feeling overwhelmed (Cuncic, 2021):

1. **Embracing Emotions:** "Resisting negative emotions only gives them more power. I choose to acknowledge and accept them."
2. **Past Acceptance:** "I recognize that I can't change the past. It's time to focus on the present and future."
3. **Accepting the Present:** "I have the capacity to accept the present moment exactly as it is, with all its imperfections."
4. **Strength through Difficulty:** "Even when facing difficult emotions, I have the resilience to endure. It may be tough, but I can handle it."

5. **Resilience:** "I will not only survive this, but I will also emerge stronger. The current pain is temporary, and it will fade."

6. **Managing Pain:** "Though this feeling is painful right now, I understand that I can endure it and come out the other side."

7. **Managing Anxiety:** "I can experience anxiety and still effectively manage the situation. My emotions don't define my abilities."

8. **Happiness despite Acceptance:** "I can accept what has happened and still find happiness in my life. The two are not mutually exclusive."

9. **Creating a New Path:** "Even in moments of discomfort, I have the power to choose a new path and make positive changes."

10. **Rational Decision-making:** "Staying rational enables me to make informed decisions and solve problems effectively."

11. **Action over Judgment:** "Taking the right actions is more productive than dwelling in judgment or blame. I choose to take constructive steps forward."

These empowering statements are your companions on your journey of radical acceptance. Keep them close, and remind yourself of their strength whenever you feel the need to embrace acceptance and move towards a more mindful and peaceful life.

Half Smiling Exercise

Half smiling is a powerful mindfulness technique rooted in DBT that can help you practice and strengthen your ability to engage in radical acceptance. It's a practical exercise that you can apply in various scenarios to develop greater emotional resilience and acceptance. Here's how to do it (Cuncic, 2021)

Half smiling involves literally forming a half-smile on your face, which can be a subtle and gentle upturning of the corners of your mouth. It may seem simple, but the act of half-smiling has profound effects on your emotional state and your ability to accept the present moment.

How to practice half smiling for radical acceptance:

- **Find a quiet space.** To start, choose a quiet and comfortable place where you won't be disturbed. Sit or lie down in a relaxed position.
- **Focus on your breath.** Close your eyes if it helps you concentrate better. Take a few slow, deep breaths to center yourself. Pay attention to the sensation of your breath entering and leaving your body.
- **Half smile.** Gently curve the corners of your lips into a half-smile. It's essential to keep this smile gentle and soft; you're not trying to force a big grin.
- **Observe your thoughts.** As you maintain the half-smile, turn your attention inward. Notice any thoughts or emotions that arise, especially those related to the situation you're struggling to accept.
- **Embrace your thoughts and emotions.** Instead of resisting or judging your thoughts and feelings, allow them to be present. This is a crucial step in practicing radical acceptance. Accept that these thoughts and emotions are part of your current reality.
- **Release tension.** Pay attention to any physical tension in your body, such as in your shoulders, neck, or jaw. As you half-smile, consciously release this tension, allowing your body to relax.
- **Stay present.** Continue to focus on your breath and the half-smile as you remain present with your thoughts and emotions.

Imagine that your half-smile is gently cradling these thoughts and feelings with kindness.

- ⊙ **Breathe through it.** If you notice resistance or discomfort arising, take a deep breath and exhale slowly. This can help you stay centered and prevent you from getting caught up in emotional turmoil.

Scenarios for half smiling practice:

- ⊙ **Dealing with past regrets.** When you find yourself ruminating about past mistakes or regrets, practice half smiling to accept that you can't change the past.
- ⊙ **Facing uncertain futures.** If you're anxious about an uncertain future, use half smiling to embrace your anxiety and accept that some things are beyond your control.
- ⊙ **Managing conflict.** In a conflict or disagreement with someone, half smile to accept the situation as it is and respond more calmly and rationally.
- ⊙ **Coping with loss.** When you're grieving a loss, half smiling can help you accept the pain and sadness as part of the natural grieving process.
- ⊙ **Dealing with chronic pain.** If you have chronic pain or illness, practice half smiling to acknowledge your pain while also finding ways to live a fulfilling life.

Remember, half smiling is a skill that improves with practice. The more you incorporate it into your daily life, the more effective it becomes in helping you achieve radical acceptance.

Willing Hands

Willing hands is a simple yet powerful technique that focuses on adjusting our body posture to enhance our ability to engage in radical acceptance. It communicates to our brain that we are in a safe and non-defensive space, encouraging a more open and accepting mindset. Here's how to practice willing hands:

Willing hands involves making deliberate changes to your body posture to signal to your brain that you are in a safe and receptive state. This physical adjustment can significantly impact your emotional state and aid in accepting the present moment. Try the following:

1. **Choose a comfortable position.** Find a quiet and comfortable space where you can sit, lie down, or stand, depending on your preference and the situation.
2. **Uncross your arms.** Start by uncrossing your arms if they are crossed. This simple act begins the process of opening up your body posture.
3. **Release tension.** Take a moment to release any tension in your body. Relax your shoulders, neck, and jaw. Breathe deeply and exhale slowly to further release physical tension.
4. **Open your palms.** Now, take it a step further by opening your palms. Here are some variations depending on your position:
   o If you are sitting, rest your hands on your legs or knees with your palms facing up.
   o If you are lying down, place your arms at your sides with your palms facing up, whether on the ground or a bed.
   o If you are standing, let your arms hang naturally at your sides with your palms facing front.

5. **Mindful Awareness:** As you adopt this open posture with willing hands, bring your attention to the sensations in your body and your emotional state. Notice any changes in how you feel and any increase in your sense of openness and acceptance.

6. **Stay present.** Whenever you encounter resistance, difficult emotions, or challenging situations, use Willing Hands to help you remain present and receptive. Allow this open posture to support your radical acceptance.

Incorporating this into your daily life can be a valuable tool for practicing radical acceptance. It's a tangible way to shift your mindset and encourage a more open and accepting approach to life's challenges. By unclasping your hands and opening your palms, you send a powerful message to yourself that you are willing to embrace the present moment with acceptance and grace.

Key Takeaways Week 4

- ⊙ Radical acceptance is about acknowledging reality without judgment.
- ⊙ Suffering often arises from our attachment to pain, not the pain itself.
- ⊙ DBT teaches us to balance our emotional and logical minds for wise decision-making.
- ⊙ Resistance to acceptance is normal, but it can be overcome with practice.
- ⊙ Avoiding emotions can lead to mental health issues; acceptance allows us to process and heal.

If you have control over yourself, you have no desire to control others.

— MIYA YAMANOUCHI

CHAPTER 5

Week 5 — Emotional Regulation

My mom had her moments of love and affection, just like any parent would. But her struggles with emotion regulation meant that I often felt like I was walking on eggshells. She would tell me she loved me and I knew she truly did love me. However, her emotional instability led her to react unpredictably, in ways that didn't seem loving at all. This usually forced me to suppress my own emotional expression, thus inhibiting my natural growth and development.

I'm sure some of you can relate to this feeling, where you constantly find yourself trying to avoid any situation that might set off a storm of emotions in a loved one. You may have developed the skill of mind-reading, trying to preemptively understand their thoughts and emotions to prevent meltdowns. It's like living in a cage of control and engulfment, isn't it?

But the good news is that dealing with these emotions and these situations for a long time doesn't mean we're destined to a certain fate. We have the strength and the freedom to break free from those old patterns and rediscover our own emotional well-being. In this chapter, we'll explore what emotion regulation is all about, and how it can be a powerful tool for nurturing our mental health and happiness.

What is Emotion Regulation?

Emotion regulation is like the compass that guides us through the ever-changing landscape of our feelings. It's the ability to understand, accept, and manage our emotions effectively, without being overwhelmed or controlled by them. Just like a ship needs a steady hand on the helm during a storm, we need to learn how to navigate the turbulent waters of our emotions.

So, how can we achieve this? Well, that's what this workbook is all about. We'll explore practical exercises, backed by research and studies, that will help you become a master of your emotions. But first, let's take a moment to reflect on why this topic is so crucial.

Growing up, I often felt like I was living in two worlds. On one hand, there was my loving, caring mother who would hug me and tell me she loved me. On the other hand, there was the unpredictable side of her, the mother who would react explosively to the smallest things. These unpredictable emotions left me feeling confused, anxious, and, at times, helpless.

I know what it's like to be consciously or unconsciously 'trained' to tiptoe around, to anticipate someone else's moods, and to try not to provoke an emotional spiral. It's exhausting, isn't it? But as I learned about DBT and emotion regulation, I discovered that I didn't have to live this way forever.

The Three Thinking Styles

Understanding the three thinking styles is a fundamental part of DBT practice, particularly in helping you gain better self-awareness and the ability to manage your emotions effectively. Let's break down what they are exactly:

- **Reasoning Self:** Think of this as the part of your mind that acts like a wise and logical advisor. It's the voice that helps you look at situations calmly, gather facts, and make smart decisions. In DBT, you'll learn how to make this part of your mind even stronger, so it can help you when you're tempted to react impulsively or based on strong emotions.

- **Emotional Self:** This is the part of you that feels the really strong emotions. Sometimes these emotions can be overwhelming. In DBT, you'll learn how to handle these big feelings by acknowledging and accepting them, but without letting them take over and make you act in ways you might regret.

- **Wise Self:** Think of this as your inner wisdom. It's like having a wise and calm friend inside you. DBT shows you how to connect with your Wise Self by practicing mindfulness and emotion control techniques. This helps you make smart and kind choices, especially when things get tough.

Understanding the nature of emotions is vital in DBT, as it forms the basis for chain analysis. Here's how the three thinking styles connect:

- **Emotions are complex.** Emotions aren't simple reactions; they involve a series of interconnected events. DBT recognizes this complexity and helps us break down our emotional responses into manageable components.

- **Chain Analysis:** This is a structured process used in DBT to examine the chain of events leading to emotional reactions and problematic behaviors. It helps identify the various factors involved in an emotional response, enabling us to gain insight into our reactions.

Chain Analysis Factors

The main factors of Chain Analysis are the following:

- ⊙ **Vulnerability Factors:** These are the predisposing factors that make a person more susceptible to emotional dysregulation. DBT teaches individuals to recognize and address vulnerability factors through self-care and skill-building.

- ⊙ **Prompting Event:** This is the specific trigger or event that sets off the emotional response. Identifying the prompting event is essential in understanding why a particular emotion arises.

- ⊙ **Interpretations:** Interpretations are the thoughts and beliefs that follow the prompting event. DBT encourages individuals to become aware of their interpretations and assess whether they are accurate or biased.

- ⊙ **Emotion Name:** Naming your emotions accurately is a significant step in emotional regulation. DBT helps individuals develop a vocabulary for their emotions, which promotes better self-understanding and communication.

- ⊙ **Biological Changes:** Emotions often come with physiological changes like increased heart rate or muscle tension. Recognizing these changes can signal the beginning of an emotional response.

- ⊙ **Action Urges:** Emotions typically come with urges to take specific actions. DBT teaches individuals to pause and consider these urges before acting impulsively.

- ⊙ **Behaviors:** These are the actions or reactions that follow the emotional response. DBT encourages individuals to evaluate whether these behaviors are effective or problematic.

⊙ **Aftereffects:** Aftereffects refer to the consequences of the emotional response and related behaviors. Understanding these helps individuals see the broader impact of their reactions.

Chain Analysis Exercises

Chain analysis exercises are practical applications of these concepts. They help us dissect and understand our emotional reactions by identifying each step in the chain of events leading to the emotion. By doing this exercise, we can gain valuable insights into our emotional patterns, develop healthier coping strategies, and work toward more adaptive responses.

By mastering these concepts and exercises, we can make significant strides in managing our emotions, improving our relationships, and leading a more fulfilling life. DBT provides a structured and compassionate framework for achieving these goals.

EXERCISE 1: Identifying Your Thinking Styles

Use the table below.

Reasoning Self	Emotional Self	Wise Self

Over the course of a few days, pay attention to your thoughts and reactions in different situations.

Write down the thoughts and emotions that come up in each column. Reflect on how each style influences your behavior and decisions.

EXERCISE 2: Exploring Chain Analysis

Chain analysis is a core DBT concept that helps us understand the sequence of events leading to emotional reactions and behaviors.

Use the chart below:

Fill in each step with examples from your own life, focusing on a specific emotional reaction.

Vulnerability Factors	Prompting Event	Interpretations	Emotion Name	Biological Changes	Action Urges	Aftereffects

Reflect on how each step in the chain contributed to your emotional response.

EXERCISE 3: Identifying and Challenging Interpretations

In the 'Interpretations' step of your chain analysis, identify any negative or irrational thoughts you had during the triggering event.

_____

_____

_____

_____

_____

_____

_____

Write down evidence that supports and contradicts these interpretations.

_____

_____

_____

_____

_____

_____

_____

_____

Use the evidence to challenge and reframe your negative thoughts.

Notice how changing your interpretations can lead to different emotional responses.

Categorizing Your Emotions

Emotions can be complex but understanding them is crucial. Let's begin by categorizing emotions into ten key categories. These are the top ten emotions that are commonly addressed in DBT (*Do We Even Need Them? Your Guide to Understanding Emotions.*, 2017):

1. Fear

- ⊙ **Definition**: Fear is that feeling of dread or unease that creeps in when you believe you're facing a threat or danger. It's your body's natural response to protect you.
- ⊙ **Examples**: Fear might surge when you're walking alone in a dark alley, confronted by a growling dog, or anticipating a critical job interview.

2. Anger

- ⊙ **Definition**: Anger is the fiery emotion that arises when you perceive injustice or frustration. It's like an emotional alarm bell, telling you that something isn't right.
- ⊙ **Examples**: Anger can flare up when someone cuts in front of you in traffic, when you feel unfairly criticized, or when you witness an act of cruelty.

3. Sadness

- ⊙ **Definition**: Sadness is the profound feeling of sorrow and grief when things don't go as planned. It's a natural response to loss or disappointment.
- ⊙ **Examples**: Sadness might wash over you after a breakup, when you lose a loved one, or when you experience a setback in your personal or professional life.

4. Happiness

- ⊙ **Definition**: Happiness is the joyful state when things are going your way. It's that warm, elated feeling of contentment and satisfaction.
- ⊙ **Examples**: You may experience happiness when you achieve a personal goal, receive good news, or simply spend quality time with loved ones.

5. Love

- ⊙ **Definition**: Love is the warm and affectionate emotion that connects us to others. It's a powerful force that fosters connections and bonds.
- ⊙ **Examples**: Love is what you feel for your family, friends, partners, and even pets. It's that overwhelming sense of care and affection.

6. Guilt

- ⊙ **Definition**: Guilt is the sense of responsibility and remorse when you believe you've done something wrong. It's your conscience telling you to make amends.
- ⊙ **Examples**: Guilt can haunt you when you break a promise, lie to someone, or hurt someone's feelings unintentionally.

7. Shame

- ⊙ **Definition**: Shame is a deep-seated feeling of inadequacy and self-disgust. It's an intensely negative emotion linked to self-worth.
- ⊙ **Examples**: Shame may surface when you make a public mistake, reveal a personal secret, or feel like you don't meet societal standards.

8. Envy

- ○ **Definition**: Envy is the feeling of wanting something someone else has. It often arises from a desire for what you perceive as missing in your life.
- ○ **Examples**: Envy can manifest when a colleague gets a promotion you wanted, or when a friend shows off a new car you can't afford.

9. Jealousy

- ○ **Definition**: Jealousy is the fear or apprehension of losing something or someone you cherish. It can be rooted in insecurity or possessiveness.
- ○ **Examples**: Jealousy can strike in relationships when you suspect your partner's affections are drifting or when a best friend gets close to someone else.

10. Disgust

- ○ **Definition**: Disgust is the strong revulsion or aversion towards something unpleasant. It's your body's way of signaling that something is unclean or harmful.
- ○ **Examples**: Disgust may arise when you encounter spoiled food, witness an act of cruelty, or come across something physically repulsive.

Now that we've identified these emotions, let's explore primary and secondary emotions.

Primary vs. Secondary Emotions

Primary emotions are your immediate, instinctive reactions to a situation. Secondary emotions, on the other hand, are your emotional reactions to your primary emotions. They often arise from how you interpret or judge your primary emotions.

For example, imagine you made a mistake at work (primary emotion: guilt). Then, you start feeling shame (secondary emotion) because you believe you're a failure due to that mistake.

Exercise on Emotions

Think of a recent emotional situation. Write down the primary emotion you felt.

_____

_____

_____

_____

_____

_____

Now, reflect on the primary emotion. Did any secondary emotions arise from it? Write them down.

_____

_____

_____

_____

_____

_____

What triggered these emotions? Understanding the triggers can help you gain insight into your emotional responses.

_____

_____

_____

_____

_____

_____

On a scale of 1 to 10, rate how intense each emotion was during the situation. This will help you gauge the impact of your emotions.

_____

_____

_____

_____

_____

_____

EXERCISE 4: Create Your Emotions Dictionary

Creating your emotions dictionary can be a powerful tool in your journey to understanding and managing your emotions. Here's how you can do it:

Use the space below as a dedicated emotions workbook space. This will be your safe space to explore your feelings.

First, write down the ten DBT emotions: Fear, Anger, Sadness, Happiness, Love, Guilt, Shame, Envy, Jealousy, Disgust.

Next to each emotion, jot down your own definition or description. What does it mean to you?

- ⊙ **Fear:**

- ⊙ **Anger:**

- ⊙ **Sadness:**

- ⊙ **Happiness:**

- ⊙ **Love:**

- ⊙ **Guilt:**

- ⊙ **Shame:**

- ⊙ **Envy:**

- ⊙ **Jealousy:**

- ⊙ **Disgust:**

Write down personal examples for each emotion. Recall situations where you experienced these emotions and describe them in detail.

_____

_____

_____

_____

_____

_____

_____

Note what typically triggers these emotions for you. Is it a specific situation, thought, or person?

_____

_____

_____

_____

_____

_____

_____

By creating your emotions dictionary, you'll develop a clearer understanding of your emotional landscape, making it easier to manage and respond effectively.

In this chapter, we looked deep into the intricate world of emotions, exploring their many facets, from fear to happiness, and everything in between. You've learned that emotions are not just reactions; they are your inner compass, guiding you through the twists and turns of life.

Key Takeaways Week 5

- Emotions are natural. Emotions are a fundamental part of the human experience. There are no 'good' or 'bad' emotions; they all serve a purpose.
- Understanding is power. By categorizing your emotions and recognizing primary versus secondary emotions, you're gaining invaluable insight into yourself. This self-awareness is the first step toward emotional regulation.
- Embrace your emotional landscape. Emotions, even the challenging ones like shame and guilt, have something to teach us. Instead of avoiding or suppressing them, let's learn to embrace them as messengers.
- You're not alone. Remember, you're not alone on this journey. Many others are navigating their emotional seas as well. Your experiences are valid, and your emotions matter.

In the next chapter, we'll take these insights to the next level and translate them into even more practical tools.

*Emotion-regulation leads to
life-regulation.*

— SAM OWEN

CHAPTER 6

Week 6 — Emotional Regulation Toolbox

We are about to begin another chapter on your path to mastering the art of emotional regulation using DBT skills. I know that the journey to emotional balance can be daunting, especially if you're carrying the weight of past experiences or dealing with overwhelming emotions. But know that I'm here to guide you, one step at a time.

In this chapter, we're going to explore the practical tools and strategies that DBT therapy has to offer that may be the best fit for you. Think of this as your emotional regulation toolbox: a place where you can find reliable methods to help you navigate the twists and turns of life's emotional rollercoaster. We'll sprinkle in some research-backed insights and relatable stories to keep things interesting, but our focus is on giving you actionable exercises and tips that you can implement right away.

I know that starting something new can be intimidating, especially when it involves emotions. If you're feeling hesitant or anxious about diving into this chapter, please know that it's entirely normal. I've been there too, and have dealt with multiple emotional challenges that wake me up in the night sweating with fear, so I understand the trepidation that can come with change.

Every step you take, no matter how small, brings you closer to a happier, healthier you. It's like building a sturdy bridge one brick at a time. And, today, we're going to lay the foundation for your emotional well-being.

So, what can you expect in this chapter? Well, I promise I won't bog you down with dry, theoretical stuff. Instead, I'll focus on practical exercises and real-world strategies that you can use in your daily life. Whether you're dealing with anger, sadness, anxiety, or just the ups and downs of everyday living, this toolbox you are building is designed to help you regain control and find that balance you've been seeking.

Using ABC PLEASE to Manage Your Emotions

I know dealing with overwhelming emotions is tough, especially if you've grown up in a challenging environment. I would like to offer you a powerful tool called ABC PLEASE. It's an approach that focuses on small goals (*Using ABC Please to Manage Overwhelming Emotions with DBT*, 2023). Let's break each component down further:

Accumulating Positive Emotions

Think of this as your happiness booster. When we're down in the dumps, we often forget what brings us joy, makes us smile, or makes us laugh. So, here's the deal: do things that make you happy. It can be as simple as chatting with a friend, listening to your favorite tunes, doing a craft you love, or even showing kindness to someone. These little doses of joy can help balance out those heavy emotions. Your mind and body collect these experiences, so don't feel guilty for experiencing them.

Building Mastery

Ever felt like life's spiraling out of control? Building mastery is like taking back the reins. Set some achievable goals. Maybe it's picking up a new hobby, tackling a chore you've been putting off, or daring yourself to step out of your comfort zone. Achieving these goals gives you a confidence boost and makes you feel more capable. The trick here is to make these goals achievable. Often, we convince ourselves that in order to snap out of a funk we need to climb a mountain, repaint the entire house, or declutter the garage. I suggest starting by making your bed. Yes, something that small. Each time you walk into your room, you will feel a sense of accomplishment. Next, try cleaning the kitchen or cleaning out that junk drawer.

Coping Ahead

Picture this as your emergency toolkit. Sometimes, you know situations that make you feel like a pressure cooker are coming. So, let's prepare! Practice some cool-down techniques like deep breathing, imagining a peaceful place, or telling yourself positive things. It's like having a shield to protect you from emotional tornadoes. For example, every time I have to deal with impending family holidays, I begin to stress weeks in advance. Not knowing how my mom is going to react to the way my kids behave or whether dinner is burnt sets my own emotions into turmoil. I lean into this coping mechanism now. I visualize the holiday going smoothly and I practice a few affirmations ahead of time. I also prepare some tactics in case the day takes a turn for the worst- if, in the midst of it all, I have to step out to practice my breathing, so be it. Protecting my emotional well-being is priority number one.

PLEASE for Your Well-being

Taking care of your body is so important. PLEASE is an acronym used to remind you to pay attention to your *physical* health. This acronym reminds us to: Treat **P**hysical i**L**lness, **E**at balanced meals, **A**void harmful substances, get enough **S**leep, and include some **E**xercise in our routines. When your body feels good, it's easier to manage emotions. This is a reminder that mental health involves treating the entire body.

Focusing on Small Goals

Okay, so the big picture can be daunting, right? That's where focusing on small goals comes in. Like we discussed in building mastery, break those huge tasks into tiny, manageable steps. Does your entire house need to be cleaned? Start with the smallest room. Allow yourself to feel that sense of accomplishment. Each small win boosts your motivation and helps you reach those big goals. It will make you want to continue on because, let's face it, tackling everything all at once usually ends in frustration and nothing getting done.

ABC PLEASE is like your trusty sidekick for managing emotions. It's about finding joy, setting and achieving goals, planning for tough times, taking care of your body, and tackling life's challenges one step at a time. Tuck this one into your toolbox and see how it fits into your life.

EXERCISE: Your ABC PLEASE Daily Plan

Think of this exercise as your personal roadmap to managing your emotions effectively. We'll create a daily plan that incorporates the ABC PLEASE skills.

Step 1: Accumulating Positive Emotions

Write down three activities or things that genuinely make you happy. They can be big or small, from enjoying a cup of tea in the morning to dancing to your favorite song.

_____

_____

_____

_____

Now, take a look at your daily schedule. Find pockets of time, even if they're brief, to engage in these activities. Make a commitment to yourself to do at least one of these things today.

Step 2: Building Mastery

Write down something you want to accomplish today. It could be as simple as making your bed or as challenging as starting a new hobby. Make sure it's something you can realistically achieve today.

_____

_____

_____

_____

Now, break that goal into smaller, manageable steps. If it's starting a new hobby, the first step might be researching what supplies you need or finding a beginner's tutorial online.

_____

_____

_____

_____

Find time in your day to work on this goal. Even if it's just 15 minutes, it's a step toward building mastery and regaining control. At the end of your day, reflect here about how you feel about your progress. Did this task make you smile? Did you feel relaxed or happy? What emotions surfaced?

_____

_____

_____

_____

Step 3: Coping Ahead

1. **Identify Potential Triggers:** Think about situations or events that usually trigger overwhelming emotions for you. It could be a stressful meeting, a family gathering, or a particular person.

2. **Develop Coping Strategies:** For each identified trigger, write down a coping strategy. For instance, if family gatherings trigger anxiety, your coping strategy might involve taking short breaks to breathe deeply or engage in grounding exercises.

Step 4: PLEASE

Assess how you're doing in the PLEASE department today. Are you feeling physically well? Are you maintaining a balanced diet? Have you been avoiding unhealthy substances? Are you getting enough sleep? Have you incorporated some form of exercise into your day? Make any necessary adjustments accordingly.

_____

_____

_____

_____

Step 5: Focusing on Small Goals

Create a short to-do list for today. Include small tasks that contribute to your larger goals or simply help you stay organized. Cross them off as you complete them.

_____

_____

_____

_____

By following your personalized ABC PLEASE Daily Plan, you'll be actively working toward managing your overwhelming emotions. Remember, it's okay to start small and gradually build up. Over time, these practices will become a natural part of your routine, and you'll find yourself better equipped to handle difficult emotions.

Feel free to come back to this exercise every day to adjust and refine your plan as needed. You can also start a separate journal with an ABC PLEASE plan that you can fill in every day. You've got this, and I'm here cheering you on every step of the way!

How to Use Opposite Actions

Imagine your emotions as a powerful force guiding your actions. Sometimes, these emotions can push us toward decisions we'd rather not make. In these moments, emotions tend to overpower our logical thinking. This is where opposite action, a valuable DBT skill, comes into play.

Let's break it down: When you're in the grip of a strong emotion, it often compels you to act in a specific way. However, instead of giving in to these emotions, opposite action encourages you to do the exact opposite.

Here's an example: Imagine you've just gone through a breakup, and you're overwhelmed with sadness. Your emotions might be urging you to stay home, away from all the reminders of your relationship. But with opposite action, you'd choose a different path. In this case, you might tell yourself to get out and do something positive, like going for a jog or seeing a movie with a friend.

Opposite action doesn't mean ignoring or suppressing your emotions; it's about recognizing and acknowledging your feelings. This emotional awareness is essential for implementing opposite action effectively.

Instead of letting your emotions dictate your actions, you create a space between your emotions and your choices.

Can Emotions Control Your Actions?

Absolutely, emotions can influence your decisions. Opposite action helps you regain control. Often, people allow emotions like anger, sadness, or fear to hijack their logical thinking, leading to potentially life-altering choices. But here's the truth: You have the power to choose not to act solely based on your feelings. You can opt for a different course of action.

Like any skill, learning opposite action takes practice. Taking some time to review situations where opposite action worked or didn't is helpful. This reflection helps you understand what happened and refine your skills.

Remember, you're a human being with emotions, but that doesn't mean your emotions must always dictate your actions. By learning and practicing DBT skills like opposite action, you can make different choices and regain control over your life.

EXERCISE 1: Identifying and Labeling Your Emotions

Take a moment to sit quietly and focus on how you're feeling right now.

Write down the emotions you're experiencing. Be as specific as possible. Instead of just 'sad,' you might write "feeling overwhelmed and hopeless."

_____

_____

_____

_____

Now, let's rate the intensity of each emotion on a scale from 0 to 100, with 0 being no intensity and 100 being extremely intense.

_____

_____

_____

_____

Once you've identified your emotions, it's time to check if they fit the facts of the situation. Our emotions can sometimes be like unreliable weather forecasts, and DBT encourages us to fact-check them. Write down that same emotion and check if you feel the reaction fits.

_____

_____

_____

_____

EXERCISE 2: Fact-Checking Your Emotions

Pick one of the intense emotions you've identified. Write it below.

_____

_____

_____

_____

Now, ask yourself, "What is the evidence for this emotion? Does it fit the facts of the situation?"

Write down the evidence that supports this emotion and any evidence that contradicts it.

_____

_____

_____

_____

Now, let's talk about the magic of opposite action. Sometimes, our emotions don't fit the facts, or they might be ineffective in helping us achieve our goals. Opposite action is about consciously acting opposite to our urges when our emotions are pushing us in unhelpful directions. Write down what opposite action may help in this situation.

_____

_____

_____

_____

EXERCISE 3: Using Opposite Action

Write down an emotion you've identified that you'd like to change.

_____

_____

_____

_____

Think about an action that would be the opposite of what you feel like doing based on that emotion.

Write down the opposite action and make a commitment to take that action, even if it feels challenging.

_____

_____

_____

_____

Lastly, let's shift our focus to the positive side of life. It's easy to get caught up in negative emotions, but there are positive events happening around us too. Write down these moments to help counterbalance unwanted emotions.

_____

_____

_____

_____

EXERCISE 4: Focusing on Positive Events

Jot down at least three positive events or experiences from your day, no matter how small they may seem.

_____

_____

_____

_____

Write down how these positive events made you feel and the impact they had on your day.

_____

_____

_____

_____

Try doing this once a day for a week and over time, create a list of positive events that you can revisit during challenging times to help change your emotional state.

_____

_____

_____

_____

Remember, changing unwanted emotions takes practice and patience. Be gentle with yourself throughout this process. And if you ever feel overwhelmed, don't hesitate to reach out for support from those you trust.

Problem Solving

It's time to explore one of the most practical skills you'll learn in DBT: Problem Solving. It's one of the best tools you can have in your toolbox for dealing with life's challenges.

Life is always unpredictable and we find ourselves in situations we wish we could change. This is where problem-solving comes to the rescue. It's all about tackling problems head-on, making things better, and regaining control over our lives.

The Steps to Effective Problem Solving

#1: Recognize the Problem

The first step is realizing that you have a problem on your hands. Sometimes, we're so caught up in our daily hustle that we don't pause to identify issues. So, take a deep breath, pause, and recognize that something needs your attention. Write it below.

_____

_____

_____

#2: Define the Problem in Detail

Once you've spotted the problem, let's get specific: What's the situation? Who's involved? What's going wrong, or what's missing? Where and when did it happen? Think about how it affects you, what you do in response, and what you want to change. The more details, the better.

_____

_____

_____

#3: Connect It to Your Goals

If the problem doesn't mess with your goals, it might not be yours to solve. So, write down how this problem interferes with what you want to achieve. This step helps you clarify if it's worth your energy.

_____

_____

_____

_____

#4: Explore Your Options

To avoid falling into the trap of black-and-white thinking, brainstorm at least three possible solutions. Get creative! More options mean a higher chance of success.

_____

_____

_____

_____

_____

#5: Consider the Consequences

Look at each option carefully. What could happen if you choose each one? Sometimes, it helps to gather more information to make informed decisions.

_____

_____

_____

_____

_____

#6: Plan Your Steps

Once you've picked an option, outline the steps needed to put your solution into action. Make a schedule for when and how you'll take these steps.

_____

_____

_____

_____

_____

#7: Evaluate the Results

You've taken action, and now it's time to see how the situation worked out. If you've successfully resolved the problem, pat yourself on the back! You've just shown off your problem-solving superpowers. But if problem solving didn't quite work, don't sweat it. Learn from the experience, go back to step 4, and keep refining your approach until you nail it. Write down three more possible solutions you could have used.

_____

_____

_____

_____

_____

Remember, problem-solving is a skill that gets better with practice. Be patient with yourself and stay motivated.

Five Options For Solving Any Problem

I would also like to review five options for solving any problem:

#1: Find a solution to the problem or make a change.

When we're faced with a problem, we need to do something about it. That means trying to figure out what's going wrong and taking action to fix it. So, we need to identify the problem. Once we've got a handle on what's going on, we need to ask ourselves a simple question: Can I do something to change or improve this situation? If the answer is yes, then it's a good idea to give it a shot. For example, let's say we're having issues with our partner. We might not be able to change them, but we can definitely change how we talk to them or interact with them. By improving how we communicate, we create an opportunity to work together and find solutions to our problems. It's all about taking practical steps to make things better.

#2: Change how you think or feel about the problem.

Sometimes when we're dealing with a problem, it's not just about fixing the situation itself; it's also about looking at how we think and feel about the problem. One way to do this is by using a few strategies. First, we can check the facts, like making sure we have the right information about what's going on. Then, we can try thinking dialectically, which means considering different viewpoints and finding some middle ground. And sometimes, we can act in ways that go against our usual reactions to see if it changes how we see things. Now, here's the interesting part. There are times when we can't change the situation to our liking, or maybe we're just not ready to take action. In those cases, we can choose to change our perspective instead. What does that mean? Well, it's about finding a way to go through a tough situation without making it worse and maybe even using it to become a stronger person on the inside. For example, let's say we're facing a challenge. Instead of trying to change the challenge itself, we focus on developing something inside us, like understanding, wisdom, or compassion. It's like using a tough situation as a kind of 'fertilizer' to help our personal or spiritual growth. So, it's not just about changing the world around us; it's also about changing how we see and grow from the challenges life throws our way.

#3: Accept the problem.

Alright, let's talk about how we can deal with a problem when it feels like there's no practical way to fix it, or maybe we're just not ready to make a change yet. One way to approach this is through something called "radical acceptance." Radical acceptance is like saying, "Okay, this is how things are right now, and I'm going to accept it without fighting it." It's the opposite of resisting or struggling against a tough situation.

Think of it like this: **Pain (how hard or painful the situation is) x Resistance (how much we fight against it) = Suffering (how much we end up hurting)**

When we practice radical acceptance, we're basically reducing the 'Resistance' part of the equation. By not constantly struggling against reality, we can actually lessen our suffering. For example, let's say your partner has a personality trait that drives you a bit crazy. Instead of hoping they'll change (which might not happen), you can accept that this is just part of who they are, and it's okay. So, radical acceptance is like letting go of the fight with reality and finding a way to make peace with it. It's a way to reduce unnecessary suffering when we can't change things immediately.

Stay Miserable

You can decide not to do anything to make your life or situation better. Instead, you might just stay stuck in feeling unhappy or uncomfortable.

Now, why would someone do this? Well, sometimes we're not ready to change things. We might not be prepared to see things differently, and we might not be able to accept the situation as it is. In those moments, it's okay to simply feel miserable. But here's the key: don't use it as a reason to be hard on yourself!

The important thing here is to stay aware. While you're feeling miserable, pay attention to *how* it feels. Does the situation stay the same, or does it maybe even get worse? How does it affect your thoughts and your actions?

Make Things Worse

There's one more choice we should talk about, even though it's not usually the best idea. Sometimes we all can do things that make the problem even worse or create even more, new problems.

Now, I have to be clear, this isn't a great option, but I mention it anyway so you're aware it exists. Most of the time, it's not what you want to do. Occasionally, you may choose this by accident, so I think it helps to be aware.

The most important thing is to pick the option that matches what you want to achieve and what you value. Think about the specific situation and what might happen if you choose each option. That way, you can make the best choice for you.

Perhaps the most profound scar left by my upbringing was the deep-seated belief that I was "too much" for others. The love from my mother had been inconsistent, a rollercoaster of affection followed by harsh criticism, rejection, or hostility whenever I sought her attention. I learned that expressing my emotional needs was dangerous and would only lead to despair and humiliation.

The ABC PLEASE skills I learned through DBT became my lifeline. These skills allowed me to regulate my emotions, establish boundaries, and assert myself without succumbing to guilt or fear, even when control and a real sense of self felt impossible.

Key Takeaways Week 6

- Focus on adding more positive experiences to your life for better emotional well-being. Use a short exercise to find and include positive activities in your daily routine.
- Improve your skills and confidence in different areas of life. Try a short exercise to identify where you can enhance your skills.
- Prepare for tough situations and emotions in advance. Learn cope ahead techniques through a short exercise to handle upcoming stressors effectively.
- Take care of your physical health because it affects your emotions. This means eating well, getting enough sleep, staying active, and avoiding substances that change your mood.
- Understand and change emotions that don't fit the situation, hinder your goals, or are too intense.
- Alter your emotions by doing the opposite of what your initial urges suggest. Practice this technique through exercises like identifying emotions, fact-checking them, and challenging your urges.
- Start problem-solving by clearly understanding the issue. Use an exercise to define and grasp the problem better.
- Explore five approaches to address problems: solving the problem, changing how you think/feel about it, accepting it, staying unhappy, or making things worse.
- Determine your desired outcomes; it's vital for effective problem-solving. An exercise can help you with this.
- Recognize the importance of brainstorming potential solutions and use an exercise to generate ideas for solving problems.

These concepts and exercises are valuable tools for improving emotion regulation, managing stress, and addressing life's challenges effectively.

Practicing these skills can contribute to enhanced emotional well-being and overall resilience.

In this chapter, we've explored the powerful tools and techniques offered by DBT to construct your personal emotional regulation toolkit. We've delved into skills like Accumulating Positives, Building Mastery, Cope Ahead, and the importance of taking care of your physical well-being through the PLEASE acronym. You've learned to recognize and change unwanted emotions, using the transformative method of Opposite Action. Additionally, we've tackled the fundamentals of effective problem-solving, equipping you with the ability to define problems, set goals, brainstorm solutions, and choose the best course of action.

As we approach the final chapter of our journey through DBT, we'll explore the realm of interpersonal effectiveness. These skills will help you navigate and nurture your relationships, enhancing your ability to communicate, set boundaries, and maintain healthy connections with others. By combining the emotional regulation techniques you've acquired in this chapter with the interpersonal effectiveness skills in the next, you'll be better equipped to lead a more balanced, harmonious, and fulfilling life.

"

Communication is an art form that is crafted throughout our lives.

— ANONYMOUS

CHAPTER 7

Week 7 — Interpersonal Effectiveness

When it comes to improving our lives and finding that sweet spot of happiness and contentment, we're often bombarded with a sea of advice and self-help resources. It can feel overwhelming, like trying to choose the best ice cream flavor at an all-you-can-eat buffet. But if there's one skill set that stands out, it's our ability to communicate effectively and navigate the sometimes turbulent waters of human interaction.

Think about it: We encounter people from all walks of life, every single day. Some are family, some are friends, some are co-workers, and some are complete strangers. And while we don't need to become the life of the party or the world's greatest conversationalist for every encounter, we do need to find a way to connect, to communicate, and to get along reasonably well with others.

Now, here's where it gets even more interesting. For folks like us who may be grappling with mental health challenges like depression, anxiety, and/or BPD, the art of interpersonal effectiveness can feel like folding a fitted sheet. It's like trying to climb Mount Everest with a backpack full of rocks.

In this chapter, we're going to explore the fascinating world of interpersonal effectiveness. We'll dive headfirst into practical exercises and activities that you can implement right away.

So, get ready to boost your communication skills, strengthen your relationships, and enhance your overall quality of life. Whether you're a natural extrovert or an introverted soul, there's something here for everyone.

What Is Interpersonal Effectiveness?

Imagine a world where you can navigate your relationships with confidence, assertiveness, and empathy, all while respecting your own boundaries and values. That's exactly what Interpersonal Effectiveness is all about. It's the art of communicating and interacting with others in a way that's both respectful and assertive. This skill is like a magic key that can unlock better connections with friends, family, coworkers, and even strangers you meet on your journey.

Let's take a quick peek at some research and studies that back up the importance of interpersonal effectiveness in our lives.

Research published in the Journal of Positive Psychology found that individuals who practice effective interpersonal skills tend to have better relationships and, as a result, experience improved mental health (Ackerman, 2019). So, developing these skills can lead to a happier and more balanced life!

Another study from the Journal of Behavioral Medicine revealed that people who use interpersonal effectiveness techniques have lower levels of interpersonal conflict and stress (Wu et al., 2023). These findings highlight the real-world benefits of mastering this skill.

What Is Emotional Effectiveness?

So, what exactly is emotional effectiveness? Think of it as your secret weapon for navigating the often turbulent waters of your emotions and the emotions of those around you. It's like having a superpower that allows you to connect with people, solve problems, and achieve your goals, all while keeping your cool.

Let's dive into some practical tips and exercises to help you boost your emotional effectiveness:

Mindfulness of Current Emotion Exercise

Find a quiet, comfortable spot and take a few deep breaths.

Close your eyes and check in with yourself. Write down what emotions you are feeling right now. Be specific. Are you feeling angry, sad, happy, anxious? Rate the intensity of that emotion on a scale from 1 to 10.

_____

_____

_____

_____

Naming Emotions Exercise

Sometimes, just putting a name to your emotion can make it more manageable.

Here's a list of emotions. Try to identify the exact emotion you're experiencing:

- SAD, blue, depressed, down, unhappy
- ANXIOUS, worried, panicky, nervous, frightened

- ⟩ GUILTY, remorseful, bad, ashamed
- ⟩ INFERIOR, worthless, inadequate, defective, incompetent
- ⟩ LONELY, unloved, unwanted, rejected, alone, abandoned
- ⟩ EMBARRASSED, foolish, humiliated, self-conscious
- ⟩ HOPELESS, discouraged, pessimistic, despairing
- ⟩ FRUSTRATED, stuck, thwarted, defeated
- ⟩ ANGRY, mad, resentful, annoyed, irritated, upset, furious

Write down three words or phrases that describe your emotion.

_____

_____

_____

_____

Pros and Cons Exercise

Using the chart below, list the potential benefits and drawbacks of expressing your current emotion in the situation you're facing. This can help you make a more informed decision about how to respond.

Pros of Acting on Emotion	Cons of Acting on Emotion

Clarifying Your Priorities

In DBT therapy, we often talk about three essential priorities: objectives or goals, relationships, and self-respect. These priorities are like the pillars that hold up the structure of your life. Let's take a closer look at each one:

- ⊙ **Objectives and Goals:** This pillar is all about setting and achieving your personal and professional objectives. It's about realizing your dreams, achieving your goals, and making your aspirations come true.
- ⊙ **Relationship:** The relationship pillar emphasizes the importance of nurturing connections with others. It's about building and maintaining healthy, loving, and supportive relationships with friends, family, and partners.
- ⊙ **Self-respect:** The self-respect pillar is all about valuing and caring for yourself. It's about setting boundaries, practicing self-compassion, and maintaining your dignity and self-worth.

Now, let's look at an exercise to help you clarify your priorities between these three pillars in different situations.

Prioritizing Your Three Pillars Exercise

Imagine you're faced with three different scenarios. For each scenario, jot down which pillar (objective/goal, relationship, or self-respect) you believe should take precedence. Don't overthink it; trust your initial instincts.

Scenario 1: You've been working long hours at your job, and your boss asks you to stay late to complete a critical project. You already promised your friend you'd attend their important event tonight.

Priority:

- ⊙ Objective/Goal-
- ⊙ Relationship-
- ⊙ Self-Respect-

Scenario 2: Your partner is upset because you've been spending a lot of time on your personal project, neglecting quality time together. They want to have a heartfelt conversation about your relationship.

Priority:

- ⊙ Objective/Goal-
- ⊙ Relationship-
- ⊙ Self-Respect-

Scenario 3: You've been feeling overwhelmed and exhausted, and a friend invites you to a social gathering that you're not particularly excited about attending.

Priority:

- ⊙ Objective/Goal-
- ⊙ Relationship-
- ⊙ Self-Respect-

Remember, there are no right or wrong answers here. Your priorities may shift depending on the situation, and that's perfectly okay.

Take your time with this exercise and remember that your priorities can change over time. The important thing is to stay true to yourself and what feels right for you in each moment.

Levels of Intensity

Determining your intensity level is like having a volume knob for your emotions and interactions, and it is a vital skill to have. Growing up, and even into my late twenties, I'd often find myself unsure of how to respond to my mom's intense reactions and requests. I would swing from guilty and people-pleasing to angry and self-righteous. It became important to find DBT skills that could help.

The Emotion Thermometer Exercise

Imagine a thermometer with different levels of intensity, just like the one we use to measure temperature. On a piece of paper, create a similar scale from 1 to 10, with 1 being the coolest and 10 being the hottest. Now, let's practice:

- **Identify your emotion.** When you feel an emotion bubbling up, jot it down on the thermometer scale according to its intensity. For example, if you're mildly annoyed, mark it as a 3, but if you're furious, it might be a 9 or 10.
- **Rate your response:** Next, think about how you typically respond to this emotion. Do you scream when you're angry, or do you calmly express your feelings? Mark your typical response on the scale.
- **Assess effectiveness.** Reflect on whether your typical response matches the intensity of your emotion. Is it an overreaction, underreaction, or just right? This exercise helps you become more aware of your emotional responses.

The 10-Second Rule Exercise

Whenever you're about to respond to something or make a request, pause for a moment. Take a deep breath and count to 10 in your head. Use this time to assess the intensity of your emotions and whether they match the situation. After those 10 seconds, decide how to respond appropriately.

Studies have shown that individuals who practice emotional regulation techniques, such as determining their intensity level, experience improved interpersonal relationships and reduced emotional distress (Lavender et al. 2016). DBT, in particular, has been found effective in helping individuals with BPD manage their emotional intensity (Chapman, 2006).

So, learning to determine your intensity level is a skill that can save you from unnecessary stress and conflicts. Practice these exercises, and over time, you'll become a pro at managing your emotional thermostat. Remember, it's all about finding that sweet spot of just-right intensity.

DEAR MAN

One of the awesome tools we have yet to explore is DEAR MAN, and it's like your trusty sidekick when it comes to achieving your goals in conversations. Let's break it down:

- **Describe:** Start by telling the other person exactly what's happening. Stick to the facts and avoid adding judgments or emotions.
- **Express:** Let your feelings out in the open using 'I' statements. This is your chance to honestly share how you feel without blaming anyone.

- **Assert:** Get straight to the point and clearly state what you want or need. Be direct and specific so there's no room for confusion.
- **Reinforce:** Explain why your request is a good idea. How will it benefit both parties? And if there's a reward involved, make sure to follow through. It makes people more likely to say 'yes'.
- **Mindful:** Stay laser-focused on your goal. Don't let yourself get sidetracked or carried away by the conversation. If necessary, calmly repeat your point like a broken record.
- **Appear Confident:** Show confidence through your tone of voice and body language. Stand tall, maintain eye contact, and speak with certainty.
- **Negotiate:** Be flexible and open to finding middle ground. Sometimes, you might need to offer alternatives or scale back your request to reach a solution that works for everyone.

Now, when using DEAR MAN, you need to have a clear goal in mind. Think about what you really want or need, considering your priorities and time constraints. Don't hesitate to ask for help when necessary, even if you're feeling a bit overwhelmed. DEAR MAN can also be your go-to tool for seeking assistance.

Here are some common goals you might have when using DEAR MAN:

- Standing up for your rights so they're taken seriously.
- Requesting something from others effectively.
- Politely refusing unwanted or unreasonable requests and making your decision stick.
- Resolving conflicts with others.
- Ensuring your opinion or point of view is heard and valued.

It's important to note that even though these skills are incredibly helpful, there's no magic formula for always getting what you want from others. Some situations might not budge, no matter how skilled you are.

If the conversation turns toxic, you might even need to do a DEAR MAN within the original DEAR MAN to address the new situation. Describe the issue, express how it's making you feel, assert what you want to change, reinforce your point, and do it all confidently and mindfully.

DEAR MAN Exercise: Making a Plan

I know each and every time I had to confront my mother about anything, my anxiety grew. I found it helpful to make a plan ahead of time. Below, let's walk through a plan using the DEAR MAN method.

Write down your current situation. What do you want to tell the person? Remember to stick to the facts.

_____

_____

_____

_____

What feelings and opinions regarding the situation do you want to make sure they understand? We always want to believe they have no idea how hard it is for you to ask for what you want.

_____

_____

_____

_____

Write down exactly how you will assert yourself by asking for what you need or saying 'no' to a request clearly. What will you say?

_____

_____

_____

_____

Write down what the person will gain from this. What are the positive effects of getting what you want or need? How will *they* feel good for doing what you want?

_____

_____

_____

_____

Being prepared ahead of time can help you be focused on your objective. Remember to be confident, maintaining eye contact. Be willing to offer and ask for alternative solutions to the problem. Write down what you are willing to settle for or give up in order to gain what you want in the situation.

_____

_____

_____

_____

In this chapter, we learned that being awesome in relationships isn't just about being polite; it's about gracefully and assertively navigating the wild world of human connections. Plus, we unlocked the superpower of emotional effectiveness: how to handle our feelings like champs!

Remember, it's not about squishing your feelings into a tiny box. It's about letting them out in the right way, like confetti at a celebration.

We talked about the three amigos of every interpersonal showdown: your goal, your relationship, and your self-respect. Sometimes, these buddies don't play nice together, and that's when things get tricky.

We gave you an exercise to help you figure out your priority in different situations. Think of it as your emotional GPS, showing you the way when things get a bit wild.

In the heat of the moment, it's easy to go full-on fire-breathing dragon mode. We chatted about dialing up or down the intensity when you're dealing with stuff. Sometimes, you need a gentle breeze, and sometimes you need a hurricane.

We unveiled the DEAR MAN toolkit! This is your secret weapon for getting what you want while keeping your relationships sparkling. A quick recap:

- **D**: Describe the issues objectively.
- **E**: Express your feelings and opinions.
- **A**: Assert your needs clearly.
- **R**: Reinforce your point with benefits or consequences.

We gave you the homework to think of real-life examples for each one—soon you'll be doing them without even thinking!

And don't forget about **MAN**:

- **M**: Stay Mindful of your objectives and priorities.
- **A**: Appear confident (think superhero cape!) in your communication.
- **N**: Be ready to Negotiate like a pro when needed.

Key Takeaways Week 7

- Interpersonal Effectiveness is all about handling your relationships effectively while respecting both yourself and others.
- Emotional Effectiveness is understanding and managing *your* emotions in your interactions with others.
- Learn to gauge the appropriate level of intensity when responding to something or making a request.
- DEAR MAN is a powerful tool for getting what you want.
- Explore examples of each element:
  - Describe: Clearly state the facts.
  - Express: Share your feelings and opinions.
  - Assert: Make your needs known.
  - Reinforce: Offer incentives or reasons for the other person to comply.
- **MAN stands for:**
  - Mindful: Stay present and attentive during the interaction.
  - Appear Confident: Project confidence, even if you don't feel it.
  - Negotiate: Be open to finding solutions that work for both parties.
- Engage in short exercises to practice these elements and tie them all together for effective communication.

In the next chapter, we're diving into validation, gentle communication skills and some hands-on exercises. Your path to being a more confident social communicator is just beginning, so keep your motivation high, and let's jump into those exercises!

66

Empathy is a strange and powerful thing. There is no script. There is no right way or wrong way to do it. It's simply listening, holding space, withholding judgment, emotionally connecting, and communicating that incredibly healing message of "You're not alone."

-BRENÉ BROWN

99

CHAPTER 8

Understanding the Power of Validation

In this chapter, we're going to explore Martha Linehan's six levels of validation and how they can transform your relationships, as well as the powerful GIVE and FAST skills that will help you navigate through life's challenges with self-respect and effectiveness.

The Six Levels of Validation

Marsha Linehan, the brilliant mind behind DBT, has emphasized the immense importance of validation. In fact, she believes it's impossible to overstate its significance. Whether you're trying to support someone you care about or learning to manage your own emotions, validation is your secret superpower.

Linehan suggests using the highest level of validation possible in any given situation. Let's break down the six levels of validation to help you understand how to harness this incredible skill (*Understanding the Levels of Validation*, 2012).

Level One: Being Present

Being present is about giving your full, undivided attention to someone. It's holding a friend's hand during a painful medical treatment, listening intently to a child's description of their day, or being there for someone when they're in need. When you're present, you're truly engaged, both with others and with yourself. It means acknowledging your internal experience without trying to escape or avoid it, even if it's uncomfortable. Remember, sitting with intense emotions is a brave act.

Workbook Exercise

Practice being present with someone you care about. Listen without judgment and notice how it makes them feel. Also, try being present for yourself. Sit quietly, acknowledge your emotions, and see how they affect your own mental state. Feel free to jot down any emotions that come through.

Level Two: Accurate Reflection

Accurate reflection is like holding up a mirror to someone's feelings. It involves summarizing what you've heard from them or even summarizing your own emotions. But remember, it's not about being artificial or critical; it's about genuinely understanding and not judging. Accurate reflection can help emotionally sensitive individuals untangle their thoughts from their emotions.

Workbook Exercise

Try accurately reflecting on your own feelings or those of a friend. Write down a recent emotional experience and then summarize it as objectively as possible.

_____

_____

_____

_____

_____

Level Three: Reading a Person's Behavior

Some folks struggle to identify their own emotions due to past experiences or learned behavior. This is where you come in. Observe their emotional state and label or guess their feelings. It's okay to be wrong; only they know how they truly feel.

Workbook Exercise

Practice reading someone's behavior and guessing their emotions. It could be a friend, family member, or even a coworker. Write down your observations and guesses, and see how they respond when you validate their feelings.

_____

_____

_____

_____

_____

Level Four: Understanding the Person's History and Biology

Our past experiences and biology shape our emotional reactions. Understanding this can deepen your level of validation. For instance, if your friend had a traumatic experience with a dog, it makes sense that they might be uncomfortable around one.

Workbook Exercise

Reflect on your own emotional reactions in the context of your past experiences and biology. Write down a situation where your past influenced your feelings, and consider how understanding that can help you validate yourself.

_____

_____

_____

_____

_____

Level Five: Normalizing Emotional Reactions

Sometimes, just knowing that our emotions are normal can be incredibly reassuring. Emotionally sensitive individuals often feel like they're "too much," but realizing that anyone would feel a certain way in a given situation can be liberating.

Workbook Exercise

Identify a situation in which you or someone you know had an emotional reaction. Explain why this reaction is perfectly normal. Write down how this knowledge helps you or them feel validated.

_____

_____

_____

_____

_____

Level Six: Radical Genuineness

At the highest level of validation, there's radical genuineness. This is when you deeply understand someone's emotions because you've experienced something similar. You're on the same emotional wavelength. Sharing your own experience as equals can strengthen relationships and enhance emotional management.

Workbook Exercise

Reflect on a time when you experienced radical genuineness from someone. How did it make you feel? How did it affect your connection with that person? How can you use this level of validation in your own relationships?

_____

_____

_____

_____

_____

Understanding and practicing these levels of validation can work wonders in your life and in the lives of those around you. Validation strengthens bonds and empowers us to manage our emotions effectively.

GIVE Skills

GIVE skills are like the Swiss Army knife of effective communication. They are especially handy when dealing with individuals who may be emotionally sensitive or challenging to connect with. Let's break them down one by one:

Gentle (Be)

Think of being gentle as having a soft touch in your interactions. Imagine you're holding a delicate butterfly in your hand—you wouldn't want to crush it, right? Similarly, be mindful of your tone, body language, and words. Avoid being harsh, judgmental, or confrontational. Instead, opt for kindness and patience.

Exercise: The Gentle Check-in

Take a moment to reflect on a recent interaction that might not have gone so well. Now, rewrite your response with a gentle tone and demeanor. What changes did you make? How does it feel different? Write your answers below.

_____

_____

_____

_____

_____

Interested (Act)

Showing genuine interest in others can work wonders in building rapport. When you actively engage with someone, it conveys that you value their thoughts and feelings. Be an attentive listener, ask open-ended questions, and show curiosity about their world.

Exercise: The Curiosity Challenge

Practice active listening with a friend or family member. Ask them about something you've never discussed before and genuinely listen to their response. How did their body language change? Did the conversation flow more smoothly? Share your observations below.

_____

_____

_____

_____

Validate (Mentioned Above)

Validation is like giving someone an emotional high-five. It's acknowledging their feelings without judgment. It doesn't mean you have to agree with everything they say, but you're letting them know their emotions are valid.

Exercise: The Validation Voyage

Think of a recent situation where someone shared their feelings with you. Write down how you validated their emotions. How did it make them feel? How did it make you feel? Share your insights below.

_____

_____

_____

_____

Easy Manner (Use An)

An easy manner is all about staying calm and composed, even in the face of chaos. Avoid getting defensive or aggressive. Instead, maintain your emotional balance and create a safe space for the other person to express themselves.

Exercise: The Zen Zone

Recall a time when you stayed calm in a difficult conversation. What techniques did you use to keep your cool? How did it affect the outcome? Share your strategies below.

_____

_____

_____

_____

_____

Did you know that research has shown that using GIVE skills can lead to improved relationships and decreased conflicts? It's true! A study found that individuals who underwent DBT training, including GIVE skills, experienced reduced anger and hostility in their relationships (Wu et al., 2023).

Morgan's Story

I'll tell you about how I used the GIVE skills with my friend Morgan when she called me to vent a few months ago. Morgan's voice sounded shaky and tired as she spilled her work problems to me- she was dealing with tons of tasks, coworkers making demands, and a boss who was always dissatisfied. You could feel the stress in Morgan's voice, and it seemed like tears were about to burst out.

My first impulse was to jump in with a bunch of solutions. I wanted to tell Morgan exactly what she should do to fix her work issues. After all, I really cared about Morgan and my first thought was that giving quick fixes would make everything better. But then I remembered the magic of GIVE skills.

Instead of bombarding Morgan with advice, I took a deep breath and reminded myself to be gentle, interested, validating, and keep things easygoing. So, I started by just listening carefully to Morgan's story. I didn't interrupt, and I gave her my complete attention. You could hear the relief in Morgan's voice when she realized that someone truly wanted to hear about her troubles.

As Morgan continued to pour her heart out, I knew it was time to validate her feelings. I told her, "Morgan, it sounds like you're going through a really tough time at work. It's totally understandable that you're feeling overwhelmed and frustrated. Anyone in your shoes would feel the same way." It was like a weight lifted from Morgan's voice when she heard those words.

Throughout our chat, I made sure to stay calm and relaxed, even though Morgan's emotions were running high. I didn't get upset along with her as she shared her problems with her colleagues and her boss. Instead, I focused on supporting Morgan by creating a safe space for her to let it all out.

By the time our conversation wrapped up, Morgan's tone had changed from despair to relief. She thanked me for being there and truly listening. Morgan admitted she'd been keeping her frustrations bottled up, worried that no one would understand. But thanks to the power of GIVE skills, she felt heard and supported.

In the following weeks, Morgan and I grew even closer. Our friendship deepened because Morgan knew that she could always come to me to express her feelings without judgment. She often says how grateful she was for our talk that day.

This story shows how using GIVE skills can transform not just individual conversations but also the dynamics of a friendship. By choosing kindness over advice, we build a stronger bond based on trust and understanding. Sometimes, the best way to support someone is to simply be a good listener, offer validation, and stay calm.

Remember, creating connections with others is all about compassion and understanding. These skills are not just tools; they're the building blocks of healthy relationships.

FAST Skills

Self-respect is the foundation of all healthy relationships, starting with the one you have with yourself. When you respect yourself, you're more likely to set boundaries, communicate effectively, and make decisions that align with your values.

FAST skills are all about maintaining self-respect while interacting with others, especially in situations where you might be tempted to give in or compromise too much. FAST is an acronym for: be **F**air, no **A**pologies, **S**tick to values, be **T**ruthful. Let's break down each component (Linehan, 2023).

Be Fair

Start by identifying a recent situation where you felt your self-respect was compromised. Write it down and describe what happened.

Now, ask the questions:

- ⊙ Am I being fair to myself?
- ⊙ Did I clearly express what I need and what I am feeling?
- ⊙ Did I listen to the other person's perspective?

Workbook Exercise

Fill in the blanks below with your thoughts and feelings from the situation:

In this situation, I believe I was fair to myself by _____. However, I could have improved my fairness by _____. Next time, I will make sure to _____.

No Apologies

Think about a time when you apologized but you didn't need to. Write down the situation and what you apologized for.

Now, ask yourself:

- ⊙ Why did I apologize?
- ⊙ What were my true feelings in that moment?
- ⊙ How could I have expressed my feelings without apologizing unnecessarily?

Workbook Exercise

Complete this sentence based on the situation you described:

In that situation, I apologized for _____. Looking back, I realize I didn't need to apologize because _____. Next time, I will express my feelings by _____.

Stick to Your Values

Take a moment to reflect on your core values. Write down the top three values that are important to you.

Now, ask yourself:

- Have I compromised my values in any recent interactions?
- How did it make me feel?
- What can I do to stick to my values while interacting with others?

Workbook Activity

Write down your top three values and brainstorm ways to uphold them in your daily interactions.

_____

_____

_____

_____

_____

_____

_____

_____

_____

Be Truthful

Think about a situation where you weren't entirely truthful. Write it down and describe why you chose not to be honest.

Now, ask yourself:

- What was my fear or motivation for not telling the truth?
- How would being truthful have improved the situation?
- What can I do to practice honesty in similar situations in the future?

Workbook Exercise

Reflect on the situation and complete this sentence:

In that situation, I was not entirely truthful because _____. In the future, I will be more honest by _____.

Studies have shown that incorporating FAST skills into your interactions can lead to improved self-esteem, healthier relationships, and reduced emotional distress (Flynn et al., 2019).

Many times throughout my young adult life, I found myself in situations where I felt pressured to agree to something my mom wanted me to do but that I didn't want to do. Instead of being truthful about my feelings, I apologized and gave in. It left me feeling resentful and like I had betrayed my own values. But after learning about FAST skills, I realized I could have handled the situation differently, sticking to my values and maintaining my self-respect.

Combining the Skills

My mother would constantly interrupt me during conversations, making it difficult for me to express my emotions or thoughts. Here's how I would combine DEAR MAN, GIVE, and FAST to address the issue:

1. **Describe:** Start by calmly describing the situation. "I've noticed that during our conversations, I often get interrupted when I'm trying to share my thoughts."

2. **Express:** Express your feelings and thoughts using 'I' statements. "I feel frustrated and unheard when this happens, and I believe it's essential for me to have a chance to speak."

3. **Assert:** Clearly state what you want or need. "I would appreciate it if you could let me finish speaking before responding."

4. **Reinforce:** Reinforce why your request is essential. "This will create a more respectful relationship for us."

5. **Mindful:** Stay focused on the issue at hand and avoid getting emotional or sidetracked.

6. **Appear Confident:** Maintain eye contact, use a calm tone, and practice good posture.

7. **Negotiate:** Be open to a discussion about how to improve communication between both of you.

Additionally, remember to be Gentle, Interested, Validate, and maintain an Easy Manner to foster a positive relationship. Be Fair in your request, avoid unnecessary Apologies, Stick to your Values, and always be Truthful to maintain your self-respect.

Let's add some extra context. Studies have shown that using a combination of DEAR MAN, GIVE, and FAST skills can significantly improve interpersonal effectiveness and reduce conflicts in various settings (May et al., 2016).

Combining DEAR MAN, GIVE, and FAST is a great tool to have for effective communication and maintaining healthy relationships. Practice these skills regularly and watch how they transform your interactions with others. I have left a space below for you to practice this skill. Take a moment and think of a situation where you want to find your voice, where you want to speak up. Jot down what you would say. Take your time and lean into the skills laid out above.

_____

_____

_____

_____

_____

In this chapter, we jumped into crucial skills and techniques that can revolutionize your relationships and communication style. Here's a quick recap:

- ⊙ **Validation vs. Invalidation:** Martha Linehan's six levels of validation are your guide to forming stronger connections with others. These levels include paying attention, reflecting back, understanding context and history, acknowledging validity, and treating people with respect. Validation is the superpower behind effective communication.
- ⊙ **GIVE skills:** These four valuable skills are your tools for nurturing and preserving relationships. Try the GIVE exercise to apply these skills and see your connections thrive.

- ⊙ **FAST skills (for self-respect):** As you navigate interpersonal effectiveness, safeguard your self-respect. The FAST exercise strengthens your self-respect and reinforces your convictions.
- ⊙ **Combining DEAR MAN, GIVE, and FAST:** The real magic happens when you combine these skills. DEAR MAN empowers assertive communication, GIVE fosters positive relationships, and FAST preserves your self-respect. Together, they're your ticket to navigate even the trickiest interpersonal situations.

As you embark upon mastering these skills, remember that practice is key. Real-life situations will be your greatest teachers. Keep your goals clear, your words kind, and your self-respect intact. Also, forgive yourself for times when you slip up and don't use these skills. Just try again next time.

You now possess the tools to build stronger connections, gracefully resolve conflicts, and maintain your self-worth in any interaction. With DEAR MAN, GIVE, FAST, and the art of validation, you're on your way to becoming an interpersonal effectiveness expert.

Key Takeaways Week 8

- ⊙ Understand the importance of validation in your interactions.
- ⊙ Martha Linehan's 6 levels of Validation:
  - Pay Attention: Give your full attention to the other person.
  - Reflect Back: Repeat or paraphrase what the other person has said to show you're listening.
  - Read Minds: Try to understand the other person's thoughts and feelings.

- Understand based on Personal Context/History: Consider the person's background and experiences.
- Acknowledge What's Valid: Recognize the legitimacy of the other person's emotions and perspective.
- Show Equality: Treat the other person with respect and as an equal.

◯ Explore ways to practice each type of validation to improve your relationships.

◯ Learn the GIVE skills for effective communication:
- Be Gentle: Approach interactions with kindness and respect.
- Act Interested: Show genuine interest in what the other person is saying.
- Validate: Acknowledge the other person's feelings and experiences.
- Use an Easy Manner: Keep the conversation light and relaxed.

◯ Self-respect is crucial in interpersonal interactions.

◯ FAST stands for:
- Be Fair: Treat yourself and others with fairness and equity.
- No Apologies: Avoid apologizing excessively or unnecessarily.
- Stick to Your Values: Maintain your personal values and boundaries.
- Be Truthful: Be honest and sincere in your interactions.

◯ Combine the DEAR MAN, GIVE, and FAST skills to create a comprehensive approach to effective communication and interpersonal effectiveness.

◯ By using these skills in synergy, you can navigate various situations and relationships with confidence and respect.

66

In the space between stimulus and response, there is a space. In that space is our power to choose our response. In our response lies our growth and our freedom.

— VIKTOR E. FRANKL

CONCLUSION

Continuing the Journey

We've journeyed together through the pages of this workbook, exploring the intricate and empowering terrain of DBT. As we come to the conclusion of this incredible expedition, it's a perfect time to pause and reflect on the profound insights we've gathered along the way.

Mindfulness: Our voyage through the world of mindfulness has shown us that it goes beyond merely being present in the moment; it's about immersing ourselves fully in the here and now, free from judgment. By embracing mindfulness, you've unlocked the power to enhance emotional regulation, discern judgmental thoughts, and make wiser, more intentional decisions in your life.

Wise Mind: The concept of finding the delicate balance between emotion mind and reasonable mind has been a guiding North star on our journey. Wise mind exercises have lit up the path, demonstrating that even in the face of life's most challenging situations, you can pause, breathe, and tap into your inner wisdom for guidance.

Distress Tolerance: Our discussions about distress tolerance have underscored the significance of not only managing but also surviving emotional distress. We've learned that acceptance is the crucial first step, and together, we've delved into a treasure trove of tools like TIP Skills, the STOP method, and the creation of a personalized Distress Tolerance Kit.

Radical Acceptance: We've embarked on the profound practice of embracing reality without judgment. We've seen how resistance to acceptance can be overcome through persistence and practice, paving the way for profound healing and unprecedented personal growth.

Emotions: Our expedition has brought us face-to-face with the profound truth that all emotions, without exception, are natural and valid. By learning to understand and work with your emotions, you've taken monumental steps toward achieving emotional well-being.

Problem-solving: We've equipped ourselves with a diverse toolkit for effective problem-solving, from the meticulous process of defining issues to the creative art of brainstorming solutions and the clarity of determining desired outcomes.

Interpersonal Effectiveness: Our exploration of interpersonal effectiveness has illuminated the importance of clarifying priorities and skillfully navigating the intricate web of human relationships. The DEAR MAN, GIVE, and FAST skills have been our trusted companions on this leg of the journey.

Combining Skills: Together, we've witnessed how these skills can harmonize and intertwine into a holistic approach to managing emotions, relationships, and life's multifaceted challenges.

As we conclude this expedition through the pages of this workbook, it's important to remember that the path to mastering these skills is not always linear. In fact, many people, myself included, find themselves embarking on the DBT path more than once. With each round, we deepen our understanding and proficiency, nurturing the flame of hope and fostering personal growth.

This workbook is not just a one-time guide: It's your map and compass for life's twists and turns. Whenever you need a refresher or a dose of motivation, know that you can return to these pages. If you have filled up the pages provided, feel free to grab a journal or any notebook and repeat the exercises there. Your experiences are valid, and your emotions matter profoundly. By applying these DBT skills, you're taking significant strides toward creating a more fulfilling and balanced life.

Before we part ways on this incredible expedition, I'd like to ask one last favor: if you've found this workbook helpful, please consider leaving a review. Your feedback will serve as a beacon, making it easier for others who may be seeking this resource to find it and embark on their own transformative journey of self-discovery and growth.

Thank you for being a part of this wonderful time. You hold within you the power to transform your life, one mindful step at a time. Embrace it, my friend, and never stop growing.

Warmest Regards,

Anna

REFERENCES

Ackerman, C. (2019, June 19). *Interpersonal effectiveness: 9 worksheets & examples*. Positive Psychology. https://positivepsychology.com/interpersonal-effectiveness/

A.J. (2023, August 21). *90 top quotes from radical acceptance*. Elevate Society. https://elevatesociety.com/quotes-from-radical-acceptance/#:~:text=%22May%20I%20love%20and%20accept

BetterHelp Editorial Team. (2018, January 23). *Mothers with borderline personality disorder: How to cope*. Better Help. https://www.betterhelp.com/advice/teenagers/mothers-with-borderline-personality-disorder-common-symptoms-and-treatment/

Chapman, A. L. (2006). Dialectical behavior therapy: Current indications and unique elements. *Psychiatry* (Edgmont), *3*(9), 62–68. https://www.ncbi.nlm.nih.gov/pmc/articles/PMC2963469/

Charlie Health Editorial Team. (2023, April 29). *ACCEPTS: A useful DBT skill for stress*. Charlie Health. https://www.charliehealth.com/post/accepts-dbt-skill#:~:text=An%20ACCEPTS%20DBT%20worksheet%20is

Cherry, K. (2019). *Psychology and life quotes from Carl Rogers*. Verywell Mind. https://www.verywellmind.com/carl-rogers-quotes-2795693

Compitus, K. (2020, October 1). *What are distress tolerance skills? Your ultimate DBT toolkit*. Positive Psychology. https://positivepsychology.com/distress-tolerance-skills/

Cuncic, A. (2021, May 26). *What is radical acceptance?* Verywell Mind. https://www.verywellmind.com/what-is-radical-acceptance-5120614

Do we even need them? Your guide to understanding emotions. (2017, November 7). Sunrise Residential Treatment Center. https://sunrisertc.com/emotions-list/

Emeritus, P. (2019). *Marsha Linehan* . Washington.edu. https://depts.washington.edu/uwbrtc/our-team/marsha-linehan/

Emotional regulation quotes-Miya Yamanouchi. (2023). Goodreads. https://www.goodreads.com/quotes/tag/emotional-regulation

Flynn, D., Joyce, M., Spillane, A., Wrigley, C., Corcoran, P., Hayes, A., Flynn, M., Wyse, D., Corkery, B., & Mooney, B. (2019). Does an adapted dialectical behaviour therapy skills training programme result in positive outcomes for participants with a dual diagnosis? A mixed methods study. *Addiction Science & Clinical Practice, 14*(1). https://doi.org/10.1186/s13722-019-0156-2

Hanh, T. N. (2023, August 18). *Inspiring quotes to live by: Embracing DBT skills for personal growth and transformation.* Grouport Therapy. https://www.grouporttherapy.com/blog/dialectical-behavior-therapy-quotes

Inspiring quotes to live by: Embracing DBT skills for personal growth and transformation. (2023, August 18). Grouport Therapy. https://www.grouporttherapy.com/blog/dialectical-behavior-therapy-quotes#:~:text=Mindfulness%20Quotes&text=%22The%20present%20moment%20is%20filled

Kabat-Zinn, J. (2019). *What is mindfulness?* Greater Good. https://greatergood.berkeley.edu/topic/mindfulness/definition

Lavender, J. M., Tull, M. T., DiLillo, D., Messman-Moore, T., & Gratz, K. L. (2016). Development and validation of a state-based measure of emotion dysregulation. *Assessment, 24*(2), 197–209. https://doi.org/10.1177/1073191115601218

Linehan, M. (n.d.). *Problem solving skill*. Dialectical Behavior Therapy (DBT) Tools. https://dbt.tools/distress_tolerance/problem-solving.php

Linehan, M. (2023a). *FAST skill*. Dialectical Behavior Therapy (DBT) Tools. https://dbt.tools/interpersonal_effectiveness/fast.php#:~:text =The%20FAST%20skill%20is%20an

Lo, I. (2023, August 8). *I have a mother with borderline personality disorder*. Medium. https://imilo.medium.com/i-have-a-mother-with-borderline-personality-disorder-107f15dc7ea3

Lorandini, J. (2019, April 16). *Opposite action for overwhelming emotions: How to make it work for you*. Suffolk DBT. https://suffolkdbtjl.com/opposite-action/#:~:text=What%20Is%20Opposite%20Action%3F

Main, P. (2022, December 2). *Carl Rogers' theory*. Structural Learning. https://www.structural-learning.com/post/carl-rogers-theory#:~:text=According%20to%20Carl%20Rogers

May, J. M., Richardi, T. M., & Barth, K. S. (2016). Dialectical behavior therapy as treatment for borderline personality disorder. *Mental Health Clinician, 6*(2), 62–67. https://doi.org/10.9740/mhc.2016.03.62

Parent with borderline personality disorder: Healing from your trauma. (2023, August 1). Eggshell Therapy and Coaching. https://eggshelltherapy.com/bpdparent/

Rowen, K. (2022, May 31). *Half-Smiling & willing hands*. DBT Center of Orange County. https://www.dbtcenteroc.com/half-smiling-willing-hands/

Tull, M. (2013, July 30). *Distress tolerance in post traumatic stress disorder*. Verywell Mind. https://www.verywellmind.com/distress-tolerance-2797294

6 life changing skills to successfully manage your next emotional crisis. (2017, September 13). Sunrise Residential Treatment Center. https://sunrisertc.com/distress-tolerance-skills/

Understanding the levels of validation. (2012, February 5). Psych Central. https://psychcentral.com/blog/emotionally-sensitive/2012/02/understanding-the-levels-of-validation#7

Using ABC please to manage overwhelming emotions with DBT. (2023, August 18). Grouport Therapy. https://www.grouporttherapy.com/blog/abc-please-dbt#:~:text=ABC%20PLEASE%20is%20an%20acronym

Vaughan, S. (2023, September 18). *DBT distress tolerance skills: Tip skill, stop skill, and more.* Psychotherapy Academy. https://psychotherapyacademy.org/section/distress-tolerance-skills/

What skills: Observe, describe, participate. (2023, September 28). DBT Self Help. https://dbtselfhelp.com/dbt-skills-list/mindfulness/what-skills/

Wu, S.-I., Liu, S.-I., Wu, Y.-J., Huang, L.-L., Liu, T., Kao, K.-L., & Lee, Y.-H. (2023). The efficacy of applying the interpersonal effectiveness skills of dialectical behavior therapy into communication skills workshop for clinical nurses. *Heliyon*, *9*(3), e14066. https://doi.org/10.1016/j.heliyon.2023.e14066

CBT

WORKBOOK

—— FOR ——

ADULTS

*Harness the Power of Cognitive Behavioral Therapy
for Anxiety, Depression, and Self Esteem*

ANNA NIERLING

For there is nothing either good or bad, but thinking makes it so.

–SHAKESPEARE

Writing With Heart—What We Learn From Life's Challenges

Have you hit those parts in life that feel like a constant struggle, weighed down by the heavy burden of anxiety and depression? Do you often find yourself battling negative thoughts that seem to have taken control of your mind? You're not alone, and there is hope. I want to welcome you to this CBT Workbook, written by someone just like you, for you.

I'm Anna, and I've been on a lifelong journey through the intricate and often confusing landscape of mental health. My path was shaped by a childhood overshadowed by the difficult challenges of my parents' mental health struggles. My mother battled Borderline Personality Disorder (BPD), while my father grappled with schizophrenia. Growing up in this environment, I became intimately familiar with the complexities and fear that accompany mental health conditions.

My earliest memories are infused with moments of uncertainty and unpredictability. My mother's BPD cast a long shadow over our household, bringing with it erratic mood swings, intense fears of abandonment, and a constant sense of walking on eggshells. I watched her navigate the turbulent sea of emotions, often feeling helpless and bewildered by the emotional whirlwind that swirled around her. My father's schizophrenia added another layer of complexity to our lives. His struggles with reality, moodiness, hallucinations, and delusions created an environment that was, at times, surreal and frightening.

As a child, I yearned for stability and normalcy, but these remained elusive goals. The chaos and unpredictability of my home life took a toll on my own mental well-being. I began to grapple with my own demons—depression and anxiety that I couldn't fully comprehend or escape. It felt like a never-ending storm, and I desperately sought a lifeline.

My path through life's challenges didn't end with childhood. In fact, it was only the beginning. The wounds of my upbringing left their mark on my adult life. The scars of witnessing my parents' struggles and experiencing the emotional turbulence of my home environment ran deep. As I navigated my way into adulthood, those wounds continued to influence my thoughts, behaviors, and emotional well-being.

I carried with me a heavy burden of anxiety and depression, and I often felt like I was fighting an uphill battle against my own mind. It was a relentless struggle, and I knew I needed help. I became aware that we are all different and that therapy needs are different for different people and some techniques may work better at certain times in our lives. Dialetical Behavioral Therapy (DBT) helped my immediate pain and suffering, but I needed more. That's when I decided to dig deeper into Cognitive Behavioral Therapy (CBT). DBT – a form of CBT- helped significantly with my social and emotional healing, but I needed a different type of therapy to help understand and challenge my thinking patterns.

My experiences with my parents' mental health conditions and my own battles with depression and anxiety continue to fuel my passion for understanding and addressing mental health. I've dedicated myself to researching, learning, and sharing the insights and techniques that have transformed my life. We all deserve to understand ourselves and what kind of therapy works for us.

In this workbook, I'll not only guide you through the principles of CBT, but also draw from my personal journey to provide relatable and compassionate support.

In my quest for relief, I stumbled upon CBT—a powerful tool that changed my life—and now I want to share it with you. This workbook is designed to be accessible and simple for those who may not have access to a CBT therapist. It's packed with exercises and activities to guide you on your journey to healing.

I've been where you are. I've struggled with my own demons, and I've found solace in the principles of CBT. Moreover, I've immersed myself in researching mental health, drawing from the wisdom of experts like Dr. Aaron Beck, who developed CBT in the 1960s. He uncovered that CBT is a proven way to help with mental health issues. Here's a brief overview (Beck, 2023):

- **Thoughts, feelings, and actions**: CBT looks at how our thoughts affect our feelings and actions. By changing our thoughts, we can change how we feel and act.
- **Focus on now and goals**: CBT concentrates on current problems and goals. It doesn't dwell on the past, but explores how past experiences affect your life today.
- **Spotting negative thoughts**: CBT helps you spot negative, automatic thoughts that pop up in response to situations. It teaches you to challenge and change them.
- **Behavior changes**: CBT uses techniques like facing fears, trying new behaviors, and organizing your time to help you improve your life.

- **Proven by science**: It's backed by scientific research and has been proven to work for many mental health issues, including depression and anxiety.
- **Mindfulness and acceptance**: It teaches you to be more aware of your thoughts and feelings without judging yourself and also to stay in the present moment.
- **Preventing relapse**: CBT helps you recognize signs of slipping back into old patterns and equips you with strategies to stay on track.

I have also studied Dr. David Burns, psychiatrist and best-selling author, whose books *Feeling Good* and *Feeling Great* have been instrumental in my own healing journey (Wikipedia Contributors, 2019).

In this workbook, I'll take you through the fundamentals of CBT in a way that's easy to understand. We'll explore the clinical science behind CBT, emphasizing that it can be effective even without a therapist. Together, we'll focus on collaboration and active participation, set goal-oriented targets, and stay rooted in the present moment.

CBT aims to teach you, empower you, and take control of your thoughts and emotions while helping you find perspective and healing. It's meant to be a journey that equips you with the tools to address those negative automatic thoughts that have held you captive for far too long. It's meant to be a type of therapy that is time-limited. It isn't like other forms of therapy, where you spend years diving into your past while working with a talk therapist.

So if you're seeking inner peace, and if you long for a life where anxiety and depression no longer call the shots, then let's embark on this journey together. Turn the page and discover the transformative power of CBT. Your healing begins now.

Watch your thoughts, they become your words; watch your words, they become your actions; watch your actions, they become your habits; watch your habits, they become your character; watch your character, for it becomes your destiny.

–LAO TZU

CHAPTER 1

Bringing CBT to Life

I want to welcome you to the first chapter on a journey toward understanding and harnessing the power of CBT to navigate the complexities of your inner world and find the inner peace you deserve. I'm honored to be your companion on this path of self-discovery and healing.

In this workbook, I aim to make the often abstract concepts of CBT easy to grasp and apply in your everyday life. I understand that not everyone has access to a CBT therapist, and that's why this workbook is designed to be your self-guided companion. You don't need a degree in psychology to understand and benefit from CBT. All you need is an open heart, a willingness to learn, and a desire for positive change.

In this chapter we'll explore what CBT is and what it's used for. I have included plenty of exercises and activities. We'll begin by teaching you how to track your moods and analyze the data, setting the foundation for your transformation.

Always remember that you are not alone on this path. Many of us have faced our own battles with mental health, and through CBT we can find the tools to navigate them more effectively.

Understanding Cognitive Behavioral Therapy

I want to start by saying that I can truly relate to the challenges you might be facing if you're dealing with mental health issues. Growing up with parents that struggled with mental health challenges, I understand the impact it can have on your life.

CBT is like a Swiss Army knife for your mental well-being. It's incredibly versatile and can help with a wide range of issues. Here are some of the key areas where CBT can make a significant difference:

- **Depression**: CBT can make a huge difference when it comes to managing depression. It helps you identify and challenge negative thought patterns, which often contribute to feelings of sadness and hopelessness. Studies have shown that CBT can bring about noticeable improvements in mood relatively quickly.
- **Anxiety**: If you're dealing with anxiety, CBT can be a lifeline. It teaches you to recognize anxious thoughts and replace them with more realistic and balanced ones. This can lead to a reduction in anxiety levels and improved overall well-being.
- **Anger**: CBT can assist in managing anger by helping you understand the triggers and thought patterns that lead to explosive outbursts. Through CBT exercises, you can learn healthier ways to cope with anger and respond to challenging situations.
- **Self-confidence**: Low self-esteem and self-doubt can hold you back in life. CBT can boost your self-confidence by challenging negative self-beliefs and helping you build a more positive self-image.

- **Hopelessness**: CBT provides you with tools to break the cycle of hopelessness by teaching you how to reframe situations and find solutions. This can restore a sense of hope and agency in your life.
- **Guilt and shame**: CBT helps you address and manage feelings of guilt and shame by examining their underlying causes and challenging distorted thoughts associated with them.
- **Addiction and cravings**: CBT is effective in addiction treatment by identifying triggers and teaching coping strategies to resist cravings and make healthier choices.
- **Strengthening relationships**: CBT can improve your communication skills, emotional regulation, and problem-solving abilities, which are essential for building and maintaining healthy relationships.

One of the fantastic things about CBT is that it often works relatively quickly. Studies have shown its effectiveness in producing positive changes in a matter of weeks or months, depending on the individual and the specific issue being addressed (Aardema et al., 2022).

So, whether you're struggling with depression, anxiety, anger, low self-esteem, addiction, or any of the other challenges I mentioned, CBT has the potential to help you make significant progress. Let's dive into CBT exercises and techniques that you can use on your own to start your journey to improved mental well-being.

Self-Assessment for Depression

Let's start by taking a closer look at your mood in terms of depression. We'll use a scale from 0–4, where 0 means "not at all" and 4 means "extremely." There are no right or wrong answers—just your honest feelings. Simply circle your answers.

Question 1: How would you rate your overall mood today in terms of depression?

(0= Not at all, 1= Slightly, 2= Moderately, 3= Very, 4= Extremely)

Question 2: How often have you felt a lack of interest or pleasure in doing things you used to enjoy?

(0= Not at all, 1= Slightly, 2= Moderately, 3= Very, 4= Extremely)

Question 3: Have you experienced significant changes in your appetite or weight recently?

(0= Not at all, 1= Slightly, 2= Moderately, 3= Very, 4= Extremely)

Question 4: Are you having trouble falling asleep, staying asleep, or are you experiencing excessive sleepiness during the day?

(0= Not at all, 1= Slightly, 2= Moderately, 3= Very, 4= Extremely)

Question 5: How would you rate your energy levels?

(0= Plenty of energy, 1= Lots of energy, 2= Little energy, 4= Extremely fatigued)

Now, add up your answers to each question above and compare your final number with the answer key on the next page.

Answer Key for Depression Test

- ⊙ **0= No symptoms:** You are not currently experiencing symptoms of depression.
- ⊙ **1–2= Slight:** You may be experiencing occasional mild symptoms. It's important to pay attention to your mood and continue monitoring your feelings.
- ⊙ **3–5= Mild:** You are experiencing mild symptoms of depression. Consider using the strategies in this book for managing these feelings.
- ⊙ **6–10= Moderate:** Your symptoms suggest a moderate level of depression. It's essential to utilize strategies in this book for managing these feelings.
- ⊙ **11–15= Severe:** You are dealing with severe depression. Please use strategies outlined in this book and lean on your support system. It may be beneficial to reach out to a mental health provider.
- ⊙ **16–20= Extreme:** Your symptoms indicate extreme depression. Besides using strategies in this book, please reach out to a mental health provider or a crisis hotline immediately.

Self-Assessment for Anxiety Exercise

Now, let's explore your mood in terms of anxiety. Use the same scale from 0–4.

Question 1: How would you rate your overall mood today in terms of anxiety?

(0= Not at all, 1= Slightly, 2= Moderately, 3= Very, 4= Extremely)

Question 2: Are you frequently worried or anxious about various aspects of your life?

(0= Not at all, 1= Slightly, 2= Moderately, 3= Very, 4= Extremely)

Question 3: Do you experience restlessness, feeling on edge, or being easily fatigued?

(0= Not at all, 1= Slightly, 2= Moderately, 3= Very, 4= Extremely)

Question 4: Are you having difficulty controlling your worries?

(0= Not at all, 1= Slightly, 2= Moderately, 3= Very, 4= Extremely)

Question 5: How would you rate your level of physical tension or muscle aches?

(0= None, 1= Little tension, 2= More tension, 3= Great tension, 4= Extremely tense)

Answer Key for Anxiety Test

- **0= No symptoms:** You are not currently experiencing symptoms of anxiety.
- **1–2= Slight:** You may be experiencing occasional mild symptoms of anxiety. Consider practicing relaxation techniques outlined in this book.
- **3–5= Mild:** You have mild symptoms of anxiety. Exploring coping strategies outlined in this book could be helpful.
- **6–10= Moderate:** Your symptoms suggest a moderate level of anxiety. It's essential to utilize strategies in this book for managing these feelings.
- **11–15= Severe:** You are dealing with severe anxiety. Please use strategies outlined in this book and lean on your support system. It may be beneficial to reach out to a mental health provider.
- **16–20= Extreme:** Your symptoms indicate extreme anxiety. Besides using strategies in this book, if possible, seek professional help immediately.

Self-Assessment for Anger Exercise

Let's explore your mood in terms of anger using a similar scale from 0–4.

Question 1: How would you rate your overall mood today in terms of anger?

(0= Not at all, 1= Slightly, 2= Moderately, 3= Very, 4= Extremely)

Question 2: Are you experiencing irritability or frustration more than usual?

(0= Not at all, 1= Slightly, 2= Moderately, 3= Very, 4= Extremely)

Question 3: Do you find yourself easily angered by minor inconveniences?

(0= Not at all, 1= Slightly, 2= Moderately, 3= Very, 4= Extremely)

Question 4: How often do you engage in physical or verbal expressions of anger?

(0= Not at all, 1= Slightly, 2= Moderately, 3= Very, 4= Extremely)

Question 5: Are you experiencing any physical symptoms of anger, such as a racing heart or clenched jaw?

(0= Not at all, 1= Slightly, 2= Moderately, 3= Very, 4= Extremely)

Answer Key for Anger Test

- ⊘ **0= No anger:** You are not currently experiencing symptoms of anger.
- ⊘ **1–2= A little anger:** You may be experiencing occasional mild irritability or frustration.
- ⊘ **3–5= Some anger:** You have mild to moderate symptoms of anger. Consider using the anger management strategies outlined in this book.
- ⊘ **6–10= Moderate anger:** Your symptoms suggest a moderate level of anger. Implement the anger management strategies outlined in this book.
- ⊘ **11–15= Severe anger:** You are dealing with severe anger issues. Continue your anger management strategies and lean on those you trust for support.
- ⊘ **16–20= Extreme anger:** Your symptoms indicate extreme anger. Besides using strategies in this book, if possible, seek professional help immediately.

Now, let's discuss statistical analyses and the accuracy of self-help tests. It's crucial to note that many self-help tests and assessments, when developed and validated properly, are almost 95% accurate (Burns, 2020).

However, it's essential to remember that moods and mental health can fluctuate over time. Just like our physical health can change, our emotional well-beings are also subject to variations. This is where the idea of tracking your mood quickly on a graph comes into play. By doing this, you can see how your mood evolves over time and identify patterns or triggers that affect your mental health positively or negatively.

Here's an exercise you can try.

EXERCISE: Mood Tracking Apps

Use a smartphone app to record your mood each day. You can rate your mood on a scale from 1–10, with 1 being the worst and 10 being the best. I would recommend searching the top three mood tracking apps of the year and narrow down your choice that way.

After a few weeks or months, review your mood app and see what patterns have emerged. Do you notice certain situations or activities that consistently affect your mood?

Many mood tracking apps can create a mood graph where they plot your mood scores over time. This visual representation can help you identify trends and progress in your emotional well-being.

We're going to go over a more extensive CBT mood tracking method in a later chapter but know that sometimes it helps to use a simple phone app occasionally to understand patterns in your moods.

Happiness Test

Happiness is a multi-dimensional concept, and this test is intended to help evaluate your current state of happiness. For each of the following five questions, rate yourself on a scale from 0–4, where 0 means "not at all" and 4 means "extremely."

Question 1: How happy and joyful do you feel right now?

(0= Not at all, 1= Slightly, 2= Moderately, 3= Very, 4= Extremely)

Question 2: How hopeful and optimistic are you about the future?

(0= Not at all, 1= Slightly, 2= Moderately, 3= Very, 4= Extremely)

Question 3: How satisfied are you with your life at this moment?

(0= Not at all, 1= Slightly, 2= Moderately, 3= Very, 4= Extremely)

Question 4: How connected do you feel to others in your life?

(0= Not at all, 1= Slightly, 2= Moderately, 3= Very, 4= Extremely)

Question 5: How much meaning and purpose do you find in your daily activities?

(0= Not at all, 1= Slightly, 2= Moderately, 3= Very, 4= Extremely)

Answer Key for Happiness Test

- **0–1= No happiness:** Scores in this range suggest a need for significant improvement in your overall sense of happiness.
- **2–4= Minimal happiness:** You may experience moments of happiness, but there is room for improvement.
- **5–9=** Some happiness: You're happy occasionally, but may feel sad or listless at other times.
- **10–14=** Significant happiness: You often feel joy and satisfaction in your life.
- **15–20=** Tremendous happiness: You experience a strong sense of joy, well-being, and contentment most of the time and in your life overall.

The Willingness Test

Willingness is critical on your journey toward improved mental health. People who see significant improvements are often those who actively engage in exercises and are willing to put in the work.

This test will help you gauge your commitment to self-directed therapy. On a scale from 0 (do not agree) to 4 (agree completely), assess your willingness for each statement.

Question 1: I'm willing to do the questions and exercises while I read this book.

(0= Do not agree, 1= Slightly agree, 2= Moderately agree, 3= Strongly agree, 4= Agree completely)

Question 2: I'm willing to do the exercises even if I'm not in the mood.

(0= Do not agree, 1= Slightly agree, 2= Moderately agree, 3= Strongly agree, 4= Agree completely)

Question 3: I'm willing to do them even if I feel hopeless and unmotivated.

(0= Do not agree, 1= Slightly agree, 2= Moderately agree, 3= Strongly agree, 4= Agree completely)

Question 4: I'm willing to do them even if I feel overwhelmed or tired.

(0= Do not agree, 1= Slightly agree, 2= Moderately agree, 3= Strongly agree, 4= Agree completely)

Question 5: I'm willing to do them even if they seem difficult at first.

(0= Do not agree, 1= Slightly agree, 2= Moderately agree, 3= Strongly agree, 4= Agree completely)

The willingness test is a reflection of your readiness to commit to the self-improvement journey outlined in this workbook. The higher your score, the more likely you are to benefit from the exercises and concepts presented here. A score of 20 indicates total willingness and a strong foundation for progress, while lower scores suggest room for improvement in your commitment to personal growth.

It really helps to find tools and strategies to navigate life's challenges. We've taken the first step together in understanding CBT and its potential to help us. As someone who's grappled with their own share of depression and anxiety, I can vouch for the transformative power of CBT. In the pages ahead, we'll delve into the 10 cognitive distortions, those tricky thinking patterns that often hold us back. These distortions can be like roadblocks on the path to healing, but don't worry, we'll work through them together, one step at a time.

Don't believe everything you think.

–JOSEPH NGUYEN

CHAPTER 2

The 10 Cognitive Distortions and How to Identify Them

In this chapter, we're diving deep into a crucial aspect of understanding and managing our mental health: cognitive distortions. These sneaky little thought patterns can wreak havoc on our well-being, and they don't discriminate; they can affect anyone, whether you've experienced mental health challenges in your family or not. Cognitive distortions can be a significant contributing factor to the development and worsening of conditions like depression. So, let's get to work on understanding them and learning how to identify and combat them effectively.

According to a study from 2021, cognitive distortions can contribute to the development and worsening of mental health conditions such as anxiety and depression (Bathina et al., 2021). These distortions are like funhouse mirrors, reflecting back a distorted image of reality and leading us to perceive the world in ways that aren't accurate.

So, in this chapter, we're going to unravel the mystery of cognitive distortions together. We'll explore what they are, delve into the 10 most common distortions, discover how they can impact our mental health, and most importantly, equip ourselves with practical tools and exercises to identify and challenge these distortions head-on.

What Are Cognitive Distortions?

Cognitive distortions, also known as thinking errors or thinking traps, are irrational or biased ways of thinking. They are patterns of thought that can lead to negative emotions and behaviors. Growing up with parents who had their own mental health challenges, I often found myself falling into these thinking traps.

Being raised in a challenging environment, I often struggled with distorted thinking patterns. For instance, my mother's BPD made me feel responsible for her emotions, leading to personalization and emotional reasoning. On the other hand, my father's schizophrenia sometimes triggered my catastrophic thinking, fearing the worst about his condition and how it could destroy our family.

The 10 Cognitive Distortions

Let's dive deeper into the 10 common cognitive distortions, along with examples for each. Understanding these distortions is fundamental to your journey toward better mental health.

All-Or-Nothing Thinking

This distortion involves seeing situations in extreme, either/or terms. You view things as either perfect or complete failures. For example:

"If I don't get this promotion, my career here has been a total waste."
"I made one mistake on the test; I'm a complete idiot."

Overgeneralization

Overgeneralization occurs when you make a broad conclusion based on limited evidence. You use words like "always" or "never." For example:

"I just got rejected; I'll always be unlovable."
"I failed at this project; I'll never succeed at anything."

Discounting the Positive

This distortion involves dismissing positive experiences, qualities, or accomplishments. You focus solely on the negative. For example:

"I got an A on the test, but that was just luck."
"They said something nice, but they were just being polite."

Jumping to Conclusions (Mind Reading/Fortune Telling)

This distortion involves making assumptions about what others are thinking or predicting future events negatively. For example:

"They didn't text me back; they must hate me."
"I'll never find love; I'll be alone forever."

Magnification/Minimization

With this distortion, you exaggerate the importance of negative events (magnification) or minimize the significance of positive events (minimization). For example:

"I spilled coffee on my shirt; it's a disaster!"
"I got a promotion, but it's not a big deal; anyone could do it."

Mental Filter

Mental filtering involves selectively focusing only on the negative aspects of a situation while ignoring the positive. For example:

"I had a great day, but that one rude comment ruined everything."

"My presentation went well, but I stumbled on one sentence and I keep thinking about it."

Emotional Reasoning

This distortion happens when you believe your emotions are proof of reality. If you feel it, it must be true. For example:

"I feel anxious, so something terrible is going to happen."
"I'm so embarrassed; I must have made a fool of myself."

Should Statements (and Hidden Shoulds)

Should statements involve setting rigid and unrealistic expectations for yourself or others. This often leads to feelings of guilt and disappointment. For example:

"I should always be happy; feeling sad is wrong. I'm broken for feeling sad."
"I must always please others; if I don't, I'm a terrible person."

Labeling

Labeling is when you attach negative labels to yourself or others based on behavior. It oversimplifies complex human nature. For example:

"I made a mistake; I'm a failure."
"They made a rude comment; they're a horrible person."

Self Blame and Other Blame

This distortion involves blaming yourself excessively for events beyond your control or blaming others without considering their perspective. For example:

"It's my fault my parents divorced; I should have been a better child."

"My friend canceled plans; they're so inconsiderate."

By reshaping your thought patterns, you have the power to transform your emotional state. This highlights why it's crucial to understand cognitive distortions. Even highly skilled psychiatrists can have their thinking influenced by these distortions. Your thoughts serve as the foundation for your emotions, and it's essential to remember that your emotions do not necessarily validate the accuracy of your thoughts. Unpleasant feelings often signal that you are harboring negative thoughts and giving them credence.

Identifying Your Distortions

It's important to understand that some therapies may not work for everyone, and simply pinpointing the origins of your issues isn't always enough. You may have heard that traditional psychotherapy often focuses on venting emotions and gaining insight, but what if these methods aren't effective for you? We need to utilize alternative approaches, like CBT, that aim for a rapid and decisive transformation in your mental landscape.

In traditional talk therapy, venting your emotions and gaining insight into your problems are primary goals. However, this approach may not work for everyone. Have you ever been at a therapy session, poured out your emotions, and been met with silence? It can lead to added anxiety, or you may even conclude that your therapist agrees with your negative thoughts.

Another good example of this is when a therapist tells you that you're a perfectionist because of your mother, but doesn't provide practical ways to change. You might be left feeling lost as to how to change and move forward.

CBT takes a different approach. It aims for a swift and decisive transformation in the way you think, feel, and behave. This practical approach focuses on identifying and challenging cognitive distortions head-on.

Understanding Emotional Distress

To truly grasp the power of cognitive distortions, remember that two conditions must be met for emotional distress:

1. **Necessary condition:** You must have a negative thought.
2. **Sufficient condition:** You must believe the negative thought.

If you have a negative thought that you don't believe—like thinking the world is about to end in five seconds—it won't upset you. But most of the time, we believe our negative thoughts, and that's where the trouble starts.

Cognitive Distortions Exercises

Scenario 1: Identifying Cognitive Distortions

Let's dive into a scenario together. Imagine this: You're waiting for a friend who's running late. Thoughts start racing through your mind, and you feel irritated.

From the 10 cognitive distortions we discussed, which might show up in your thoughts? Fill in both the thoughts and then the distortions you spot.

_____

_____

_____

_____

In this scenario, you might find distortions like "mind reading" (assuming your friend is deliberately late), "catastrophizing" (believing that being late means your friendship is in trouble), and "emotional reasoning" (feeling irritated, so you believe that something terrible must be happening).

Scenario 2: Identifying Cognitive Distortions

Now, imagine you receive a rejection email after a job interview. What cognitive distortions might go through your mind? Identify the thoughts and distortions that come up.

_____

_____

_____

_____

In this scenario, you may notice distortions like "personalization" (assuming the rejection is entirely your fault), "fortune telling" (predicting that you'll never get a job again), and "all-or-nothing thinking" (believing that one rejection defines your entire worth).

Scenario 3: Identifying Cognitive Distortions

Lastly, envision a situation where you're in a crowded room, and you start feeling anxious. What cognitive distortions do you notice in your mind? Identify the thoughts and distortions you spot.

_____

_____

_____

_____

_____

In this scenario, you could identify distortions such as "mind reading" (thinking that everyone is judging you), "hidden shoulds" (believing that if you appear anxious, it's the end of the world, so you should appear calm and collected), and "labeling" (calling yourself a loser for feeling anxious).

Negative Thoughts Exercise

Throughout the day, I would like you to pay attention to your thoughts. When you catch yourself feeling upset or anxious, ask yourself:

- What negative thought triggered this emotion? (If you're not sure, choose a possible thought that could have triggered it.)

_____

_____

_____

_____

_____

- Do I truly believe this negative thought?

_____

_____

_____

_____

This exercise will help you become more aware of your thought patterns and set the stage for challenging and changing them in the future. It is a great idea to keep a journal handy and write as often as you catch these emotions, thoughts, and feelings arising.

Self-Monitoring Exercise

When we're caught up in the whirlwind of negative thinking, it can be challenging to recognize just how frequently these thoughts occur. Self-monitoring helps shine a light on these patterns, making them easier to identify and ultimately change.

Download a tally/tracker app: Start by downloading a tally or counter app on your phone. You can find various free apps on app stores that make tallying simple.

Set up your tally: Create a new tally for tracking negative thoughts. Name it something like "Negative Thoughts Tracker."

Push the button: Throughout your day, every time you catch yourself having a negative thought, quickly tap the button on your tally app. Make it a habit to do this as soon as you recognize the thought.

Record daily totals: At the end of each day, record the total number of negative thoughts you've tracked.

Initially, you might be surprised by the number of negative thoughts that pop into your head. That's entirely normal. Remember, awareness is the first step toward change.

Many people notice a remarkable shift within two to three weeks of consistently tracking their negative thoughts. It's as if your mind starts to recognize the patterns and naturally begins to reduce these thoughts.

A Few Tips for Success

- ⊙ **Be consistent:** Try to use the tally app every day, even if it feels repetitive or you have a day with a particularly high number of negative thoughts.
- ⊙ **Be non-judgmental:** Remember, the goal here is awareness, not self-criticism. It's okay to have negative thoughts; what matters is how you choose to respond to them.
- ⊙ **Celebrate small victories:** Each day with fewer negative thoughts is a step in the right direction. Celebrate your progress along the way.

The exploration of the 10 common cognitive distortions has shed light on the various ways our thought patterns can lead to negative emotions and behaviors. By identifying these distortions, we have taken concrete steps to building a healthier and more balanced mental framework. As we transition into the next chapter, we will explore practical strategies for implementing a mood tracker. This invaluable tool will help us gain deeper insight into our emotional fluctuations and provide a solid foundation for our journey toward emotional well-being.

In the following pages, I will introduce you to the Straightforward Technique that will empower you to effectively challenge your thought patterns, identify patterns, and make informed choices to enhance your emotional resilience.

For many, negative thinking is a habit which over time becomes an addiction.

−PETER MCWILLIAMS

CHAPTER 3

Mood Trackers and the Straightforward Technique

It is time to equip you with practical tools to help you better understand and manage your emotions. In this chapter, I'll introduce two essential elements: the Daily Mood Tracker and the Straightforward Technique.

The Daily Mood Tracker

Imagine having a map that shows you the terrain of your emotional world. The Daily Mood Tracker is precisely that map. This tool is like a trusty sidekick that will accompany you on your journey, helping you keep tabs on your mood fluctuations. It's a simple but powerful way to track your emotional ups and downs, helping you spot patterns and triggers you might not have noticed before.

I'll guide you through the process of setting up your Daily Mood Tracker and making the most out of it. With each passing day, you'll gain a better understanding of your emotional landscape, which is a crucial step toward effectively managing your mental health.

The Straightforward Technique

I will also introduce you to the Straightforward Technique, developed by Dr. David Burns (Lam, 2022). It's a practical approach that can help you challenge and reframe negative thought patterns. Sometimes our minds can get stuck in a loop of negative thinking, and it can feel like there's no way out. This technique is your escape hatch from that mental maze.

I'll break down the steps, provide examples, and offer exercises to help you apply the Straightforward Technique in your own life. It's a tool that empowers you to take control of your negative thoughts and feelings, arming you with the skills to steer your emotional ship in the right direction.

Let's get started with some exercises.

Creating Your Daily Mood Tracker

On each day that you're feeling upset in some way, you will begin by marking the date and the upsetting event or thought that occurred. You will then view the list of emotions and circle the ones that resonate with how you're feeling in each moment.

DATE:
UPSETTING EVENT:
CIRCLE EMOTIONS:

SAD, blue, depressed, down, unhappy
ANXIOUS, worried, panicky, nervous, frightened
GUILTY, remorseful, bad, ashamed
INFERIOR, worthless, inadequate, defective, incompetent

LONELY, unloved, unwanted, rejected, alone, abandoned

EMBARASSED, foolish, humiliated, self-conscious

HOPELESS, discouraged, pessimistic, despairing

FRUSTRATED, stuck, defeated

ANGRY, mad, resentful, annoyed, irritated, upset, furious

SHOCKED, stunned, disoriented, bewildered, betrayed

DECEIVED, let down, powerless, helpless, vulnerable

DISGUSTED, repulsed, jealous, envious

OVERWHELMED, inundated, insecure, uncertain, doubtful

GUILT-RIDDEN, self-critical, numb, detached, dissociated

SCARED, exhausted, drained, confused, irrational, sensitive

TENSE, on edge, jittery, lonely, isolated, cut off

VICTIMIZED, inadequate, insufficient, lacking

The Straightforward Technique for Cognitive Distortions

This exercise is designed to be used in conjunction with the Daily Mood Tracker to help you address those automatic negative thoughts and cognitive distortions that often contribute to unpleasant emotions. Once you track your moods, you can apply this technique to address the thoughts contributing to those negative emotions.

Our thoughts have a powerful impact on our emotions and behaviors. When we're caught up in automatic negative thoughts, it can be difficult to see things clearly and objectively. This exercise will guide you through identifying those negative thoughts, challenging them, and replacing them with more rational responses. By practicing this regularly, you can gradually shift your thought patterns toward a healthier mindset.

Exercise Steps

1. Describe the trigger (1st column):

⊙ In this column, write down what happened or the situation that led to the unpleasant emotion. Be specific and concise. If you don't know what caused the thought, skip this step.

2. Describe your feelings (2nd column):

⊙ Write down the emotions you felt in response to the trigger and indicate their intensity on a scale from 0–100%. For example, "Anxiety: 90%."

3. Automatic negative thoughts (3rd column):

⊙ Identify and write down the automatic negative thoughts that popped into your mind in response to the trigger. These are the thoughts that contribute to your unpleasant emotions. Do not describe your feelings here, just the thoughts you're having.

4. Cognitive distortions (4th column):

⊙ In this column, list multiple cognitive distortions present in each automatic thought. You can use abbreviations like OG for overgeneralization or MF for mental filtering. Recognizing these distortions is key to challenging them effectively. If you can't find any cognitive distortions within a thought, it's likely because it's a description of an event or feeling rather than a thought. Here is a list of cognitive distortions to refresh your memory:

- all-or-nothing thinking
- overgeneralization
- mental filters
- discounting the positive
- jumping to conclusions (mind reading or fortune telling)
- magnification or minimization

- emotional reasoning
- should statements
- labeling
- personalization and blame

5. Rational responses (5th column):

⊙ Challenge the automatic negative thoughts with rational, balanced responses. For each thought, ask yourself if there's evidence to support it or if it's an exaggeration. Counter it with a more balanced perspective.

6. Belief in rational responses (6th column):

⊙ Rate your belief in the rational responses you've written down on a scale from 0% (completely disbelieve) to 100% (fully believe). It's important to fully and genuinely believe these rational responses.

Here is an example chart:

Describe the Trigger	Describe Your Feelings in a %	Automatic Negative Thoughts	Cognitive Distortions	Rational Responses	Belief in Rational Responses
I was fired from my job.	unworthiness: 90% fear: 85% embarrassment: 90%	I can't do anything right. I am stupid. I screwed up that bid, I am worthless.	all-or-nothing thinking labeling labeling	I did a great job, maybe there are cutbacks. This job doesn't offer me the growth I need.	55% 85%
My wife asked for a divorce.	anxious: 95%	Nobody will ever love me again.	overgeneralization	I am great and worthy of love.	96%

CBT WORKBOOK FOR ADULTS

Describe the Trigger	Describe Your Feelings in a %	Automatic Negative Thoughts	Cognitive Distortions	Rational Responses	Belief in Rational Responses

Let's explore some tips for writing down negative thoughts.

Separate Events From Thoughts

This means that when describing what led to your negative emotion, you should clearly distinguish between the actual event or trigger and the thoughts that followed.

Imagine your emotions and thoughts as two separate threads in the fabric of your experiences. To untangle them effectively, it's crucial to understand the distinction between the trigger, which is the objective situation or circumstance, and the subsequent thoughts that arise.

The event or trigger is the objective situation or circumstance that happened. It's something that can often be observed or described by others.

The event or trigger is like the raw data of an experience, something that exists in the external world and can be observed or documented by others. It's the "what" that occurred, devoid of personal interpretations or judgments. This objective aspect serves as the starting point for understanding your emotional responses.

For example, imagine you receive a critique at work from your supervisor during a team meeting. The critique itself, such as your supervisor pointing out a mistake in a project, is the event or trigger. It's a factual occurrence that can be documented or described to others. It's the same critique that everyone in the meeting heard.

Now, the thoughts that follow this event can vary greatly from person to person. Some might think, "I made a mistake; I need to improve," while others might think, "I'm a complete failure; I'll never get anything right." These thoughts represent the subjective interpretations or reactions to the same trigger—the critique. By distinguishing the event from the thoughts, you can better examine and address your personal responses and cognitive distortions that may be influencing your emotional reaction.

The thoughts are your subjective interpretations or reactions to the event. These are the internal dialogues or mental responses that occurred as a result of the event. By keeping them separate, you can better identify which thoughts are contributing to your negative emotions and work on challenging and changing those specific thoughts.

Exclude Emotions From Thoughts

In the column where you write down your automatic negative thoughts, it's essential to focus solely on the thoughts themselves and avoid including the emotions or feelings directly.

Emotions can certainly be intense and overwhelming, but they are the result of your thoughts. By isolating the thoughts, you can better analyze and address the cognitive distortions that may be influencing your emotional state.

For example, don't write down 'I'm thinking I'm anxious" in the 'thought' column. Write down the thought that is making you anxious (for example, "I'll never succeed at anything.")

This separation helps you gain clarity on the thought-emotion connection and enables you to challenge the thoughts more effectively.

Keep It Concise

When jotting down your negative thoughts, aim to be succinct and to the point. Avoid overly long or elaborate descriptions.

Limit each thought to one or two sentences at most. Being concise ensures that you capture the essence of the thought without unnecessary elaboration, making it easier to work with during the exercise.

Use Complete Sentences

Writing out your thoughts as complete sentences is essential for clarity and effective analysis. Complete sentences provide context and structure to your thoughts. They make it easier to see the thought patterns, cognitive distortions, and rational responses clearly.

By using complete sentences, you also practice expressing your thoughts more precisely, which can be valuable in daily life when dealing with negative thinking.

Avoid Rhetorical Questions

Rhetorical questions are those that don't require an answer and are often used to express a point or emphasize a feeling. Instead of using these in the negative thought column, rephrase them as declarative statements. For instance, if you catch yourself thinking, "Why am I so worthless?" you can rewrite it as "I'm totally worthless" or "I shouldn't be so messed up."

This transformation makes it easier to identify and challenge distorted thoughts, as they are presented as statements to be analyzed rather than questions.

By following these expanded guidelines, you can enhance the effectiveness of the exercise and gain greater insight into your thought patterns, making it easier to challenge and change them to promote better mental health.

Encourage yourself to do this exercise at least once a day for 30 days, or even more often if negative thoughts arise throughout the day. Writing down your thoughts using this structured approach will prevent them from getting jumbled in your mind and help you gain better control over your thought patterns. Sometimes, you may find yourself experiencing a strong emotion without being able to identify the exact negative thoughts driving that emotion. These elusive thoughts, often referred to as "silent thoughts," can be challenging to uncover. In such cases, a helpful strategy is to create or imagine potential negative thoughts that could be contributing to your feelings.

For instance, let's say you're feeling upset, but you can't pinpoint the specific negative thoughts that might be causing your distress.

Consider a scenario where you're about to give a public talk, and you're overwhelmed by anxiety. In this situation, if you struggle to identify the exact negative thoughts triggering your anxiety, you can try inventing some negative thoughts that are commonly associated with public speaking anxiety. These imagined thoughts serve as your "silent thoughts."

For example, you might jot down thoughts like, "I'm awful at public speaking," or "I'll embarrass myself in front of everyone." These silent thoughts act as placeholders for the potential underlying negative beliefs or fears that could be contributing to your emotional state. By acknowledging and addressing these silent thoughts, you can gain insight into your emotional reactions and work toward managing them effectively.

We've explored valuable techniques for tackling those pesky cognitive distortions that often cloud our thinking and contribute to negative emotions. I introduced you to the Straightforward Technique, which provides a structured approach to identifying, challenging, and reframing automatic negative thoughts. By using this technique, you've taken a significant step toward building a healthier and more rational mindset.

Additionally, we discussed the importance of keeping a Daily Mood Tracker. This simple yet effective tool allows you to gain insight into your emotional patterns, helping you identify triggers and monitor your progress as you work on reframing cognitive distortions. By tracking your moods daily, you're equipping yourself with valuable information that will guide you on your journey to emotional well-being.

As you continue to practice these techniques, remember that change takes commitment and practice. Be patient and compassionate with yourself as you navigate the process of challenging and reshaping your thought patterns. With persistence and dedication, you can begin to experience a shift toward more positive and balanced thinking.

In the next chapter, we'll delve into two powerful tools—the "Magic Button" and the "Magic Dial." These tools will empower you to deal with negative emotions as they arise, providing you with practical strategies to regain control and find emotional balance. By combining these techniques with the cognitive distortion reframing skills you've developed in this chapter, you'll be well-equipped to tackle the challenges that come your way.

It's not about managing your emotions, it's about managing your reaction to your emotions.

–YUNG PUEBLO

CHAPTER 4

The Magic Button and the Magic Dial

Let's take a trip into the intriguing concepts of the Magic Button and the Magic Dial. These ideas are not just abstract theories; they are powerful tools that can help us regain control over our emotional responses and create a more balanced and harmonious inner world. We're not talking about actual buttons or dials, of course, but rather metaphorical tools that empower us to better manage our emotions.

Throughout this chapter, I'll break down these concepts in a way that's easy to understand and apply. We won't get lost in jargon or complex theories; instead, we'll focus on practical exercises and strategies that you can use in your own self-directed therapy journey.

The Magic Button

The Magic Button is not a literal button, but rather a metaphor used in CBT to help us understand and manage our emotional reactions to various situations. It represents the idea that, if we could have a button that instantly changed our emotional responses or eliminated negative thoughts and feelings, we could improve our well-being and mental health.

The Magic Button symbolizes the desire for quick and effortless control over our emotions. It's the fantasy of being able to instantly turn off feelings of anxiety, anger, sadness, or any other distressing emotion.

The Magic Button Reflection Exercise

The Magic Button Reflection Exercise is designed to help you gain insight into your emotions and explore the potential consequences of instantly eliminating them. This exercise can be a valuable tool in practicing emotional awareness and considering the role of emotions in your life.

Sit in a quiet and comfortable space. Close your eyes and take a few deep breaths to center yourself. Begin by identifying the negative emotion you are currently experiencing. Is it anxiety, depression, guilt, anger, or something else? Write down the emotion and acknowledge its presence without judgment.

_____

_____

_____

_____

With your eyes closed, imagine that there is a magical button right in front of you. This button has the power to instantly make the negative emotion you identified in step 1 completely disappear. Take a moment to visualize this button. What does it look like? How does it make you feel knowing that it can eliminate your negative emotion?

Now, ask yourself: Do you want to push the Magic Button? Most people instinctively say "yes" because it's natural to desire relief from distressing emotions. However, resist the urge to press it just yet.

Open your eyes and write down the following questions and take some time to reflect on each one:

What would happen if I pressed the Magic Button and my negative emotion instantly disappeared?

_____

_____

_____

_____

_____

How would my life change in the short-term and long-term?

_____

_____

_____

_____

_____

Are there any potential downsides or consequences to eliminating this emotion so quickly?

_____

_____

_____

_____

_____

Could I lose any opportunities for personal growth, self-understanding, or insight by getting rid of this emotion immediately?

_____

_____

_____

_____

_____

_____

Write down your thoughts, feelings, and insights regarding the consequences of pressing the Magic Button. Be honest with yourself about how you feel about the prospect of instantly eliminating the negative emotion.

_____

_____

_____

_____

_____

_____

Take a few moments to reflect on what you've discovered. Remember that emotions, even negative ones, serve a purpose in our lives. They can provide valuable information, drive personal growth, and lead to self-discovery. While it's natural to desire relief from distressing emotions, this exercise encourages you to think about the potential consequences of immediate emotional suppression.

The Magic Button Reflection Exercise helps you gain a deeper understanding of the role emotions play in your life and encourages you to consider alternative ways of coping with them. It can be a useful tool for building emotional resilience and making more informed decisions about how to manage your emotions effectively.

The Magic Dial Exercise

The Magic Dial Exercise is a powerful cognitive tool that allows you to explore the positive aspects and potential benefits of your negative thoughts and feelings. By reframing your emotions, you can achieve a more balanced perspective and make informed decisions about how to manage them effectively.

Feeling Now (1–100)	Feeling Goal (1–100)	Feeling After (1–100)

While filling out the chart above, use the following instructions:

- ⊙ In the "Feeling Now" column, list the negative emotions or thoughts you are currently experiencing. Be honest and specific about what you're feeling.
- ⊙ For each negative emotion or thought listed, ask yourself the following two questions:

What are some benefits or advantages of this negative feeling? How might it be helping me (and potentially others)?

_____

_____

_____

_____

_____

_____

_____

What does this negative feeling show about me and my core values that's beautiful, positive, and even awesome?

_____

_____

_____

_____

_____

_____

- Now that you've answered these questions, are there any potential benefits and positive aspects of this feeling that reveal parts of yourself that you want to keep? If you were to turn the dial down on that feeling, would you turn it down all the way to zero, or would you keep it at 10 percent or even 30 percent of it's current strength. Some people want to turn the dial all the way down to zero for certain feelings but realize that they want to keep a few other feelings around at low levels.
- Fill in the Feeling Goal Column. In this column, write down the desired level of the negative emotion or thought you'd like to achieve after considering the benefits and positive aspects. This is where you set a more balanced goal for your feelings.
- After completing the questions and setting your "Feeling Goal," take a moment to reconsider your negative emotions and thoughts. Try to reframe them based on the benefits and positive aspects you've identified.
- Revisit the Straightforward Technique from before- go through the thoughts that triggered those feelings, identify their distortions, and reframe them.
- In the "Feeling After" column, write down your revised feeling percentages after applying the reframing techniques.
- Continue this process for each negative emotion or thought you listed in the "Feeling Now" column.

As an example, I wanted to go ahead and do this exercise myself to show how it is done a bit more clearly.

The Magic Dial Exercise as Done by Anna

Feeling Now	Feeling Goal	Feeling After
Anxious 70/100	Anxiety 10/100	Anxiety 40/100
Overwhelmed 85/100	Overwhelmed 5/100	Overwhelmed 35/100
Angry 65/100	Angry 30/100	Angry 25/100
Frustrated 70/100	Frustrated 0/100	Frustrated 40/100

What are some benefits or advantages of this negative feeling? How might it be helping me (and potentially others)?

My frustration and anger can be motivating forces. They can push me to take action, address issues, or make improvements in my life or my surroundings. These emotions can drive me to change situations that are causing distress. Overwhelm can lead to a desire to simplify and organize my life, which can improve efficiency and reduce stress in the long run. It can also encourage me to seek help or delegate tasks, fostering collaboration and support from others. Frustration and anger can be signals that my boundaries have been crossed. They can encourage me to assert myself and communicate my needs, which can lead to healthier relationships and interactions with others.

CBT WORKBOOK FOR ADULTS

What do negative feelings show about me and my core values that's beautiful, positive, and even awesome?

> **These feelings show my resilience, compassion, and commitment to my core values. They highlight my self-awareness, motivation for positive change, and capacity for deep connections with others. These emotions are opportunities for personal growth and creativity in problem-solving, reflecting my inner strength and dedication to becoming the best version of myself.**

Examples of Positive Reframing:

1. Guilt:

- Benefit: shows you have a moral compass
- Benefit: demonstrates that you care about others
- Benefit: indicates a willingness to be accountable for your actions

2. Hopelessness:

- Benefit: protects you from getting your hopes up and then facing disappointment
- Benefit: allows for a realistic assessment of a situation
- Benefit: encourages caution and preparation for potential challenges

3. Sadness and depression:

- Benefit: reflects the love and connection you had with a loved one
- Benefit: demonstrates your passion and attachment to your job or aspirations
- Benefit: allows for introspection and personal growth

4. More examples of reframing your feelings:

⊙ Here are more examples of positive and valuable aspects you can find within a feeling:

- "This feeling is painful but helps me understand something about myself."
- "This feeling shows I'm accountable by examining my own flaws instead of blaming others."
- "This thought protects me from future disappointments."
- "This thought reflects my high standards and commitment to excellence."
- "This thought shows how much I care about others."

By completing this exercise, you can develop a more nuanced understanding of your emotions. You'll gain insight into the potentially positive aspects of your feelings, allowing you to make informed decisions about whether to "press the button" to eliminate them entirely or to use the "magic dial" to achieve the emotional state you may really desire. Remember, emotions are complex, and this exercise can help you embrace their richness and value in your life.

In this chapter, we've delved into the intriguing concepts of the Magic Button and the Magic Dial, two powerful tools within CBT. As we've explored the desire for instant emotional control represented by the Magic Button and the nuanced reframing of emotions through the Magic Dial, we've gained valuable insight into our inner worlds. Recognizing that emotions are complex and multifaceted, we now embark on the next leg of our journey—a chapter dedicated to CBT for Self-Esteem and Negative Thoughts. Here, we'll build on the foundation we've laid, equipping ourselves with practical strategies to enhance our self-esteem and effectively manage those negative thoughts that often stand in the way of our well-being and personal growth. As we continue to explore the transformative power of CBT, remember that understanding and mastering our emotional worlds is a continuous journey, and every step forward brings us closer to a more fulfilling and empowered self.

Transformation starts in your mind. What you allow in, good or bad, is what will grow.

–ANONYMOUS

CHAPTER 5

CBT for Self-Esteem and Negative Thoughts

CBT focuses on the connection between your thoughts, feelings, and behaviors. It's all about understanding how your thoughts can shape your emotions and actions. This is a game-changer when it comes to self-esteem and negative thoughts because it empowers you to take control of your mental well-being.

In this chapter, we're going to dive deep into CBT exercises that you can apply to combat negative self-esteem and those relentless negative thoughts that keep holding you back. These exercises are designed to help you challenge and reframe those harmful thought patterns, build a healthier sense of self-worth, and ultimately lead a more fulfilling life.

So, if you've ever felt weighed down by self-doubt, if you've ever wanted to break free from the chains of negative thinking, then let's give these a try.

Unmasking the Inner Critic Exercise

Take a few minutes to sit in a quiet, comfortable space. Allow your inner critic to speak freely and jot down those automatic thoughts as they flow. These thoughts might come rapidly, and they might be harsh, but that's okay.

Once you've got your thoughts on paper, let's pick three to work on together. We'll reframe them to understand what your inner critic might be trying to tell you. Remember, this is a journey of self-discovery and self-compassion.

Example 1: "I suck with money."

Reframe: "I didn't get a lot of education about finances growing up, so I want to learn now." Or "I'm sometimes good with money. I've been paying off my credit card little by little."

What your inner critic might be trying to tell you: Perhaps your inner critic is highlighting an area of your life where you could benefit from improvement. Recognizing this is the first step to positive change. Instead of dwelling on your perceived inadequacy, embrace the opportunity to seek financial guidance and improve your money management skills.

What is one thing your inner critic says to you, and how can you reframe it?

_____

_____

_____

_____

_____

_____

_____

_____

What might your inner critic be trying to tell you?

Example 2: "I'm a failure in relationships."

Reframe: "I struggle in social situations and that makes dating difficult. I went on a date this week and am empowering myself with ways to be more social."

What your inner critic might be trying to tell you: Your inner critic might actually be pointing out that you value connections with others and want to improve your relationships. Rather than feeling like a failure, use this as motivation to work on your communication skills, empathy, and understanding of others.

What is one thing your inner critic says to you, and how can you reframe it?

_____

_____

_____

_____

_____

_____

What might your inner critic be trying to tell you?

_____

_____

_____

_____

_____

Example 3: "I'll never achieve my dreams."

Reframe: "I've taken a huge step toward achieving my dream of writing my first novel by setting goals for this year. Today, I accomplished writing ten pages, which feels like a significant accomplishment!"

What your inner critic might be trying to tell you: Your inner critic is likely expressing your desires and dreams. Instead of feeling defeated, use this as a starting point to create a realistic plan for achieving your goals. Break them down into smaller, manageable steps and take one step at a time.

What is one thing your inner critic says to you, and how can you reframe it?

_____

_____

_____

_____

_____

_____

What might your inner critic be trying to tell you?

_____

_____

_____

_____

_____

Befriending Your Inner Critic

Now that you've reframed these thoughts, let's talk about befriending your inner critic. Responding to negativity with more negativity only fuels inner conflict and frustration. Instead, consider the following:

1. **Welcome your inner critic:** Rather than resisting or ignoring it, acknowledge your inner critic's presence. It's trying to protect you, even if it doesn't always do so in the best way.

2. **Listen to your inner critic:** Take the time to understand what your inner critic is saying. What are its concerns? What fears or worries is it trying to voice?

3. **Collaborate with your inner critic:** Recognize that your inner critic is there to help you, even if its methods are misguided. Work together to find more constructive ways to address your concerns.

4. **Replace it with a friendly voice:** As you befriend your inner critic, consider replacing its harsh words with a more compassionate and motivating inner voice. Treat yourself as you would treat a friend; with kindness and encouragement.

Remember, the next time your inner critic surfaces, try these steps instead of battling it. Embrace the opportunity to learn and grow, and you'll find that your inner critic can become a valuable ally on your journey to mental well-being.

The Socratic Method

On your journey toward improving your mental health, one powerful technique is cognitive restructuring. The Socratic method does just that. This process involves identifying and changing irrational thoughts that can negatively impact your emotions and behaviors. Socratic questioning encourages you to engage in a reflective and rational examination of your thoughts (Kruse, 2022).

Exercise Instructions

Take a moment to find a quiet and comfortable space where you can focus on your thoughts without distractions. Remember, this exercise is just for you, so feel free to be open and honest with yourself.

Step 1: Identify a Challenging Thought

Start by identifying a thought that's been bothering you or causing you distress. It could be related to a specific situation, a recurring pattern of thinking, or a belief about yourself. Write down this thought.

_____

_____

_____

_____

_____

_____

_____

_____

Step 2: Break Down Your Thought

Now, let's dissect this thought using Socratic questioning. Ask yourself the following questions and write down your answers:

What is the evidence against this thought?

⊙ Consider any facts, past experiences, or logical reasons that contradict your thought.

_____

_____

_____

_____

_____

_____

_____

_____

What is the evidence for this thought?

⊙ Explore any reasons or experiences that may support your thought.

_____

_____

_____

_____

_____

_____

Am I basing this thought on fact or feeling?

○ Reflect on whether your thought is grounded in objective reality or if it's driven by emotional reactions.

_____

_____

_____

_____

_____

_____

_____

_____

_____

Do I have all the evidence, or am I making assumptions?

○ Think about whether you have all the necessary information to make an accurate judgment, or if you're making assumptions.

_____

_____

_____

_____

_____

_____

_____

_____

Am I looking at all the evidence, or just what supports my thoughts?

> ⊙ Consider whether you've been selectively focusing on information that confirms your thought while ignoring contradictory evidence.

_____

_____

_____

_____

_____

_____

_____

Am I having this thought out of habit, or does the evidence support it?

> ⊙ Reflect on whether this thought is a recurring pattern for you, and if so, whether it's based on evidence or simply a habit.

_____

_____

_____

_____

_____

_____

Did someone pass this thought on to me, and if so, is this a reliable source?

⊙ Think about whether this thought was influenced by someone else's opinions or beliefs, and evaluate the reliability of the source.

_____

_____

_____

_____

_____

_____

_____

_____

Is my thought a likely scenario or a worst-case scenario?

⊙ Assess whether your thought is an extreme or unlikely interpretation of a situation.

_____

_____

_____

_____

_____

_____

Step 3: Evaluate and Restructure

After answering these questions, take a step back and review your responses. You'll likely notice that the process of questioning your thoughts has led to a more balanced and rational perspective. Now, try to reframe your original thought in a more constructive and realistic way. Write it once again and see if you notice any changes.

_____

_____

_____

_____

Step 4: Practice and Repeat

Keep your workbook handy, as you may find it beneficial to revisit this exercise whenever you encounter challenging thoughts. Over time, this practice can help you develop a healthier thought pattern and improve your overall mental well-being. Remember to be kind to yourself as you navigate this process.

Straightforward Cost Benefit Analysis Exercise

The cost benefit analysis is a traditional decision-making method that has been incorporated into cognitive restructuring within CBT. In a nutshell, it can be employed to confront outdated and unhelpful thought patterns, making way for the adoption of fresh, more beneficial thoughts.

Write down a specific thought you're interested in changing.

_____

_____

_____

_____

List the pros and cons of the thought and rate how important each thought is, not what it suggests, on a scale from 1 (not very important) to 10 (very important). For example, if your thought is "I am worthless," you aren't rating if you are worthy, you are rating how helpful that thought is.

Pros	Importance (1–10)
TOTAL	

Cons	Importance (1–10)
TOTAL	

Once you've assessed the advantages and disadvantages of your present, work on creating alternative helpful thoughts. What are some additional thoughts you can think of?

_____

_____

_____

_____

_____

_____

Paradoxical Cost Benefit Analysis Exercise

The Paradoxical Cost Benefit Analysis is a powerful tool to gain insight into the reasons why certain patterns or behaviors persist in our lives. Remember that change can be challenging, but understanding the forces that keep you stuck is a crucial step toward personal growth and healing.

Step 1: Identify the Problem

Start by identifying the issue or behavior you want to explore. It could be a pattern, habit, or belief that you feel may be holding you back. Write it down in clear, concise terms.

_____

_____

_____

_____

_____

Step 2: List the Positive Advantages

Now, let's dig deep into the positive aspects or advantages of this problem. It may seem counterintuitive, but every behavior or pattern often has some perceived benefits. Be honest with yourself and list them down. For example, if your problem is excessive procrastination, the benefits might include avoiding stress or temporarily feeling more relaxed.

_____

_____

_____

_____

_____

_____

Step 3: Reflect on the Advantages

Take a moment to reflect on the list of positive advantages you've just created. Ask yourself: "Given all these advantages, why should I change?" This question is crucial because it highlights the reasons why you might be resistant to change. Be compassionate with yourself during this process, acknowledging that these perceived benefits are valid concerns in your mind.

_____

_____

_____

_____

_____

Step 4: Consider the Disadvantages

Now, let's flip the perspective. Write down the negative consequences or disadvantages of maintaining this problem or behavior. Continuing with the procrastination example, this could involve missed opportunities, increased stress, or strained relationships.

_____

_____

_____

_____

_____

_____

Step 5: Compare the Lists

Compare the two lists side by side: the positive advantages and the negative disadvantages. This step helps you gain a clearer understanding of the complex dynamics at play. You'll see the reasons that make it challenging to let go of the problem, as well as the potential benefits of change. Feel free to write down the reasons you find it challenging to let go and what the benefits of change could be.

_____

_____

_____

_____

_____

_____

Step 6: Reflect on Your Goals

Take a moment to think about your long-term goals and aspirations. How does this problem or behavior align with your vision for the future? Consider whether the advantages of maintaining it are worth sacrificing your larger goals.

_____

_____

_____

_____

_____

_____

Step 7: Challenge Your Resistance

As you reflect on your goals, challenge the resistance that may be holding you back. Recognize that change is a process, and it's okay to feel conflicted. Embrace self-compassion as you work toward making positive changes in your life.

Self-Esteem

I understand how challenging it can be to navigate the world with a backdrop of negative thoughts and feelings about yourself. Low self-esteem is like a shadow that follows us around, casting doubt on our worth and abilities. It can stem from a variety of sources:

- ⊙ **Childhood experiences:** The environment we grow up in can heavily influence our self-esteem. If your environment was filled with instability or emotional challenges during your formative years, this may lead to feelings of inadequacy or insecurity that stay with you.

- ⊙ **Negative self-talk:** Low self-esteem often arises from a habit of negative self-talk. Constantly criticizing yourself or expecting perfection can erode your self-worth over time.
- ⊙ **Comparison:** Comparing yourself to others, especially in the age of social media, can be a self-esteem killer. It's easy to feel like you don't measure up when you're constantly bombarded with others' highlight reels.
- ⊙ **Traumatic experiences:** Experiencing trauma or abuse can have a profound impact on self-esteem. It can lead to feelings of shame, guilt, and worthlessness.

How CBT Can Help

CBT is an incredibly effective tool for rebuilding your self-esteem because it helps you recognize and change those negative thought patterns and behaviors.

CBT for low self-esteem entails a dual approach aimed at reshaping unproductive thought patterns and behaviors that keep us trapped. By addressing the essential elements of diminished self-assurance, self-sabotaging thoughts, and ineffective actions, we can disrupt the cycle of declining self-esteem.

Remember, self-esteem is a journey, and it takes time and effort. Be patient with yourself as you work through these exercises. Your path to better self-esteem is unique, but with CBT and a compassionate approach, you can make significant progress.

My Strengths Exercise

When you acknowledge and harness your strengths, you often experience greater happiness and increased self-esteem. For those who find it challenging to identify their strengths, the practice of strength-spotting can prove to be an effective therapeutic method.

Take some time to reflect on this list. Circle what resonates with you. I have left blank squares for you to add attributes you feel fit you best. Continue to come back to this list and add more as you feel they come into your life.

CREATIVITY	EMPATHY	RESILIENCE	DETERMINATION
ADAPTABILITY	LEADERSHIP	COMPASSION	OPTIMISM
PATIENCE	HONESTY	FUNNY	ORGANIZED
CURIOUS	CONFIDENT	INDEPENDENT	LOGICAL
ASSERTIVE	AMBITIOUS	FLEXIBLE	SMART
BRAVE	KIND	MODEST	WISE
FORGIVING	FAIR	EMPATHETIC	ARTISTIC
CONFIDENT	DISCIPLINED	LOGICAL	PERSISTENT

Labeling Exercise

In this exercise, we're going to explore the labels we often use to describe ourselves and others, such as "stupid," "defective," or "failure." These labels can have a significant impact on our self-esteem and mental well-being. By examining and redefining these terms, we can begin to challenge negative self-perception and build a healthier self-image.

Instructions

Take a moment to reflect on times when you have labeled yourself or others as "such a loser," "defective," or a "failure." Think about the situations or reasons behind these labels.

Define the terms: Write down your personal definitions of these terms based on your own experiences and perceptions. For example:

What does it mean to be a "a loser" in your eyes?

_____

_____

_____

_____

_____

How do you define someone as "defective"?

_____

_____

_____

_____

_____

When do you consider yourself or others a "failure"?

_____

_____

_____

_____

Challenge your definitions: Now, let's examine these definitions more closely. Consider the following questions:

Is it fair to label someone as a "loser" or "defective" based on occasional mistakes or flaws?

_____

_____

_____

_____

_____

Are there specific criteria or a threshold that determines when someone is a "failure"?

_____

_____

_____

_____

_____

Do these labels take into account the complexities of human experiences and the possibility of growth and change?

_____

_____

_____

_____

_____

Self-compassion exercise: Write down a list of positive qualities and strengths you possess. This can include skills, achievements, or personal characteristics. Use this list to counterbalance the negative labels you explored earlier.

_____

_____

_____

_____

_____

_____

In this chapter, we've explored the transformative power of CBT in the context of self-esteem and negative thoughts. You've learned how to identify and challenge those self-deprecating beliefs and replace them with more realistic and empowering ones. As you move forward, remember that the journey to improved mental well-being is a continuous one. In the next chapter, we'll delve deeper into how CBT can help you navigate the intricate landscape of depression and sadness, offering you practical tools and insights to regain control over your emotions and find a path toward greater emotional resilience and happiness.

Depression doesn't take away your talents, it just makes them harder to find.

–LADY GAGA

CHAPTER 6

CBT for Depression and Sadness

In this chapter, we're going to delve into how CBT can be a powerful tool for managing and overcoming depression and sadness.

Depression and sadness can often feel overwhelming, like a never-ending rain cloud hanging over our heads. Sometimes, it's hard to see any light at the end of the tunnel. However, one important lesson I've learned on my journey is that cognitive distortions often play a significant role in intensifying our feelings of despair. They trick our minds and cloud our thinking.

But here's the thing: It's crucial to recognize that sadness, at times, is a natural and valid emotion. Just like the rain helps flowers grow, sadness can also serve a purpose in our lives.

Depression

It's like a heavy raincloud that lingers over your head, casting a shadow on every aspect of your life. Depression is not just feeling sad; it's a persistent, deep-seated feeling of hopelessness, emptiness, and despair. It can affect your energy, motivation, and overall ability to enjoy life.

Sadness

Sadness, on the other hand, is a normal human emotion. It's like a passing rain shower, a natural response to difficult or challenging situations. Sadness is temporary and often triggered by specific events or circumstances. It's okay to feel sad from time to time; it's a part of life.

I want to take this time to remind you of the Magic Dial and the Straightforward Technique exercises we discussed in previous chapters. These are valuable tools when dealing with depression and sadness. When our cognitive distortions are trying to tell us things about ourselves that are not true, these exercises can help us reframe. Utilize both of them before beginning these next exercises in order to gain the most from them.

Daily Activity Schedule and Self-Assessment Exercise

Step 1: Creating Your Daily Activity Schedule

Schedule	Task Wishlist	Actual Completed	Task	Task Toughness Rating
Morning Routine				
Mid-Morning Routing				
Lunchtime				
Afternoon				
Evening Routine				
Nighttime				

Morning Routine (7:00 A.M. to 9:00 A.M.)

- List the activities you want to accomplish during your morning routine, such as getting out of bed, showering, having breakfast, or meditating.
- Assign each task a rating based on how tough you think it will be on a scale from 1 (easy) to 10 (very tough).

Mid-Morning (9:00 A.M. to 12:00 P.M.)

- Plan out the tasks and activities for this time slot. This could include work, studying, exercise, or any other responsibilities.
- Rate the toughness of each task.

Lunchtime (12:00 P.M. to 1:00 P.M.)

- Include activities related to your lunch break, such as eating, going for a walk, or taking a mental break.
- Rate their toughness.

Afternoon (1:00 P.M. to 5:00 P.M.)

- Continue scheduling tasks and responsibilities for the afternoon, including any appointments or meetings.
- Rate the toughness of each task.

Evening Routine (5:00 P.M. to 8:00 P.M.)

- Plan activities for winding down in the evening, like cooking dinner, spending time with family, or engaging in hobbies.
- Rate the toughness of these activities.

Nighttime (8:00 P.M. to 10:00 P.M.)

- Include activities you typically do before bedtime, such as reading, journaling, or practicing relaxation techniques.
- Rate the toughness of each task.

Step 2: Tracking Your Day

Throughout the day, as you complete each activity, record what you actually did in each time slot. Be honest with yourself about whether you followed your schedule or if you deviated from it.

Step 3: Self-Assessment

⊙ At the end of the day, review your schedule and the actual activities you completed.

⊙ For each task, compare the rating you assigned for toughness before doing it to how you actually felt while doing it. Did you find it easier or tougher than you anticipated?

_____

_____

_____

_____

_____

_____

Reflect on the reasons behind any deviations from your planned schedule. Were there any unexpected challenges or triggers for your mental health issues?

_____

_____

_____

_____

_____

Consider how your mood and energy levels fluctuated throughout the day. Did certain activities have a positive or negative impact on your mental well-being?

_____

_____

_____

_____

_____

_____

Step 4: Goal Setting

Based on your self-assessment, identify areas where you can make adjustments to your daily routine to better support your mental health. Set realistic goals for the following day to help you manage your time and emotions effectively.

Remember, this exercise is a tool for self-reflection and self-improvement. It can help you better understand your daily challenges and find strategies to cope with them. Be kind and patient with yourself as you work through this process, just as you would be with someone you care about.

Anti-Procrastination Technique

Procrastination can be a tough opponent, but we're going to tackle it head-on with this practical exercise. Get a sheet of paper and a pen ready, because it's time to take action.

Task That's Been Procrastinated	Steps Needed to Complete Task	Anticipated Difficulty of Each Step 1/10	Anticipated Satisfaction of Completing Task 1/10	Actual Difficulty Level of Completing Task 1/10	Actual Satisfaction Level 1/10

Step 1: Identify the Task

In the first column, write down the task you've been procrastinating on. Be specific and clear about what needs to be done.

Step 2: Break It Down

Now, in the next column, list each step required to complete the task. Breaking it down into smaller, manageable parts makes it less daunting.

Step 3: Predict Difficulty

In the third column, predict how difficult each step will be on a scale from 1–10, with 1 being the easiest and 10 being the most challenging. This step is crucial for setting realistic expectations.

Step 4: Predict Satisfaction

In the fourth column, estimate how satisfying it will be to complete each step on a scale from 0–100, with 0 being not satisfying at all and 100 being extremely satisfying. Think about the sense of accomplishment you'll feel.

Step 5: Get Started

Now it's time to take action. Begin working on the task and record your actual experience in the last two columns:

- ⊙ In the fifth column, note how difficult the task actually was. Compare it to your initial prediction.
- ⊙ In the sixth column, record how satisfying completing the task turned out to be.

Reflect and Adjust

After completing the task, take a moment to reflect on the exercise. Did your predictions about difficulty and satisfaction match the reality of the task? What did you learn from this experience?

_____

_____

_____

_____

_____

_____

Owning Your Accomplishments Exercise

This exercise aims to shift your focus from what you haven't accomplished to what you have achieved each day. By acknowledging your daily accomplishments, you can boost your self-esteem and build a more positive self-image.

Instructions

◯ **Daily reflection:** For seven days, at the end of each day take a few minutes to reflect on your day's activities. Be kind to yourself as you do this, knowing that it's okay if you didn't achieve everything you had planned.

Monday

Tuesday

Wednesday

Thursday

Friday

Saturday

Sunday

- **List your accomplishments:** Write down a list of things you did during the day, no matter how small or insignificant they may seem. These could include:

  - getting out of bed
  - taking a shower
  - preparing a meal
  - sending a message to a friend
  - going for a short walk
  - completing a work or school task
  - engaging in a hobby or self-care activity

- **Acknowledge your efforts:** After listing your accomplishments, take a moment to acknowledge the effort it took to complete each task. Recognize the extra strength and courage you put forth.

- **Give yourself credit:** Assign yourself credit for each accomplishment. You can use a scale like 1–10, with 10 being the highest. Be generous with your scores and avoid self-criticism.

- **Reflect on your list:** Review your list and the assigned credits. Take a moment to appreciate your daily achievements and recognize that you are making progress, no matter how slow it may feel.

- **Set realistic expectations:** If you find yourself consistently setting high expectations that lead to disappointment, consider whether your goals are realistic. Adjust them as needed to set yourself up for success.

Pleasure Predicting Sheet Exercise

Instructions

1. **Create your pleasure predicting sheet:** Start by making a list of activities that you can do either by yourself or with others. These activities can be simple daily routines, hobbies, social events, or anything you have planned. Don't forget to include activities that you're looking forward to or have been wanting to try.

2. **Predict satisfaction levels:** Next to each activity on your list, predict how satisfying it will be on a scale of 0 (least satisfying) to 100 (most satisfying). Be honest with yourself, and trust your instincts. Consider factors like your personal preferences, past experiences, and expectations.

3. **Participate in the activities:** Over the course of the week or month, engage in these activities one by one. Try to be fully present and immerse yourself in each experience. Take note of how you feel during and after each activity.

4. **Compare predictions to reality:** After completing each activity, take a moment to reflect. How satisfying was the activity compared to your initial prediction? Did it exceed your expectations, fall short, or match your prediction? Use a scale from 0–100 to rate your actual satisfaction.

5. **Reflect and learn:** As you go through this exercise, consider what you've learned about yourself and your ability to predict your own happiness. Are there any patterns in your predictions? Did you tend to underestimate or overestimate your satisfaction? What can you learn from this process?

List of Activities	Predicted Satisfaction 0–100	Emotions While Participating	Actual Satisfaction 0–100

Example: Let's say you predicted that going for a nature walk would be a 70 in terms of satisfaction. After the walk, you felt refreshed, inspired, and more at ease, rating it at an 85. This exercise not only helps you understand the activities that bring you joy, but also teaches you to trust your intuition when predicting future experiences.

Remember, the purpose of this exercise is to encourage self-reflection and help you identify activities that genuinely bring you pleasure, learning, or personal growth. It's all about building a toolbox of self-care activities tailored to your unique needs.

Worst, Best, Average Exercise

Two common cognitive distortions are labeling and overgeneralization, where we unfairly judge ourselves based on limited or extreme criteria. In this exercise, we'll work on challenging these distortions and building a more balanced view of ourselves.

Step 1: Identify Negative Self-Labels

Think about a negative self-label you often use, such as "I'm a bad mother/friend/partner." Write it down.

_____

_____

_____

Step 2: Define Positive Characteristics

Now, let's counteract this distortion by identifying positive characteristics of a good mother, friend, or partner. For example:

- ⊙ A good friend is supportive, trustworthy, empathetic, and dependable.
- ⊙ A good mother is nurturing, patient, loving, and attentive.
- ⊙ A good partner is respectful, passionate, patient, and loving.

Write down at least five positive characteristics for the role you've chosen to focus on.

_____

_____

_____

Step 3: Self-Assessment

Using a scale of 0–100, evaluate yourself in this role when you're at your:

- ⊙ worst
- ⊙ average
- ⊙ best

For each level, consider how closely your self-perception aligns with the positive characteristics you identified in Step 2. Be honest but gentle with yourself.

_____

_____

_____

_____

Step 4: Choose an Area for Improvement

Now that you have a clearer understanding of your self-perception at different levels, select a specific area where you'd like to improve. For example, if you rated yourself lower as a friend when you're at your worst, you might choose an area like "being more supportive during tough times."

Step 5: Create an Improvement Plan

Outline a plan for improvement in your chosen area:

Set a clear and achievable goal. For instance, "I will check in with my friends once a week."

_____

_____

_____

_____

Break your goal down into smaller, manageable steps. "I will start by sending a text message every Monday."

_____

_____

_____

_____

Create a timeline for each step, setting realistic deadlines.

_____

_____

_____

_____

Identify potential obstacles and brainstorm solutions. For example, "If I get busy, I'll set a reminder on my phone."

_____

_____

_____

_____

Step 6: Take Action

Start implementing your improvement plan. Be patient with yourself and celebrate your progress, no matter how small.

Future Projection: Finding Joy and Self-Esteem Exercise

Are you ready to take a trip into the future? Let's embark on a journey of self-discovery, where you'll meet a future version of yourself who is filled with joy and self-esteem.

Step 1: Setting the Scene

Find a quiet, comfortable space where you won't be disturbed. Close your eyes and take a few deep breaths. Imagine a serene place, like a peaceful garden or a calm beach, where you feel safe and relaxed. Picture yourself sitting there, feeling the warmth of the sun on your skin, the gentle breeze in your hair, and a sense of tranquility all around you.

Step 2: Meeting Your Future Self

In your mind's eye, visualize a version of yourself from the future. This future you is brimming with confidence, joy, and self-esteem. Imagine how they carry themselves, the sparkle in their eyes, and the positivity radiating from them.

Step 3: Engage in a Conversation

Start a conversation with your future self. Ask them questions about how they overcame their struggles and found happiness. Here are some prompts to get you started:

"Future me, how did you build such high self-esteem?"

_____

_____

_____

"What steps did you take to find joy and contentment?"

_____

_____

_____

_____

"Tell me about the moment when you realized things were getting better."

_____

_____

_____

_____

"What advice would you give to your present self right now?"

_____

_____

_____

_____

Step 4: Listen and Learn

As you engage in this imaginary conversation, pay close attention to the wisdom and insights your future self shares with you. Absorb their positive energy and let it fill your heart.

Step 5: Make a Commitment

Now, with your future self as your guide, make a commitment to yourself. Promise that you will work toward building a brighter future filled with joy and self-esteem. Write this commitment down.

_____

_____

_____

_____

Step 6: Return to the Present

Slowly open your eyes and take a few more deep breaths. Bring yourself back to the present moment knowing that you have connected with a future version of yourself who has found healing and happiness.

Step 7: Reflect and Take Action

Take a moment to reflect on the insights you gained during your conversation with your future self. What steps can you take right now to start making progress toward that happier, more confident you?

_____

_____

_____

_____

_____

_____

_____

Past Projection/Memory Rescripting Exercise

This exercise will help you confront and reframe painful memories, giving you the chance to express feelings that may have been bottled up or change the experience. It's a vital step toward finding peace within yourself.

Step 1: Choose a memory. Take a moment to reflect on a specific memory that continues to haunt you. It could be an incident where someone hurt you, a missed opportunity, or a moment when you felt powerless or inadequate. The key is to select a memory that still carries emotional weight. Write it down.

_____

_____

_____

_____

_____

_____

Step 2: Visualize the memory. Now, imagine yourself transported back to that moment. Reconstruct the scene as vividly as possible in your mind. Feel the emotions, notice the sights, sounds, and sensations. Let yourself be fully immersed in the memory.

_____

_____

_____

_____

_____

_____

Step 3: Engage in a conversation. In your mind's eye, initiate a conversation with the person involved in the memory. Speak your truth. Write down what you were unable to communicate at that time. Be honest and raw—this is your safe space to say what you needed to say.

_____

_____

_____

_____

Step 4: Rewrite the narrative. As you engage in this conversation, visualize the person's response being more empathetic, understanding, and compassionate than it was in reality. Imagine them validating your feelings, offering support, or apologizing for their actions. This is your chance to rewrite the narrative in a way that brings you healing.

_____

_____

_____

_____

Step 5: Release and forgive. As you conclude the conversation, let go of the emotional burden that the memory has carried. Imagine releasing it like a balloon and watching it float away, leaving you feeling lighter and freer. Take a moment to forgive yourself and the other person involved, knowing that this exercise is about your healing, not theirs.

_____

_____

_____

Step 6: Reflect and journal. Open your eyes and return to the present moment. Take some time to reflect on your experience. Write down your thoughts and emotions. How did the exercise make you feel? Did it provide any sense of closure or relief?

_____

_____

_____

_____

_____

_____

_____

_____

_____

_____

In the journey of self-discovery and healing, you've just completed a chapter on CBT and its application in dealing with sadness and depression. Drawing from my own experiences, I understand the weight of these emotions all too well. The exercises you've engaged with in this chapter are designed to empower you on your path to self-directed therapy. Remember, it's okay to struggle, and it's okay to seek help through self-guided approaches like CBT. As we transition into the next chapter, which delves into CBT techniques for managing anxiety and stress, know that you're not alone in this journey, and your resilience shines through every step you take toward a brighter, healthier future.

"

Man is not worried by real problems so much as by his imagined anxieties about real problems.

–EPICTETUS

CHAPTER 7

CBT for Anxiety and Stress

Anxiety and stress are like two unwelcome companions who seem to always show up uninvited to life's party. They're the butterflies in your stomach when you're facing a big presentation, the racing thoughts that keep you up at night, and the constant feeling of unease that follows you around like a shadow. That being said, they are both emotions we tend face in our lives, and knowing how to deal with them is key. So what exactly is stress and anxiety (*Stress and Anxiety: How They Differ and How to Manage Them*, 2022)?

- ⊙ **Anxiety:** This can manifest in many forms, from generalized anxiety disorder to panic disorder, social anxiety, or specific phobias. It's characterized by excessive worry, restlessness, and physical symptoms like a racing heart or sweaty palms. Anxiety can make you feel trapped in your own mind, always on high alert for danger even when it's not there.

- ⊙ **Stress:** It's a natural response to challenging situations in life. It's the body's way of preparing for a fight-or-flight response, which can be helpful in short bursts. However, when stress becomes chronic, it can take a toll on your physical and mental well-being, leading to symptoms like tension, irritability, and fatigue.

Now, let's connect the dots between stress, anxiety, and guilt. Often, these emotions are closely intertwined. Stress can fuel anxiety, and both can trigger feelings of guilt. You might find yourself worrying excessively about things beyond your control, leading to a sense of guilt for not being able to handle it all. It's a vicious cycle, and it's essential to break free from it.

Cognitive Distortions and Your Inner Dialogue

We now understand that cognitive distortions can make anxiety and stress worse. We all have them to some degree, and identifying and challenging them is a key step toward relief.

Before we dive into the exercises in this chapter, I want to emphasize the importance of reviewing the techniques we've explored in previous chapters. The Magic Dial and Straightforward Technique exercises are like building blocks, helping you develop the skills necessary to tackle these next ones.

Uncovering Stress Triggers and Challenging Negative Thoughts

Step 1: Pause and Recognize Stress

The first step in managing stress is to recognize when it's happening. It's all too easy to get caught up in the whirlwind of our thoughts and emotions without even realizing we're stressed. So the next time you catch yourself saying "I'm so stressed," hit the brakes.

Step 2: Reflect on the Lead-Up

When you catch yourself in the midst of stress, pause for a moment and reflect on what led up to this feeling. Ask yourself:

What was happening right before I felt stressed?

_____

_____

_____

_____

_____

How was I feeling at that moment?

_____

_____

_____

_____

_____

What thoughts were going through my mind just before I uttered those words?

_____

_____

_____

_____

_____

_____

Step 3: Examine Your Beliefs

Now, let's dig a bit deeper. Consider the thoughts that were racing through your mind. For example, you might have been thinking, "I'll never get this done. I'm a failure!" These thoughts are often driven by underlying beliefs.

Take a moment to identify the beliefs behind these thoughts. Maybe it's a belief about perfectionism, fear of failure, or the need for approval. Remember, this thought isn't a truth about you, so we need to understand where it is coming from.

_____

_____

_____

_____

_____

Step 4: Identify Cognitive Distortions

Our minds can play tricks on us, especially when we're stressed. It's essential to recognize these cognitive distortions. Review your beliefs and the thoughts that triggered your stress. Can you spot any cognitive distortions in there? Be gentle with yourself; we all have them from time to time.

_____

_____

_____

_____

_____

Step 5: Challenge and Reframe

Now it's time to challenge those negative thoughts and replace them with more balanced and realistic ones. Ask yourself:

Is there evidence to support these thoughts, or am I jumping to conclusions?

_____

_____

_____

_____

How else can I look at this situation? In our example, we used "I will never get this done, I am a failure." Maybe we could look at it as, "I am overwhelmed, I have a lot on my plate, and if I take it one step at a time as well as potentially delegate some tasks I can achieve my goal because I know I am not a failure."

_____

_____

_____

_____

_____

What would I tell a friend or my own child who had similar thoughts and feelings?

_____

_____

_____

Try to reframe your thoughts in a way that reflects a healthier perspective. For example, instead of "I'll never get this done. I'm a failure!" you could reframe it as "I'm facing a challenging task, but I can break it down into smaller steps and make progress."

Step 6: Practice Self-Compassion

Lastly, remember to be kind and compassionate to yourself throughout this process. We all have our ups and downs, and nobody is perfect. Negative thinking patterns can really do a number on us. When you find yourself feeling sad, anxious, or stressed, take a moment and look at how you are speaking to yourself. If it isn't how you would speak to your child or anyone else you love, change that narrative.

Repeat this exercise as often as needed to build your skills in identifying stress triggers, challenging negative thoughts, and promoting mental well-being.

_____

_____

_____

_____

_____

_____

_____

_____

_____

_____

The "What If" Exercise

Negative thoughts have a way of sneaking into our minds, and they can really take a toll on our mental health. It's important to remember that these thoughts are not always based in reality, and they can be influenced by our past experiences and fears. In this exercise, we're going to tackle these negative thoughts head-on.

Step 1: The "What If" Process

Pick one negative thought from your mood journal you began in Chapter 3. For this exercise, let's say you've chosen, "I'll never succeed in my career." Write it down.

Take a moment to consider what the worst-case scenario might be if this thought were true. In our example, it might be, "I'll be stuck at a dead-end job forever."

Now, take it a step further. Ask yourself again, "What's the worst that could happen if I'm stuck at a dead-end job forever?" Continue this process until you reach the most extreme worst-case scenario.

_____

_____

_____

_____

_____

Once you've reached the worst-case scenario, it's time to assess how likely it is to happen. In reality, the chances of this worst-case scenario occurring may be quite low.

_____

_____

_____

_____

_____

Finally, ask yourself if you could live with the worst-case scenario if it did happen. Most often, you'll find that even in the worst of circumstances, you have the resilience and strength to cope and adapt.

_____

_____

_____

_____

_____

Step 2: Challenge and Reframe

Now that you've walked through this exercise, take a moment to challenge the negative thought you started with. For example, you might reframe your thought like this: "While success in my career may take time and effort, I am a persistent person. I am capable of learning and growing. Even if I face setbacks, I can adapt and find new opportunities." Reframe your thought now.

_____

_____

_____

_____

_____

_____

Remember, this process is about gaining perspective and building resilience. Negative thoughts can feel overwhelming, but breaking them down like this can make them seem less daunting. Give this exercise a try whenever you catch yourself trapped in negative thought patterns. Over time, it can help you gain control over your thoughts and feelings, leading to improved mental well-being.

Worry Journaling and Empowerment Breaks

This exercise can help you manage those incessant worries and turn them into opportunities for growth and self-compassion.

Step 1: Set Aside Worry Time

Set aside a specific time each day for worrying. Choose a time that works best for you, but make sure it's when you can be alone and won't be rushed. Let's start with 10 minutes.

Find a quiet, comfortable spot where you won't be disturbed. It could be a cozy chair or even a park bench. Make it your worry haven.

Step 2: Embrace Your Worries

During your designated worry time, allow yourself to worry without holding back. If you constantly criticize yourself, do it wholeheartedly during these 10 minutes. Write down everything that's bothering you, all those negative thoughts and self-doubts. Be mindful that worry is normal; you don't need to feel shame or guilt. This exercise is meant to give you space for worry so it doesn't consume all of your time.

_____

_____

_____

_____

As you express your worries, write down how they make you feel. It's okay to experience discomfort, sadness, or frustration. Emotions are a part of you and acknowledging them is crucial.

_____

_____

_____

_____

Step 3: Empowerment Break

Once your 10 minutes of worry are up, it's time for a switch. Move to a different space or take a short walk. This is your empowerment break. Use this time to engage in a positive and productive activity that brings you joy, peace, or a sense of accomplishment. Feel free to walk, stretch, make tea, or even do yoga.

During your empowerment break, remind yourself of your worth and value. Focus on your strengths and the things you're grateful for. Use this time to recharge and shift your attention away from worry.

Take some time to reflect on how your body feels after time spent in this space.

_____

_____

_____

_____

_____

Step 4: Reflect and Adjust

At the end of each day, revisit your worry journal and the notes from your empowerment breaks. Take note of any progress, changes in your thought patterns, or insights you gained.

_____

_____

_____

_____

As you become more adept at managing your worries, consider gradually reducing the time you allocate to worry sessions. The ultimate goal is to spend less time worrying and more time living a positive, fulfilling life.

Remember, this exercise is all about giving yourself permission to acknowledge your worries and then step away from them into your empowered space.

Anxiety Distraction Toolkit

In this exercise, we're going to create your very own anxiety distraction toolkit. These are quick, accessible, and easy-to-use techniques that will help you divert your focus when anxiety starts creeping in. Think of it as your personal armor against anxiety.

Step 1: Brainstorm Your Distraction Techniques

Take a moment to think about the things that have helped distract you from anxiety in the past. Everyone is different, so your distractions might be unique to you. Here are some ideas to get you started:

- **Deep breathing:** Practice simple breathing exercises to calm your nervous system.
- **Coloring or drawing:** Engage in a creative activity to shift your focus.
- **Listening to music:** Create a playlist of your favorite calming songs.
- **Mindfulness meditation:** Use guided meditation apps to ground yourself.
- **Exercise:** Go for a walk, run, or do some yoga to release tension.
- **Puzzle games:** Solve crossword puzzles, Sudoku, or play brain games.

- **Journaling:** Write down your thoughts and feelings to gain clarity.
- **Aromatherapy:** Use essential oils or scented candles for relaxation.
- **Reading:** Dive into a book that captures your interest.
- **Sensory items:** Keep stress balls, fidget spinners, or textured objects handy.
- **Hydration:** Keeping a large cup or bottle of water near you is always a great idea.

Step 2: Create Your Toolkit

Now that you have a list of distraction techniques, select the ones that resonate with you the most. Remember, it's essential to have a variety of options, as what works best can vary depending on the situation and your mood.

- **Small journal:** The first item in your toolkit should be a small journal. On the first page, list the items you have in your kit and a brief description of how to use them. We do this because when anxiety hits, we don't always have the mental space to remember what works best or how. For example:

  - Deep breathing: Take slow, deep breaths. Inhale for a count of four, hold for four, exhale for four. Repeat until a feeling of calm comes over you.
  - Coloring or drawing: When that feeling of anxiety begins, start to color or draw. You should be focusing on how the drawing tool feels in your hand, the patterns, and the colors.
  - Listening to music: Grab your calming playlist, one you created to put you at ease. Immerse yourself in the tones, lyrics, and vibrations.

- **The right bag:** How you decide to carry your items is important. Maybe a cute backpack or a tote that you keep at work or in your car. For example, I made three toolkits and keep one beside my bed, one in my desk drawer at work, and one in my car. The bags I use for each are different.
- **Choose your items:** Now the fun part! Fill your bag with the items you find work well for you. Take your time with this and put some thought into it.

Step 3: Practice and Adjust

Your anxiety distraction toolkit is a valuable resource, but it's essential to practice using the techniques in this book regularly- especially mood tracking - even when you're not feeling particularly anxious. This way, they become second nature to you.

As you use your toolkit, pay attention to what works best for you. Some distractions may be more effective than others, and that's perfectly normal. Tweak and customize your toolkit over time to include techniques that resonate with you personally.

Transforming Your Inner Landscape

In this exercise, we'll combine the techniques of image substitution and visualize success to help you reframe and cope with challenging memories or situations from your past. This exercise is designed to provide you with a tool to reprocess and have less stress and anxiety in difficult situations.

Step 1: Identify the Negative Memory

Begin by choosing a specific memory or situation from your past that continues to impact your mental health negatively. It could be an incident related to your upbringing, your experiences with your parents, or any other event that triggers negative emotions.

_____

_____

_____

_____

_____

_____

_____

Step 2: Describe the Negative Memory

Write down a detailed description of the negative memory. Be as specific as possible about what happened, where it occurred, and how it made you feel. Use this description as a starting point for your transformation.

_____

_____

_____

_____

_____

_____

_____

Step 3: Visualize a Safe Haven

Now, close your eyes and take a few deep breaths to calm your mind. Imagine a serene and safe place where you can find comfort and solace. This could be a peaceful beach, a quiet forest, or any location where you feel secure and relaxed. Describe this place in detail.

_____

_____

_____

_____

Step 4: Replace the Negative Image

As you focus on this safe haven, bring the negative memory to the forefront of your mind. Picture the negative memory as if it's a movie playing on a screen in this safe place. Now imagine a remote control in your hand.

Step 5: Image Substitution

Using the remote control, pause the negative memory on the screen. Take a moment to write down the negative emotions that arise. Then, with intention, press the "play" button to transform the scene. Replace the negative elements of the memory with the peaceful imagery of your safe haven.

_____

_____

_____

_____

For example, if the negative memory involved a parent's outburst, visualize them speaking calmly and kindly in this new version. Focus on changing the emotions, reactions, and outcomes in a way that brings comfort and resolution. Write down if you can feel a shift in how those memories hold space now.

Step 6: Embrace the New Imagery

Allow yourself to be immersed in this transformed memory. Feel the sense of relief, peace, and safety wash over you as you experience the new version of the memory. Take as much time as you need to fully absorb the positive feelings associated with this visualization.

Step 7: Visualize Future Success

Now, expand your visualization to the future. Imagine yourself in a scenario where you have overcome the negative impact of this memory entirely. Picture yourself thriving, happy, and at peace. Consider how you have grown and healed from this experience.

Step 8: Embrace Your Future Self

As you visualize your successful future self, jot down the emotions you're experiencing. Feel the joy, confidence, and contentment that come with this imagined success. Embrace this positive energy and hold on to it as motivation for your ongoing healing journey.

Step 9: Journal Your Experience

Write down the transformation you experienced during this exercise. Reflect on the emotions and sensations you felt during the image substitution and future success visualization. This journaling can serve as a powerful reminder of your ability to reframe and heal from past experiences.

_____

_____

_____

_____

_____

_____

_____

_____

_____

_____

By now, you've learned valuable techniques and strategies to challenge negative thought patterns and develop healthier coping mechanisms. As you move forward to the next chapter on using CBT for anger, remember that healing is a process, and it's okay to take it one step at a time. The exercises ahead will guide you in understanding and managing your anger in a healthy way, building on the foundation you've laid here. Be patient with yourself, and remember that each small step you take is a significant stride toward a happier, more balanced life.

It is wise to direct your anger toward problems, not people; to focus your energies on answers, not excuses.

–WILLIAM ARTHUR WARD

CHAPTER 8

CBT for Anger

I grew up in a household where anger was a frequent visitor due to both my parents dealing with mental health challenges. As you can imagine, this made for a difficult environment, and I have struggled with my own mental health as a result.

When it comes to anger, I know all too well the tumultuous emotions it can stir up within us. Anger, whether it's a sudden burst or a slow simmer, is a powerful and complex emotion. It can manifest in various ways, and it often leaves us feeling overwhelmed and out of control.

In this chapter, we're going to explore how CBT can be a valuable tool in helping you manage your anger. It is a practical and effective approach that can empower you to gain better control over your emotions, even when dealing with justifiable anger.

Let's start by acknowledging that anger isn't always a bad thing. It can be a healthy response to certain situations. Picture it like a dial on a magical control panel- think of the Magic Dial in a previous chapter. Sometimes, you need to turn it up to protect yourself or assert your boundaries. That's perfectly okay. The key is learning how to turn it down when it becomes overwhelming or destructive.

Before diving into the exercises in this section, it's essential to understand what triggers your anger and how you experience it. Do certain situations or people consistently set you off? Do you feel a surge of heat in your chest, a tightening in your jaw, or a knot in your stomach when anger takes hold? Taking a moment to reflect on these questions can be the first step toward gaining mastery over your emotions. I encourage you to do the Magic Dial exercise before beginning some of the exercises in this chapter. The foundational tools we explored earlier- such as Magic Dial and the Straightforward Exercise- can provide you with insights into your emotional responses and help you set the stage for the exercises to come. It's like preparing the canvas before you start painting your emotional landscape.

Spelling Out the Anger Exercise

Anger is a complex emotion, often triggered by specific events or situations. This exercise will guide you through a process of spelling out your anger, breaking it down step-by-step, and helping you develop healthier coping mechanisms. We'll also explore any cognitive distortions that may be contributing to your anger.

Step 1: Identify the Trigger

Begin by identifying the specific trigger that made you angry. Write down the details of the situation, including where and when it happened.

Example: "The trigger for my anger was when my coworker made a hurtful comment during a team meeting."

_____

_____

_____

Step 2: Identify the People Involved

List the individuals involved in the triggering situation, and briefly describe their roles.

Example: "My coworker, Sarah, was the person who made the hurtful comment."

Step 3: Why Were You Angry?

Dig deep and reflect on why this trigger made you angry. What about the situation or the person's actions pushed your buttons? Be honest with yourself.

Example: "I was angry because Sarah's comment felt like a personal attack. It hurt my feelings and embarrassed me in front of the team."

Step 4: Identify Cognitive Distortions

Now, let's explore if there were any cognitive distortions at play. Remember that cognitive distortions are irrational and negative thought patterns that can intensify anger. Some common distortions include:

- **Catastrophizing:** Assuming the worst-case scenario.
- **Personalization:** Taking responsibility for things beyond your control.

⊙ **All-or-Nothing Thinking**: Seeing situations in black and white, without gray areas.

Examine your thoughts related to the trigger and identify any cognitive distortions. Write them down.

Example: "I was catastrophizing by thinking that everyone in the meeting now sees me as incompetent."

_____

_____

_____

Step 5: Reframe Distorted Thoughts

Challenge and reframe those distorted thoughts. Ask yourself if there's a more balanced and rational way to view the situation.

Example: "While Sarah's comment was hurtful, it doesn't mean everyone thinks I'm incompetent. People make mistakes, and it's okay."

_____

_____

_____

Step 6: Choose Action Steps

Think about what you can do to address your anger constructively. Consider healthy ways to cope with your feelings and manage the situation.

Example: "I can schedule a private conversation with Sarah to express how her comment made me feel. This way, we can work on better communication and understanding."

_____

_____

_____

Step 7: Express Yourself

If you feel it's necessary, write down what you would like to say to the person or people who caused your anger. This can be a therapeutic way to process your emotions, even if you don't intend to share these thoughts with them.

Example: "Sarah, I want you to know that your comment during the meeting hurt me. I believe open communication can help us avoid misunderstandings in the future."

_____

_____

_____

Breathe Out Anger, Breath In Calm Exercise

We all experience anger from time to time. It's a natural emotion, and it's okay to feel it. However, holding on to anger for too long can be detrimental to our mental well-being. This exercise will help you release pent-up anger and invite calmness back into your life.

Step 1: Visualize Your Anger

Close your eyes and take a few deep breaths. Imagine your anger as a vivid color inside you. It's likely to be red, but it can be any color that resonates with your emotions. Picture this anger as a swirling, fiery mass in a specific part of your body.

Step 2: Focus on Your Breath

Now shift your attention to your breath. Take a slow, deep breath in through your nose, counting to four as you inhale. Feel the air filling your lungs and expanding your chest.

Step 3: Breathe Out the Anger

As you exhale, imagine that you are expelling the anger from your body. Visualize this fiery mass of anger leaving your body with each breath out. Picture it dissipating into the air, becoming smaller and less intense with every breath.

Step 4: Inhale Calm

As you continue to breathe, imagine a calming white light surrounding you. With each inhalation, this light enters your body, filling the space that was occupied by anger. Feel the soothing, peaceful energy of this light washing over you.

Step 5: Self-Affirmation

While you breathe out the anger and breathe in the calming light, repeat a self-affirmation to yourself. You can say something like, "It's okay to let go of this anger, even though I have the right to be angry." Keep repeating this affirmation as you continue the exercise.

Step 6: Continue for 10 Minutes

Set a timer for 10 minutes, and continue this practice. Focus on your breath, the release of anger, and the influx of calmness. Let go of any judgments or expectations during this time.

Step 7: Reflect

After the exercise, take a moment to reflect on how you feel. Notice any changes in your emotional state or physical sensations. Write down your thoughts and feelings.

_____

_____

_____

_____

_____

_____

_____

_____

_____

Remember, this exercise is a tool to help you manage and release anger in a healthy way. It's essential to acknowledge your emotions and give yourself permission to feel them, but also to let go when they no longer serve you.

Reframing Anger Exercise

Anger is a natural emotion that we all experience at various points in our lives. It can be triggered by past traumas, misunderstandings, or current stressors. This exercise aims to help you reframe your past experiences with anger, allowing you to gain new insights and understanding without reliving the intense emotions associated with it.

Step 1: Choose a Memory

Take a moment to reflect on a time when you felt anger. It could be an incident from your past that still lingers in your memory. Choose a specific event that you are willing to explore without becoming overwhelmed. Write it down.

_____

_____

_____

_____

_____

_____

Step 2: Recall the Details

Now, recall the details of the event. What was happening at that time? Who was involved? Try to remember as many specifics as you can without getting lost in the emotions of the moment. Write down the details to help you visualize the situation clearly.

_____

_____

_____

_____

_____

_____

Step 3: Third-Person Perspective

Imagine stepping outside of yourself and looking at the situation from a third-person perspective, as if you were a neutral observer. Visualize the scene as if it were a movie playing in front of you.

Describe what you looked like in that moment. How did your body language, facial expressions, and actions reflect your anger?

_____

_____

_____

_____

_____

_____

_____

Observe the other person involved. What did their body language and expressions convey?

_____

_____

_____

_____

_____

_____

_____

Take note of any environmental factors or background details that may have contributed to the situation.

_____

_____

_____

_____

Step 4: Reflection

Now that you have this external perspective, reflect on what you notice differently. Consider the following questions:

Were there any misunderstandings or misinterpretations on your part or the other person's part?

_____

_____

_____

How might the situation have been influenced by your past experiences or triggers?

_____

_____

_____

Can you identify any patterns in your behavior or reactions during moments of anger?

_____

_____

Step 5: Empathy and Compassion

Take a moment to practice self-compassion and empathy. Understand that anger is a natural response to certain situations, but it doesn't define who you are as a person. Also, consider the other person's perspective and the challenges they may have faced.

Step 6: Learn and Grow

Finally, think about how you can apply the insights gained from this exercise to your life moving forward. Are there healthier ways to cope with anger? Can you communicate your feelings and needs more effectively? Use this exercise as a stepping stone toward personal growth and healing.

_____

_____

_____

_____

_____

_____

_____

_____

_____

_____

_____

_____

Drawing the Anger Exercise

Anger can be like a storm brewing within us, ready to unleash its fury. But what if we could take a step back and externalize that anger? Visualizing your anger can help you gain perspective and cultivate compassion for yourself. Here's an exercise to help you do just that.

Close your eyes for a moment and try to connect with the anger you're feeling. Where do you feel it in your body? Is it a burning sensation, a heavy weight, or something else? Take note of these physical sensations.

_____

_____

_____

_____

_____

_____

Now try to visualize your anger as an entity or object. What does it look like? Is it a shape, a color, or even an abstract form? Don't overthink it; let your imagination flow.

_____

_____

_____

_____

_____

_____

Open your eyes and pick up your drawing materials. Begin to draw what you saw in your mind's eye. Don't worry about making it perfect or artistic; this is for your eyes only.

If you like, you can add details to your drawing that represent the source of your anger or any words or phrases that come to mind.

Once you complete the drawing, answer the following: How do you feel toward this representation of your anger? Are you angry at it? Do you resent it? Or can you find some compassion and understanding for it?

_____

_____

_____

_____

_____

_____

_____

_____

Take a moment to sit with your drawing. Observe how you feel now that you've externalized your anger. Has your perspective changed? Can you find it in yourself to be more compassionate and accepting toward it?

_____

_____

_____

_____

_____

_____

_____

_____

Write down your thoughts and feelings about the exercise. How did it make you feel? Did you gain any insights about your anger or yourself?

_____

_____

_____

_____

_____

_____

_____

_____

_____

_____

Remember, healing takes time, and it's okay to revisit this exercise whenever you need to process your anger. Over time, you'll develop a deeper understanding of your emotions, and you'll find new ways to cope and grow.

In this chapter, we've delved into the power of CBT as a tool for managing anger. We've discussed how our thoughts, emotions, and behaviors are all interconnected and how identifying and challenging negative thought patterns can help us gain better control over our anger responses. You've learned various techniques and exercises to help you apply CBT principles to your own life and address anger issues constructively.

Remember, anger is a natural emotion that everyone experiences from time to time. It can be a signal that something is bothering you or a boundary has been crossed. However, when anger becomes overwhelming or unmanageable, it can strain your relationships and overall well-being.

As we move into the next chapter, we'll explore how CBT can be a powerful tool not only for managing your emotions, but also for improving your relationships. The skills you've developed in this chapter will serve as a foundation for better communication and emotional regulation in your interactions with others.

Take care of yourself and stay committed to your growth. You're stronger and more resilient than you may realize.

66

We can improve our relationships with others by leaps and bounds if we become invested in ourselves along the way.

–JOYCE MEYER

CHAPTER 9

CBT for Relationships

One of the most significant lessons I've learned is the importance of fostering meaningful relationships in our lives. Whether it's with friends, family, or a partner, healthy relationships are the cornerstone of our emotional well-being. But let's be real; relationships can be tough. When you throw depression, anxiety, anger, guilt, or low self-esteem into the mix, things can get even more complicated.

In this chapter, we're going to explore how CBT relates to our relationships. CBT is a powerful tool that can help us understand and improve the way we interact with others.

Why Meaningful Relationships Matter So Much

Meaningful relationships are the heart and soul of our lives, influencing our well-being and happiness in profound ways:

- ⊙ **Emotional fulfillment**: They provide us with emotional support, helping us navigate life's challenges and share its joys.
- ⊙ **Validation and self-worth**: These connections validate our worth and make us feel valued and loved.
- ⊙ **Sense of belonging**: They give us a sense of belonging, making us feel like we're an integral part of a community.

- **Personal growth**: Healthy relationships encourage personal growth and self-discovery.
- **Stress reduction**: They act as a buffer against stress, offering comfort and understanding during difficult times.
- **Happiness**: They contribute to our overall happiness by creating meaningful memories and moments of joy.

How Our Personal Experiences Shape Our Connections

Our past experiences, especially those in our formative years, greatly influence how we approach and engage in relationships:

- **Family dynamics**: Our upbringing and family dynamics significantly shape our attachment styles and expectations in relationships. For instance, growing up in a nurturing environment can lead to secure attachment, while a turbulent upbringing may result in anxious or avoidant attachment.
- **Trauma and resilience**: Experiences of trauma or adversity can impact our ability to trust and connect with others. Trauma survivors may struggle with intimacy, while resilience can foster healthier connections.
- **Role models**: The relationships we witnessed as children, such as our parents' interactions, serve as models for our own behavior in relationships. We may replicate or strive to avoid these patterns.
- **Communication patterns**: How we communicate and resolve conflict is often shaped by early experiences. Open and healthy communication in childhood tends to lead to better communication skills in adulthood.

How CBT Can Enhance Our Relationships

CBT is a powerful tool for improving relationships by addressing thought patterns, emotions, and behaviors:

- **Recognizing negative thought patterns**: CBT helps identify and challenge negative thought patterns that can undermine relationships, such as self-doubt or mistrust.
- **Emotion regulation**: It teaches techniques to manage intense emotions, preventing emotional outbursts that can strain relationships.
- **Improved communication**: CBT can enhance communication skills, allowing for more effective and empathetic interactions with others.
- **Behavioral changes**: It empowers individuals to modify behaviors that may be causing issues in relationships, such as avoidance or aggression.
- **Conflict resolution**: CBT equips individuals with strategies to handle conflicts constructively and find mutually satisfying resolutions.
- **Boundary-setting**: It helps establish healthy boundaries in relationships, fostering a balance between personal autonomy and connection with others.
- **Empathy and perspective-taking**: CBT encourages empathy and the ability to see situations from others' perspectives, enhancing understanding and reducing conflict.

Talk Show Host Exercise

In this exercise, we'll explore a way to develop your empathy and improve your interpersonal skills by adopting the friendly and inquisitive demeanor of a talk show host. This exercise is designed to help you connect with others on a deeper level, making them feel valued and understood. It can be especially beneficial if you've had personal experiences with depression and anxiety, as it allows you to approach conversations with empathy and kindness.

- ⊙ **Choose a conversation partner:** Select someone you'd like to connect with on a deeper level. It could be a friend, family member, colleague, or even a stranger you've just met.
- ⊙ **Set the stage:** Find a comfortable and quiet place to have a conversation with your chosen partner. Ensure that you won't be interrupted during your conversation.
- ⊙ **Adopt the talk show host persona:** Imagine you are a friendly and empathetic talk show host. While being subtle, your goal is to create a safe and inviting space for your conversation partner to share their thoughts and feelings.
- ⊙ **Open with warmth:** Begin the conversation with a warm and friendly greeting. Smile, make eye contact (if in person), and use a kind tone of voice to convey your interest in the conversation.
- ⊙ **Ask open-ended questions:** Instead of talking about yourself, focus on your conversation partner. Ask open-ended questions that encourage them to share more about their thoughts, feelings, and experiences. For example:

  - "I'm really curious about your journey. Can you tell me more about what you've been through?"
  - "What has been on your mind lately?"
  - "How do you cope with challenges or difficult emotions?"

- ⊙ **Active listening:** As your partner begins to open up, practice active listening. This means giving them your full attention, nodding to show you're engaged, and maintaining eye contact.

Avoid interrupting or offering solutions unless they specifically ask for advice.

- ⊙ **Express empathy and validation:** Show empathy and understanding by acknowledging your partner's emotions. Use statements like:

  - "It must have been tough for you."
  - "I can see why you might feel that way."
  - "Thank you for sharing this with me. It means a lot."

- ⊙ **Encourage further sharing:** Keep the conversation flowing by asking follow-up questions based on what your partner has shared. This demonstrates your genuine interest in their story.

- ⊙ **Reflect on the experience:** After your conversation, take a moment to reflect on how you felt during the interaction. Did you feel more connected to your conversation partner? Did you learn something new about them?

_____

_____

_____

_____

_____

_____

- ⊙ **Practice regularly:** Make a commitment to practice this exercise regularly with different people. The more you adopt the talk show host persona, the better you'll become at building empathetic connections with others.

Boundaries Exercise

Setting and maintaining healthy boundaries is an essential skill for maintaining your mental and emotional well-being, especially if you grew up in an environment like mine. It's not always easy, but it's incredibly important for your own peace of mind. In this exercise, I will help you identify a boundary you need to set, understand why it's important to you, explore alternative approaches, and address any negative thoughts or cognitive distortions that might arise.

Step 1: Identify the Boundary

Think about a specific situation or relationship in your life where you feel your boundaries are being crossed or neglected. This could be with a friend, family member, coworker, or anyone else. Write down the details of this situation:

Who is the person involved?

_____

_____

_____

What specific behaviors or actions are causing you discomfort or harm?

_____

_____

_____

How does this make you feel?

_____

_____

_____

Step 2: Understand the Importance

Now reflect on why it's important for you to set this boundary. What will setting this boundary help you achieve? What are the benefits of having this boundary in place? Write down your thoughts and feelings:

What are your goals or desired outcomes from setting this boundary?

_____

_____

_____

_____

_____

How will it improve your mental and emotional well-being?

_____

_____

_____

_____

What positive changes do you hope to see in your life as a result?

_____

_____

_____

_____

_____

_____

Step 3: Explore Alternative Approaches

Consider different ways to address the situation or relationship without violating your own boundaries. Think of alternative actions or responses that could be more constructive or healthy for you:

What other ways can you communicate your needs or concerns to the person involved?

_____

_____

_____

_____

_____

Are there compromises or agreements that could be made to respect both parties' boundaries?

_____

_____

_____

_____

How can you assert yourself while maintaining respect and understanding?

_____

_____

_____

Step 4: Address Negative Thoughts and Cognitive Distortions

Sometimes, setting boundaries can trigger negative thoughts or cognitive distortions. Identify any negative thoughts that come up when you think about setting this boundary and try to reframe them:

List any negative thoughts that arise when considering setting this boundary.

_____

_____

_____

_____

Challenge these thoughts by asking yourself if they are based on facts or assumptions.

_____

_____

_____

_____

Replace negative thoughts with more realistic and positive affirmations.

_____

_____

_____

_____

Step 5: Commitment and Action

Now that you've identified the boundary, understood its importance, explored alternatives, and addressed negative thoughts, it's time to take action. Commit to setting and maintaining this boundary for your well-being:

Write down your plan of action. What steps will you take to communicate and implement this boundary?

_____

_____

_____

_____

_____

Set a specific timeframe for initiating this boundary.

_____

_____

_____

_____

_____

Remember that it's okay to seek support from friends, family, or a therapist during this process.

Take Stock of Your Social Network

This exercise is intended to be a tool to help you assess and adjust your connections with others and create a more balanced and supportive social environment.

Step 1: Draw Your Social Circle

In the space provided, draw a large circle in the center. This circle represents your innermost social circle. Imagine it as your "trust zone."

Step 2: Create Rings

Inside this circle, draw a few more concentric circles, each one smaller than the previous. These rings represent different levels of closeness in your social network. From the inside out, label them as follows:

1. Bull's-eye: People you can be completely transparent with. Usually, this will be a very small number.
2. Best friends
3. Close friends
4. Friends
5. Acquaintances
6. Familiar faces
7. The rest of the world

Step 3: Populate Your Social Circle

Now, start filling in the names of people in your life within each of these categories. Be honest with yourself, and don't judge your choices. This is your own assessment, and it's for your benefit.

Step 4: Reflect and Recalibrate

Take a moment to reflect on your social circle. Notice how many people you have in each category. Do you feel like you have a balance that works for you, or are there areas where you want to make changes?

_____

_____

_____

_____

_____

Step 5: Consider Your Priorities

Now, consider these questions:

Are there people in the "bull's-eye" or "best friends" categories that you'd like to get closer to? How can you strengthen those relationships?

_____

_____

_____

_____

Are there individuals in your "friends" or "close friends" circles who should be in a more inner ring, but you haven't allowed them to get closer due to fear or past experiences?

_____

_____

_____

_____

Are there people who you've been investing too much time and energy in and are not receiving the same from in return? Should they move to more outer rings of your circle?

_____

_____

_____

_____

_____

Step 6: Action Plan

For each category, make a list of actions you can take

To build trust and transparency with those in the inner circles.

_____

_____

_____

_____

_____

_____

To strengthen relationships with friends who should be closer.

_____

_____

_____

_____

_____

_____

To set boundaries with people who might be taking too much from you without giving back.

_____

_____

_____

_____

_____

The Five Secrets Exercise

In life, we all encounter difficult conversations and conflicts with others. These situations can be especially challenging when dealing with loved ones who have mental health issues. This exercise will empower you to approach these conversations with understanding, empathy, and patience.

Step 1: The Disarming Technique

Begin by finding some truth in what the other person said, even if it seems totally unreasonable or unfair. This technique helps diffuse tension and opens the door to productive communication.

Exercise: Think of a recent conflict or conversation with someone close to you. Write down at least one aspect of their perspective that you can acknowledge as valid or understandable, even if you don't fully agree.

_____

_____

_____

_____

_____

_____

Step 2: Empathy

Empathy is a powerful tool for building bridges in relationships. Try to see the world through the other person's eyes. Paraphrase their words (thought empathy) and acknowledge how they are likely feeling (feeling empathy) based on what they've said.

Exercise: Recall a recent interaction with someone where you disagreed or felt disconnected. Write down what they said (thought empathy) and how they might have been feeling (feeling empathy). Put yourself in their shoes as much as possible.

_____

_____

_____

_____

_____

_____

_____

Step 3: Inquiry

Asking gentle, probing questions is essential to understanding the other person's perspective and emotions better. It shows your genuine interest in their thoughts and feelings.

Exercise: Think of a past conversation or conflict. Write down a few open-ended questions you could have asked to gain a deeper understanding of the other person's viewpoint and emotions.

_____

_____

_____

_____

_____

_____

Step 4: "I Feel" Statements

Expressing your thoughts and feelings directly is crucial for effective communication. Use "I feel" statements instead of "you" statements, which can come across as blaming.

Exercise: Reflect on a recent disagreement. Write down how you could rephrase any accusatory or blaming statements into "I feel" statements that express your emotions without placing blame.

Step 5: Stroking

Even during heated arguments, it's essential to convey an attitude of respect and find something genuinely positive to say about the other person.

Exercise: Recall a recent disagreement or argument. Write down something positive or appreciative about the other person, even if it feels challenging to do so.

I hope this chapter has been helpful. In our journey to healthier relationships, CBT can be a powerful tool. With the right techniques and a bit of practice, we can improve our connections with loved ones, friends, and even ourselves.

Be patient with yourself, keep practicing, and remember, you have the power to transform your life, one step at a time.

So, turn the page and let's keep going. Your story is still being written, and there are more chapters ahead.

We can be addicted to our thoughts. We cannot change anything if we cannot change our thinking.

–SANTOSH KELWAR

CHAPTER 10

CBT for Habits and Addictions

Through the years, I learned that the monsters we face aren't always the same, but the pain they bring is universal. Habits and addictions, whether they involve food, substances, or other behaviors, can become the chains that bind us, keeping us from living the lives we want.

But I want you to know something essential: You are not alone in this journey. You're not the only one who has tried to quit smoking, only to find yourself lighting up again when stress hits. You're not the only one who has stood in front of the refrigerator, battling an urge to eat when you're not even hungry. You're not the only one who has reached for that drink or that pill just to numb the pain.

CBT is a powerful tool that can help you break free from the grip of habits and addictions, just as it has helped countless others, including myself.

You see, CBT is for the brave soul who wants to take control of their life, who's tired of being a prisoner to their own impulses.

Throughout these pages, I'll provide you with practical exercises. Together, we'll work to understand your triggers, challenge your thought patterns, and develop healthier coping strategies.

The Raisin Meditation for Mindful Eating Exercise

Step 1: Find Your Space

Find a comfortable and quiet place to sit. If you have a dedicated meditation space, use it. Ensure you won't be disturbed for the next 10–15 minutes.

Step 2: Ground Yourself

Take a few deep breaths and focus your attention on your body. Feel your feet on the ground and your back against the chair. Allow yourself to relax and release any tension.

Step 3: Introduce the Raisin

Hold a raisin in the palm of your hand. Examine it closely with your eyes, paying attention to its shape, color, and texture. Notice any ridges or wrinkles on its surface.

Step 4: Engage Your Senses

Bring the raisin up to your nose and take a deep breath. Notice any scent or aroma that the raisin gives off. Let the fragrance fill your senses.

Step 5: Place It in Your Mouth

Slowly place the raisin in your mouth, but refrain from chewing it just yet. Focus on the sensations of the raisin resting on your tongue and the inside of your mouth. Let it sit there for a few seconds.

Step 6: Begin Chewing Mindfully

Begin to chew the raisin slowly and mindfully. Pay close attention to the sensation of each chew. Feel the texture and savor the flavor of the raisin as it gradually breaks down.

Step 7: Swallow Mindfully

Swallow the raisin and notice the sensation of it moving down your throat. Be present in this moment.

Step 8: Reflect on Your Experience

Take a moment to reflect on your experience. How did it feel to eat the raisin mindfully? Did you notice any new sensations or flavors that you wouldn't have noticed otherwise?

_____

_____

_____

_____

_____

Here are some additional questions for reflection:

How did the raisin meditation make you feel?

_____

_____

_____

_____

_____

Were you able to stay focused on the raisin, or did your mind wander?

_____

_____

_____

_____

_____

Did you discover any new aspects of the raisin that surprised you?

_____

_____

_____

_____

_____

How might practicing mindful eating benefit your overall relationship with food?

_____

_____

_____

_____

_____

Habit Plan Exercise

Creating a habit plan is a powerful tool to help you develop new, healthy habits that can contribute to your overall well-being. In this exercise, I'll guide you through the process of connecting your new habit to an existing one and then rewarding yourself for successfully completing the task. This approach can make it easier to incorporate positive changes into your daily routine.

Step 1: Connect Your New Habit to an Existing Habit

Think of a habit you already have in your daily routine. It could be something as simple as brushing your teeth, having your morning coffee, or taking a shower. Now, identify the new habit you want to develop. To connect them effectively, complete the sentence below:

After [existing habit], I will [new habit].

For example:

- *After I finish my morning coffee, I will meditate for 10 minutes.*
- *After I shower in the evening, I will write down three things I'm grateful for.*

By linking your new habit to something you already do regularly, you'll be more likely to remember and integrate it into your daily life.

Step 2: Reward Success

Rewarding yourself for successfully completing your new habit is a key part of reinforcing it. Rewards can be small but meaningful, and they should align with your new habit. Here's how to complete this step:

After [new habit], I will [reward].

For instance:

- *After I meditate for 10 minutes, I will treat myself to a cup of herbal tea.*
- *After I write down three things I'm grateful for, I will spend 15 minutes reading a book I enjoy.*

Your rewards should be enjoyable and sustainable, helping to create a positive association with your new habit. Avoid rewards that might contradict your efforts or be too difficult to maintain consistently.

Now it's your turn to create your habit plan. Fill in the blanks below:

Step 1: Connect Your New Habit to an Existing Habit

After _____ [existing habit], I will _____ [new habit].

Step 2: Reward Success

After _____ [new habit], I will _____ [reward].

Use this habit plan as a tool to build a better, healthier, and more fulfilling life for yourself, one step at a time.

STOP Exercise

The STOP Technique is an acronym representing four key steps (*Mindfulness STOP Skill*, 2023):

- **Stop:** The first step is of utmost importance, representing a vital pause—a brief interruption in your actions or reactions. It entails deliberately stopping impulsive responses and establishing a mental and emotional gap for thoughtful decision-making.

- ⊙ **Take a breath:** Mindful breathing acts as a potent tether to the here and now, fostering a profound connection between the mind and body. The breath offers a reliable and readily available focal point, encouraging relaxation and providing a sense of stability during stressful moments.

- ⊙ **Observe:** This stage motivates individuals to examine their thoughts, emotions, and the world around them without passing judgment. It entails nurturing a non-reactive awareness, enabling a more profound comprehension of one's inner and outer experiences.

- ⊙ **Proceed mindfully:** This phase entails proceeding with purpose and consciousness following the pause, mindful breath, and observation. It underscores the application of mindfulness to both decision-making and actions.

Step 1: Stop—Interrupting Impulsive Reactions

Take a moment to reflect on a recent situation where you reacted impulsively. It could be an argument with a friend, a frustrating work scenario, or anything that triggered an immediate and emotional response.

Now, write down that situation. Describe how you felt and the impulsive reaction you had.

_____

_____

_____

_____

Now, ask yourself:

What would have happened if I had paused before reacting impulsively?

_____

_____

_____

_____

_____

_____

_____

How could taking a moment to stop have changed the outcome of this situation?

_____

_____

_____

_____

_____

_____

Can you think of an alternative, more intentional response?

_____

_____

_____

_____

Step 2: Take a Breath—Cultivating Mindfulness

Take a few deep breaths right now. Pay attention to the sensation of each breath, the rise and fall of your chest, and the rhythm of your inhales and exhales.

As you do this, think about a recent stressful situation. How might taking a few deep breaths have helped you remain calm and focused in that moment?

_____

_____

_____

_____

_____

_____

_____

Step 3: Observe—Developing Self-Awareness

Now, let's practice observation. Recall a recent situation where you felt overwhelmed by emotions. Take a moment to list the emotions you experienced during that time. Be honest and specific.

_____

_____

_____

_____

_____

How did these emotions affect your thoughts and actions?

_____

_____

_____

_____

_____

What physical sensations did you notice in your body while experiencing these emotions?

_____

_____

_____

_____

_____

How could observing these emotions without judgment help you gain more control over them in the future?

_____

_____

_____

_____

_____

_____

Step 4: Proceed Mindfully—Enhancing Decision-Making

Think about a challenging circumstance you've faced recently. Imagine applying the STOP Technique to this situation.

How might pausing, taking a breath, and observing your emotions have influenced your decisions and actions?

_____

_____

_____

_____

_____

_____

_____

_____

Can you identify an alternative course of action that might have been more effective and less emotionally driven?

_____

_____

_____

_____

_____

_____

Stimulus Control Exercise

Stimulus control is all about modifying your environment to reduce triggers and cues that lead to unwanted behaviors. By identifying these triggers and making changes in your surroundings, you can regain control over your habits and addictions.

Step 1: Identify the Trigger

Take a moment to reflect on the habit or addiction you're trying to change. What situations, places, people, or emotions tend to trigger this behavior? For instance, let's say you're trying to quit smoking, and one trigger is stress.

_____

_____

_____

_____

_____

Step 2: Use a Trigger Chart

Use the following chart to record each time you engage in the unwanted behavior. This will help you spot patterns and understand your triggers better.

Date/Time	Location	Who Was Present	Emotional State	Triggers You Can Identify

Step 3: Analyze Patterns

After some time, review your entries. Look for commonalities among the triggers. Are there specific places, people, or emotions that consistently lead to the unwanted behavior?

_____

_____

_____

_____

_____

_____

Step 4: Modify Your Environment

Now that you've identified your triggers, it's time to make changes. Consider the following:

- ⊙ Remove or avoid triggers: If possible, distance yourself from people or situations that consistently trigger your habit. For example, if certain friends encourage your addiction, limit your time with them.
- ⊙ Create a supportive environment: Surround yourself with people who understand your goals and can provide positive reinforcement.
- ⊙ Replace triggers with healthier alternatives: Find healthier ways to cope with the emotions or situations that trigger your habit. Instead of reaching for a cigarette when stressed, try deep breathing exercises or going for a walk.

Step 5: Establish New Habits

As you modify your environment and reduce triggers, replace your unwanted behavior with healthier habits. Consistency is key here. It may take time to establish new routines, so be patient with yourself.

In this chapter, you've learned that by understanding the connection between your thoughts, feelings, and actions, you can take meaningful steps toward breaking free from the grip of addiction and forming healthier habits.

But let's be honest; change is rarely linear, and the journey in mental health is often accompanied by setbacks. So, as we move into our final chapter, remember that it's okay to stumble along the way. It's not about perfection; it's about progress. The fact that you're reading this workbook and actively working on yourself is already a significant step forward.

The comeback is always stronger than the setback.

–ANONYMOUS

CHAPTER 11

What if I Have Setbacks?

I want you to know that I get it. I really do. Life has a way of messing things up just when we think we are getting the hang of it, and sometimes those old negative thoughts and feelings creep back in, even when we thought we had them all figured out. Trust me, I've been there too. I want to be honest with you. Healing, therapy, and growth does come with setbacks. You should expect them, and being prepared is what will help.

This chapter is all about understanding and navigating those moments when you feel like you're slipping back into a dark place. It's about acknowledging that setbacks are a normal part of the journey. You see, mental health is not a linear path. It's more like a series of hills and valleys. Sometimes you'll be on top of the world, and other times you'll find yourself in a deep, dark valley.

It's okay to stumble, and to feel like you're taking a step back. It doesn't mean you're failing; it means you're human.

In this chapter, we're going to explore why setbacks happen, what they might look like for you, and most importantly, how to bounce back from them.

We'll look at some practical exercises and strategies that will help you build resilience and face those moments when the clouds of negativity start to gather.

It's okay to fall; what matters is that you keep moving forward. Let's turn those setbacks into opportunities for growth, self-discovery, and ultimately, healing.

Christine's Story

At the young age of 51, Christine suffered a heart attack, and it changed how she viewed life. After some dark days, she found the world of CBT, and this is how it changed her entire point of view:

After suffering a heart attack at 51, I decided to make a genuine effort to prioritize my health and well-being. My goal is to cultivate strength and fitness, as I recognize the importance of maintaining good health and physical capability. It's not just about my own well-being; it's also about being present and active in the lives of my children and future generations.

However, as the years have passed, my journey toward better fitness and healthier eating has faced numerous setbacks. While some individuals might rebound swiftly from such challenges, I found myself consistently falling into a pit of self-pity whenever I encountered obstacles. I would dwell on my misfortune or perceived lack of willpower, often reverting to my old habits, forgetting the positive changes I had diligently worked on for months.

It was only when I started CBT that I realized I wasn't alone in responding this way to adversity. As it turns out, my specific pattern of self-sabotage is quite common and even has a recognized term: "all-or-nothing thinking."

This term describes a mindset rooted in extremes. It's the belief that things are either a resounding success or an utter failure, that a performance is either flawless or completely flawed. This rigid way of thinking doesn't allow for setbacks, often leading to harsh self-criticism and negative judgments of both oneself and others.

The first time I encountered the concept of all-or-nothing thinking, it felt like someone had gained access to my thoughts and cracked them wide open. Throughout my entire life, I had been trapped in this pattern, labeling even the tiniest setbacks or minor stumbles as complete failures. This reinforced my belief that I lacked self-control and was destined for failure. At times, I was on the brink of success, only to throw my hands up in despair and crash back down the mountain.

Once I grasped the essence of all-or-nothing thinking, a profound shift occurred within me. I felt empowered and resilient. Simply recognizing this counterproductive thought pattern and understanding how it worked against me was sufficient to give me the strength to keep going.

When I Was (Not) Resilient Exercise

This exercise will help you reflect on situations when you were resilient and situations when you struggled to access your resilience. By understanding these moments, you can gain valuable insights into your strengths and how to lean into them during setbacks.

Part 1: When I Was Resilient

Describe a situation where you were resilient:

What was the situation and the context?

_____

_____

_____

_____

_____

_____

What resilient qualities were you able to access (like perseverance or self-confidence)?

_____

_____

_____

_____

_____

_____

What helped you access those qualities?

_____

_____

_____

_____

A situation where you failed to access your resilience:

Describe a situation where you struggled to be resilient:

What was the situation and the context?

_____

_____

_____

_____

_____

_____

What resilient qualities were you NOT able to access?

_____

_____

_____

_____

_____

_____

What prevented you from accessing those qualities?

_____

_____

_____

_____

_____

What were the consequences of not being able to access these qualities?

_____

_____

_____

_____

_____

Part 2: Reflecting on the Scenarios

Now, let's delve deeper into the two scenarios you've just described:

Scenario 1: When You Were Resilient

Consider what words describe how you were at the time.

_____

_____

_____

_____

What identity did you have or were you carrying with you?

_____

_____

_____

_____

_____

Scenario 2: When You Failed to Be Resilient

Reflect on what words describe how you were during this situation.

_____

_____

_____

_____

_____

_____

What cognitive distortions were you carrying with you that you can identify at this time?

_____

_____

_____

_____

_____

_____

By examining these two scenarios, think about what this tells you about your resilience:

Are there specific qualities that seem more developed in your resilient moments?

_____

_____

_____

Do you notice any patterns in what helped or hindered your resilience?

_____

_____

_____

_____

_____

_____

_____

_____

How do these insights into your resilience journey make you feel? Do you think you can lean into them in moments of setbacks?

_____

_____

_____

_____

_____

_____

One of the crucial aspects of preparing for your CBT journey is understanding that setbacks are a natural part of the process. Just like any journey, you might encounter obstacles along the way. However, it's essential to be prepared for these setbacks and not let them discourage you. In fact, setbacks can provide valuable learning opportunities and can be an integral part of your growth and healing.

Exercise: Externalization of Voices Technique

This exercise will help you identify and manage the negative or critical thoughts that may arise during setbacks in your CBT journey.

Identify negative thoughts: Think about a specific setback or challenge you've encountered in your CBT practice. What negative thoughts or cognitive distortions came up for you during this time? Write them down as accurately as possible.

_____

_____

_____

_____

_____

_____

Create a character: Imagine that these negative thoughts are coming from a separate character or entity outside of yourself. Give this character a name, persona, and appearance. It could be an exaggerated version of your inner critic or someone entirely fictional.

_____

_____

_____

_____

_____

_____

Dialogue with the character: Now, write a dialogue between yourself and this character. Imagine that you are having a conversation with them. Ask questions like, "Why are you saying these things?" or "What are you trying to protect me from?" Be honest and open in your conversation.

_____

_____

_____

_____

_____

_____

_____

_____

Challenge the character: As you continue the dialogue, challenge the negative thoughts and criticisms presented by this character. Use your newfound insights you have learned in this workbook to counter these thoughts with more balanced and rational perspectives.

_____

_____

_____

_____

_____

_____

Reframe and empower: Transform the character's negative statements into positive affirmations or constructive feedback. Encourage and empower yourself through this dialogue.

_____

_____

_____

_____

_____

_____

Reflect and summarize: After the dialogue, reflect on what you've learned. Write down any key insights or realizations. Summarize how you plan to apply this newfound understanding to deal with setbacks in your CBT journey.

_____

_____

_____

_____

_____

The beauty of CBT lies in its adaptability and resilience-building qualities. So when setbacks inevitably come knocking on your door, don't be disheartened. Instead, embrace them as opportunities for growth. As we've discussed, the first step is to identify those negative thought patterns that tend to resurface during tough times. Then, apply the techniques we've learned to challenge and reframe those thoughts. Think of it as a mental workout—the more you practice, the stronger you'll become.

CONCLUSION

As I bring this CBT workbook to a close, I want you to understand the deeply personal connection that fueled its creation. As I mentioned, growing up in a household where both my parents grappled with their mental health challenges, I intimately experienced the profound impact these struggles can have on individuals and families alike. Through the years, I witnessed various therapeutic approaches make a positive difference in the lives of myself and my loved ones, but CBT in particular has etched a special place in my heart. It's been the catalyst for a transformative journey that has reshaped my own life in ways I never thought possible.

With that background in mind, this workbook was conceived from a place of compassion and empathy. It was born out of an earnest desire to extend the transformative power of CBT to others who may be traveling a similar, often rocky path toward healing.

Remember, healing is a journey, and setbacks are as much a part of that journey as the progress you'll make. Just as I've encountered my fair share of obstacles, you may face your own challenges along the way. And that's normal. What's key to recognize is that you now possess a comprehensive toolkit filled with practical exercises and empowering techniques. These tools are designed to guide you through those difficult moments, helping you navigate your thoughts and emotions with skill and resilience.

Don't hesitate to return to these pages as frequently as you need to. We covered exercises to help with anger, fear, anxiety, sadness, depression, addiction, and so much more. We spent significant time exploring cognitive distortions, including what they are and how we can identify them.

I want you to think of this workbook as your trusted friend on the road to self-discovery and healing. Keep that mood tracker journal active; it's a valuable ally in understanding and managing your emotional landscape.

As you go through this workbook, choose the exercises that resonate most with you and repeat them. Embrace them, practice them, and as you grow and heal, don't be afraid to explore the other valuable resources the book contains. Your journey is unique, and this workbook is here to support you every step of the way.

If you've found this workbook to be a source of guidance and comfort, I would be deeply grateful if you could take a moment to share your thoughts in a review. Your feedback can get this resource into the hands of those, just like us, who are seeking the guidance and support they need on their own healing journeys.

In closing, I want to thank you for placing your trust in both me and the remarkable power of CBT. With the utmost empathy, understanding, and respect, I wholeheartedly wish you strength, resilience, and a future filled with brighter tomorrows.

Warm regards,

Anna

REFERENCES

Aardema, F., Bouchard, S., Koszycki, D., Lavoie, M. E., Audet, J.-S., & O Connor, K. (2022). Evaluation of inference-based cognitive-behavioral therapy for obsessive-compulsive disorder: A multicenter randomized controlled trial with three treatment modalities. *Psychotherapy and Psychosomatics*, *91*(5), 1–12. https://doi.org/10.1159/000524425

Aaron T. *Beck*. (2023). Beck Institute. https://beckinstitute.org/about/dr-Aaron-t-beck/

Alamy. (n.d.). *Inspiring motivation quote with text The comeback is always stronger than the setback*. Retrieved December 19, 2023, from https://www.alamy.com

Anger worksheets. (2012). Therapist Aid. https://www.therapistaid.com/therapy-worksheets/anger/none

Bathina, K. C., Thij, M., Lorenzo-Luaces, L., Rutter, L. A., & Bollen, J. (2021). Individuals with depression express more distorted thinking on social media. *Nature Human Behaviour*, *5*, 1–9. https://doi.org/10.1038/s41562-021-01050-7

Beck, J., & Cotterell, N. (n.d.). A cognitive-behavioral approach to relationships. In *Beck Institute*. https://beckinstitute.org/wp-content/uploads/2021/06/A-Cognitive-Behavioral-Approach-to-Relationships.pdf

Bell, C. (2023, November 1). *15 best CBT apps of 2022*. Choosing Therapy. https://www.choosingtherapy.com/best-cbt-apps/

B, J. (n.d.). *It s not about managing your emotions, it is about managing your reaction to your emotions*. Yung Pueblo. Retrieved December 12, 2023, from https://www.pinterest.ca/pin/321374123415188851/

Burns, D. (2020). *Feeling Great*. PESI Publishing Group.

Cognitive restructuring: Socratic questions (worksheet). (n.d.). Therapist Aid. https://www.therapistaid.com/therapy-worksheet/socratic-questioning

Dahl, D. (2022, September 19). *79 mad quotes that won t make you angrier*. Everyday Power. https://everydaypower.com/mad-quotes/

Daisy. (2019, May 22). *It starts in your mind*. SPOTEBI. https://www.spotebi.com/workout-motivation/it-starts-in-your-mind/

Hall, L. (2022, June 1). *Relatable quotes about depression that remind us all we re not alone*. Country Living. https://www.countryliving.com/life/inspirational-stories/a40122265/depression-quotes/

Kelwar, S. (n.d.). *We are addicted to our thoughts. We cannot change anything if we cannot change our thinking." -Santosh Kelwar... | Inspirational quotes motivation, Real talk, Me quotes*. Pinterest. Retrieved December 19, 2023, from https://www.pinterest.ca/pin/763923155517523462/

Kooienga, M. (2023, April 7). *Mindful eating: The raisin activity and guided meditation*. Nutrition Stripped. https://nutritionstripped.com/mindful-eating-the-raisin-activity-and-guided-meditation/#:~:text=Begin%20to%20chew%20the%20raisin

Kruse, S. (2022, April 13). *The Socratic method: Fostering critical thinking*. The Institute for Learning and Teaching. https://tilt.colostate.edu/the-socratic-method/#:~:text=What%20is%20the%20Socratic%20Method

Lam, R. (2022, December 5). *A simple and effective CBT technique to empower mindset*. https://www.feelinggoodinstitute.com/technique-video/the-feeling-good-therapist--stop-negative-thinking-with-the-straight-forward-technique#:~:text=The%20technique%20involves%20answering%20three

La Vasan, T. (2018, April 17). *8 inspiring quotes about change*. Red Online. https://www.redonline.co.uk/wellbeing/g518163/best-quotes-about-change/

McWilliams, P. (n.d.). *Peter McWilliams quote*. A-Z Quotes. Retrieved December 12, 2023, from https://www.azquotes.com/quote/1046720

Mindfulness STOP skill. (2023, December 1). Cognitive Behavioral Therapy Los Angeles. https://cogbtherapy.com/mindfulness-meditation-blog/mindfulness-stop-skill

Nyugen, J. (n.d.). *Don t Believe Everything You Think*. Goodreads. https://www.goodreads.com/en/book/show/60726415

Rahman, I. (2022, January 19). *CBT for anger: How it works, techniques, & effectiveness*. Choosing Therapy. https://www.choosingtherapy.com/cbt-for-anger/

Schaffner, A. K. (2020, October 15). *Living with the inner critic: 8 helpful worksheets*. PositivePsychology. https://positivepsychology.com/inner-critic-worksheets/#:~:text=Real%2DLife%20Examples

Stiles, K. (2021, July 30). *Quotes about anxiety*. Psych Central. https://psychcentral.com/anxiety/quotes-about-anxiety

Stress and anxiety: How they differ and how to manage them. (2022, February 17). Healthline. https://www.healthline.com/health/stress-and-anxiety#:~:text=What%20are%20stress%20and%20anxiety

Substance use worksheets. (2023). Therapist Aid. https://www.therapistaid.com/therapy-worksheets/substance-use/none

Sutton, J. S. (2021, December 6). *Resilience counseling: 12 worksheets to use in therapy*. PositivePsychology. https://positivepsychology.com/resilience-counseling/#activities

Wikipedia Contributors. (2019, May 17). *David D. Burns*. Wikipedia. https://en.wikipedia.org/wiki/David_D._Burns

ACT

WORKBOOK

— FOR —

ADULTS

Acceptance and Commitment Therapy for Anxiety, Depression, and Addiction with Simple Techniques

ANNA NIERLING

HOW TO USE THIS BOOK

Whether you're on a self-directed path to personal growth or a therapist looking for valuable exercises to incorporate into your practice, this book is designed to guide you toward a more mindful and fulfilling life.

The Tenets of ACT and How They Work Together

In this book, we will explore the core tenets of Acceptance and Commitment Therapy (ACT). These principles are not isolated; they interconnect and build upon each other. I recommend following the chapters in order, as they are intentionally structured to help you gradually integrate ACT into your life. Even if you choose to start with some of the first exercises in each chapter and then progress through the rest, I encourage you to revisit and complete all exercises from each chapter once you've finished the book. Your personal toolbox will benefit from this holistic approach, as different exercises may resonate with you at different times.

ACT skills can enhance your life, whether you're already engaged in another form of talk therapy or not. These techniques are complementary and can serve as valuable tools to empower you on your journey to self-discovery and emotional well-being.

It's vital to understand that ACT is not about avoiding, escaping, or distracting from painful thoughts and feelings. Many people have found that ACT can help them feel better and manage their constant chattering mind. The primary goal of ACT is to liberate you from the tyranny of your mind, allowing you to focus on what truly matters in your life. While you should experience moments of relief along the way, it's important to approach these exercises with the intention of freeing up your time, energy, and attention. Remember, feeling better is a bonus, not the primary goal.

Pain is part of being human, even emotional pain.

–RACHEL EDDINS

INTRODUCTION

Do you ever find yourself lying awake at night, your mind racing with worries about the future, and an overwhelming sense that you're not doing enough? Are you constantly striving for happiness, only to feel like it's just out of reach? Are panic attacks and anxiety consuming your attention and energy? If you've ever felt this way, you're not alone. I've been there too. I want to share with you a therapy approach, Acceptance and Commitment Therapy (ACT), and how it transformed my life and can do the same for you.

Hi, I'm Anna, and I've spent years studying and researching mental health disorders. My journey into this field began when my mom was diagnosed with bipolar disorder. The diagnosis was later changed to borderline personality disorder (BPD), and throughout those years, I dedicated myself to helping my mother manage despite the challenges of the initial misdiagnosis. Additionally, I was raised by a father grappling with schizophrenia, a constant undercurrent in our lives, and one that persists to this day as he faces the ongoing challenges of medication adjustments and maintenance. Watching my parents' struggles and trying to support them ignited my passion for understanding and improving mental well-being.

I hold a bachelor's degree in psychology, and over the years, I've explored therapies such as Cognitive Behavioral Therapy (CBT) and Dialectical Behavior Therapy (DBT). Additionally, I have published three books on these subjects, including a book on Borderline Personality Disorder (which can potentially be fully cured with DBT). While DBT and CBT helped me tremendously, I often felt that something was missing—a missing piece of the puzzle that could truly set me free from my relentless anxiety and worries.

That missing piece turned out to be ACT, a "third-wave" therapy that focuses on psychological flexibility. ACT changed my life in ways I couldn't have imagined. It allowed me to slow down, savor the present moment, and find meaning and fulfillment in my life, rather than constantly chasing after an elusive happiness.

In this workbook, I'll introduce you to ACT in a relatable and accessible way. Together, we'll explore the core concepts of this transformative therapy, understand how it adds to traditional CBT, and learn how it can help you live a richer, more meaningful life.

ACT isn't about erasing pain or magically becoming happy all the time-this is not reality. Instead, it's about accepting the pain that inevitably comes with life and learning to take effective action guided by your deepest values. It's about being fully present and engaged in your life, even in the face of discomfort.

We'll also challenge some common misconceptions about happiness. Contrary to popular belief, happiness isn't our natural state, and feeling unhappy doesn't mean you're broken.

It's fascinating how our minds are wired to suffer psychologically. It all goes back to our cave-person days when our ancestors had to be hyper-aware of danger. Imagine being chased by a tiger. You had to be on high alert to notice and avoid any potential threats, otherwise, you'd end up as dinner. So, over time, our minds have evolved to constantly compare, evaluate, criticize, and focus on what's lacking. It's like a survival mechanism. And hey, think about it, if you were rejected by your tribe back then, you were basically left vulnerable to becoming a roaming animal's dinner.

In other words, our minds have evolved to notice, predict, and avoid danger, leading us to focus on what's lacking or what could go wrong. Understanding this can be a vital step toward finding true happiness and fulfillment.

How else is ACT unique? You see, it doesn't rely on the assumption of healthy normality like Western psychology does. Western psychology is built on the idea that humans are naturally psychologically healthy, and as long as they have a healthy environment, lifestyle, and social context, they will experience happiness and contentment. According to this perspective, psychological suffering is considered abnormal, like a disease or syndrome caused by unusual pathological processes.

Why does ACT think this assumption might be wrong? Well, let's look at the numbers. Every year, nearly 30% of adults experience a recognized psychiatric disorder. In fact, the World Health Organization estimates that depression is currently the fourth most significant, expensive, and disabling disease worldwide. And guess what? By the year 2025, it's projected to become the largest (World Health Organization, 2023). Just think about it: in any given week, one-tenth of adults are dealing with clinical depression, and one in five individuals will experience it at some point in their life.

Clearly, even though our standard of living is higher than ever before in recorded history, psychological suffering is all around us.

Russell Harris, author of *The Happiness Trap* states: "The harder we chase after pleasurable feelings and try to avoid the uncomfortable ones, the more likely we are to suffer from depression and anxiety."

ACT has been scientifically proven to help with various mental health challenges, including anxiety, depression, anger, addiction, guilt, shame, eating disorders, chronic pain, and more. It can enhance your relationships, boost your self-esteem, and provide you with the tools to navigate life's ups and downs with resilience and grace (Keng et al., 2011).

So, if you're ready to embark on a journey toward a more meaningful and fulfilling life, I invite you to dive into the pages of this workbook. Together, we'll explore the principles of ACT, practice many exercises, and discover a new way of approaching your thoughts, emotions, and experiences. It's time to embrace your life, warts and all, and start living it to the fullest. Let's get started on this transformative path to psychological flexibility and personal growth.

Life is a series of natural and spontaneous changes. Don't resist them; that only creates sorrow. Let reality be reality. Let things flow naturally forward in whatever way they like.

–LAO TZU

CHAPTER 1

Embracing the Freedom Beyond Control

One of the most significant challenges we all face is our relentless quest to control our feelings and thoughts. Picture yourself in a haunted house, desperately trying not to jump or get scared when monsters lurk around every corner. Or imagine being in a room filled with yawning people, and you're struggling to stifle a yawn of your own. Why is it so tough to control our emotions and thoughts in these situations?

Let's break it down:

Imagine a bear charging straight at you, but you're told not to feel anxiety. Your favorite meal is right in front of you, and the mouthwatering aroma tempts your senses, but you're forbidden from salivating. As you slice an onion, tears threaten to escape, yet you're compelled to hold them back. Now, take a look at a picture of a pink elephant, but try your hardest not to think about the fact that it should be grey. These exercises, as strange as they may sound, mirror the everyday struggle we face when attempting to manage our inner world.

But it's not just these playful challenges. Society bombards us with messages about how we should think and feel. We're constantly told to "think positive," to "stop feeling sorry for ourselves," and to believe that "big boys and girls don't cry." These well-meaning messages often come from people who may be grappling with their own emotional struggles in secret. We're taught to bottle up our painful feelings, to hide them from each other, because we're led to believe that expressing these emotions makes us appear weak, silly, or broken.

In this chapter, we'll dive deep into the fundamental reasons why controlling our feelings and thoughts can be such a Herculean task. We'll help you understand that the relentless pursuit of control may not always serve your best interests. Instead, we'll embark on a journey together to embrace these emotions, let go of the need for constant control, and discover true meaning and fulfillment in our lives through the principles of ACT. I will be your guide, leading you through exercises and insights that will help you break free from the unnecessary constraints of control and open yourself up to a life filled with authenticity and purpose.

Obeying Your Thoughts and Feelings

To obey our thoughts and feelings means to unquestionably accept and buy into them. It's akin to taking them at face value and allowing them to dictate our actions and emotional state. When we obey, we often believe that the thoughts and feelings are entirely true and that we must act accordingly. Here are some key points to consider:

- ⊙ **Believing the truth:** When a painful thought or feeling arises, we may automatically assume that it's entirely accurate. For example, if you experience anxiety, you might think, *"There's something wrong with me,"* or *"I'm going crazy."* This unquestioning belief in the truth of our thoughts and feelings can lead to unnecessary distress.
- ⊙ **Rigid rules:** Oftentimes, we tend to set strict rules for ourselves based on our thoughts and feelings. We might place unrealistic

expectations or standards on ourselves, thinking that following them will allow us to manage or get rid of our anxiety or other negative emotions.

- ⊙ **Escaping into our heads:** Obedience to our thoughts and feelings can lead us into a cycle of overthinking and rumination. This means we get caught up in constantly analyzing and dwelling on our thoughts and emotions. Instead of finding solutions or relief, we end up becoming more distressed and stuck in our own discomfort.

Struggling With Our Thoughts and Feelings

On the flip side, struggling with our thoughts and feelings involves actively resisting them or attempting to stuff them down. While this approach may seem like a way to gain control, it often leads to increased suffering. Here's what struggling looks like:

- ⊙ **Excessive resistance:** When we struggle, we employ various strategies to stop our thoughts and feelings from dominating us. These strategies can include distraction, avoidance, or suppression. Although they may offer short-term relief, they can hinder progress in the long term.

- ⊙ **Ineffectiveness:** Struggle strategies refer to the various methods or approaches we employ to cope with difficult emotions or situations. However, these strategies can become problematic when they prove to be ineffective, particularly when we are trying to suppress feelings of rejection or grief. In such circumstances, our efforts to resist or fight against these emotions only serve to intensify our distress, making the situation even more challenging to handle.

- ⊙ **Distraction as struggle:** Even seemingly harmless activities like constant distraction can become a struggle strategy. While distraction can be useful at times, it's essential to recognize when we are using it to avoid confronting our thoughts and feelings.

ACT aims to help us find a more balanced and mindful approach to our thoughts and feelings. Rather than automatically obeying or struggling with them, we learn to observe and acknowledge them without judgment. This allows us to make more intentional choices about how we respond.

Where Is the Delete Button?

In the quest for understanding ACT, it's crucial to grasp one fundamental concept: There's no delete button for our thoughts. Our minds are wired in a way that often compels us to fill in the blanks, even when they're incomplete. Think about those famous lines: "Mary had a little _____" or "Happy birthday to _____." Most likely, your brain immediately filled in the blanks, even though there's no specific information provided.

Our brain doesn't change by simply erasing thoughts or trying to get rid of them. Instead, it evolves by laying down new neural pathways on top of the old ones. This is a key insight that ACT brings to the table. It's not the negative thoughts themselves that are the problem; it's our relationship with them. We often feel obligated to obey our thoughts or consider them as the absolute truth. This sense of being "hooked" by our thoughts, or fused with them, is what ACT seeks to address.

Consider this analogy: Even things you forget stay with you to some extent. This phenomenon is known as the reacquisition effect. It's why, for example, you might find it easier to relearn something you once knew but forgot, rather than learning it from scratch. Similarly, our thoughts, especially the negative ones, tend to linger in our minds, making it challenging to simply delete or dismiss them.

When life is calm, and we're in a controlled environment, we often believe we have more emotional control than we actually do. We might have relaxation techniques or coping mechanisms that seem effective at the time. However, when faced with a high-stress situation, like a job interview, a date, or a heated argument, it becomes much harder to employ these techniques effectively.

ACT recognizes that life is messy and unpredictable. It acknowledges that we can't always control our thoughts or the circumstances we find ourselves in. Instead of striving for absolute control, ACT encourages us to develop the skills to observe our thoughts without judgment, to recognize when we're getting caught up in them, and to make choices aligned with our values, even in the face of difficult emotions.

EXERCISE: Exploring Your Past Tools for Well-Being

In this exercise, we will reflect on the various techniques and strategies you have used in the past or are currently using to improve your emotional well-being. By examining their effectiveness and potential costs, you can gain insight into which approaches have provided short-term relief but may not have yielded long-term benefits.

List Your Past and Current Techniques

Take some time to make a comprehensive list of all the techniques, practices, or strategies you have tried or are currently using to feel better emotionally. This could include activities like meditation, yoga, positive thinking, journaling, video games, drinking, and any others that come to mind.

_____

_____

_____

_____

_____

Evaluate Long-Term Effectiveness

For each technique you've listed, reflect on how effective it has been in the long run. Consider whether it has consistently improved your emotional well-being over time, or if its impact tends to be short-lived. You may want to use a scale from 1 to 10 to rate their long-term effectiveness, with 1 being not effective at all and 10 being highly effective.

Technique	Effectiveness 1-10	Short lived or Long term improvement

Consider the Costs

Explore the potential costs associated with each technique. Costs can be both tangible and intangible. Tangible costs might include financial expenses, while intangible costs could involve the impact on your relationships, physical health, or overall life satisfaction. Be honest about the negative consequences, if any, that have arisen from using these techniques.

_____

_____

_____

_____

Identify Short-Term Relief vs. Long-Term Benefits

Reflect on how many of the techniques on your list primarily provide short-term relief from emotional pain but do not contribute to long-term well-being. Try to identify patterns or themes among these techniques. What common characteristics do they share? Are they primarily distractions, numbing activities, or quick fixes?

_____

_____

_____

_____

By completing this exercise, you will gain a better understanding of the strategies you have employed to improve your emotional well-being and their overall impact. This awareness can be valuable as you continue to explore ACT and seek more sustainable ways to find meaning and fulfillment in your life, beyond mere short-term relief.

EXERCISE: Exploring Daily Avoidance Patterns with Flexibility in Mind

In this exercise, we will explore the daily activities and behaviors that you engage in to avoid unpleasant feelings. ACT is deeply rooted in the idea of flexibility. It's not about following strict rules, but about learning to adapt and make choices that fit your life and values.

Step 1: Identify Avoidance Behaviors

Start by creating a journal or a list where you can record the various activities or behaviors you engage in to avoid unpleasant feelings. These could be things like procrastination, overeating, excessive screen time, avoidance of difficult conversations, or any other avoidance strategy you notice in your life. You are welcome to utilize the area provided.

_____

_____

_____

_____

Step 2: Reflect on the Purpose

Next to each avoidance behavior, reflect on why you think you engage in it. What unpleasant feelings or thoughts are you trying to escape or avoid by doing these things? Be as specific and honest as possible. Understanding the purpose behind your avoidance patterns is crucial for personal growth.

Step 3: Challenge Your Patterns

Now, let's apply the principles of flexibility from ACT. Do your best to answer the following questions for each avoidance behavior.

Is this avoidance behavior helping me live a fulfilling and meaningful life?

_____

_____

_____

Am I willing to accept the discomfort that comes with these unpleasant feelings, knowing that they are a natural part of being human?

_____

_____

_____

What values and long-term goals am I sacrificing by avoiding these feelings?

_____

_____

_____

Can I find more flexible and mindful ways to handle these unpleasant feelings?

_____

_____

_____

Step 4: Create a Flexibility Plan

Based on your reflections, identify one or two avoidance behaviors that you'd like to address. Develop a flexibility plan for each chosen behavior:

For example, if you tend to procrastinate because it helps you avoid the anxiety of starting a challenging task, your flexibility plan might look like this:

1. Acknowledge the anxiety when it arises.
2. Remind yourself of your values and long-term goals (e.g., completing the task will help you grow in your career).
3. Divide the task into more manageable and smaller steps.
4. Practice self-compassion and self-acceptance, knowing that it's okay to feel anxious.

Your Flexibility Plan

_____

_____

_____

_____

_____

_____

_____

_____

_____

_____

Step 5: Take Action

Implement your flexibility plan and track your progress in your journal. Notice any shifts in your relationship with these avoidance behaviors and the associated unpleasant feelings. Be patient with yourself as you work towards more flexible and mindful responses.

Remember that ACT is a journey of self-discovery and growth. It's not about eliminating all unpleasant feelings but learning to respond to them in a way that aligns with your values and leads to a more fulfilling life. Flexibility is the key to unlocking this transformation.

Key Takeaways

- **The challenge of controlling thoughts and feelings**: We often struggle to control our thoughts and feelings. This struggle is compounded by societal messages that encourage us to suppress or hide our emotions.
- **Obedience to thoughts and feelings**: Obedience involves unquestioningly accepting and acting on our thoughts and feelings as if they are entirely true. This can lead to distress, rigid rules, and overthinking.
- **Struggling with thoughts and feelings**: Struggling entails actively resisting or attempting to suppress thoughts and feelings. While it may offer temporary relief, it often leads to increased suffering, ineffectiveness, and excessive distraction.
- **ACT's mindful approach:** ACT promotes a balanced and mindful approach to thoughts and feelings. It encourages us to observe and acknowledge them without judgment, allowing for more intentional choices in response.

⊙ **No delete button for thoughts:** ACT teaches us that we can't delete our thoughts; our minds naturally fill in the blanks. The focus is not on eliminating negative thoughts, but on changing our relationship with them. Instead of getting hooked, ACT encourages us to observe our thoughts, recognize when we're getting caught up, and make value-aligned choices, even in tough situations.

As we conclude this chapter, we have only scratched the surface of the fascinating world of ACT. The journey we have embarked upon has introduced us to the fundamental principles and concepts that underpin this remarkable field. But hold on tight, because the next chapter will take us deeper into the captivating realm of the science behind ACT. Get ready to explore the intricate mechanisms, groundbreaking research, and mind-boggling discoveries that will leave you in awe.

Between stimulus and response there is a space. In that space is our power to choose our response. In our response lies our growth and our freedom.

–VIKTOR E. FRANKL

CHAPTER 2

Unveiling the Science Behind ACT

We can't dig into the science of ACT without discussing Relational Frame Theory (RFT), a fascinating psychological framework that explores the connections between language, cognition, and behavior. It delves into the intricate web of how we relate to ourselves, our thoughts, and the world around us. RFT lays the foundation for ACT, providing us with valuable insights into the power of language and the stories we tell ourselves.

Making Sense of RFT

RFT is a powerful framework developed by Steven Hayes and Aaron Brownstein, and it plays a significant role in ACT. This theory revolves around the way humans understand the relationships between words and their meanings, and how this understanding goes both ways (Ackerman, 2018).

Think of how we understand words and their meanings as a two-way street, something unique to humans. Consider the word 'Mama.' A child understands that 'Mama' means their mother, and when seeing their mother, they can also recognize her as 'Mama' when prompted. This is known as reciprocal recognition—connecting the object/person/place with the name or word. Another example is a child learning that 'brushing teeth' is something we do before 'bedtime.' If you say 'bedtime,' the child might think of brushing their teeth. Conversely, if you say 'brush teeth,' they might think it's time for bed soon. They've linked these concepts in both directions. Animals, however, usually have a one-way understanding. They might hear a command and know to perform a certain action, but they don't have the ability to reverse this. If you show them the action, they can't always identify the command that goes with it. It's more like a single direction in understanding rather than a conversation back and forth.

To better grasp the concept of two-way relationships, think about comparisons like "The house is bigger than a blueberry" and "The sun is bigger than the house." A small child who understands these relationships can then deduce that the sun is bigger than a blueberry. This process extends to understanding one's own place in these relationships. If a child knows they are smaller than the house, they can conclude that they are also smaller than the sun.

Language as Relating, Not Just Associating

One important idea from RFT is that language goes beyond simply associating words with meanings. It involves learning to connect words in complex and dynamic ways. This ability to make connections is what makes human thinking intricate and genuine. Our minds utilize language to understand the intricate aspects of the world because we constantly form connections in our minds.

One interesting thing about human thinking is how one thought can automatically lead to another, even if they seem unrelated. For instance, when you think about how sweet your child is, it can unexpectedly bring up thoughts about your mother's shortcomings. These connections between thoughts are formed because our minds can create complex cognitive networks by linking one idea to another.

One of the goals of ACT is to acknowledge that thoughts can trigger unrelated thoughts, and instead of trying to break down these dense and complex networks, we learn to work with them.

EXERCISE: Object Relations Exploration

In ACT, we learn to be more mindful of our thoughts, feelings, and experiences, and to observe them without judgment. This exercise is designed to help you understand how your mind creates relations between different objects and concepts, ultimately illustrating the interconnected nature of your thoughts and emotions.

Choose Two Objects

Take a moment to choose two unrelated objects in your surroundings or think of any two objects that come to mind. These could be anything–for example, a coffee cup and a book, a tree and a bicycle, or even abstract concepts like love and fear. Write them down.

_____

_____

How is One Better Than the Other?

Now, consider the first object you selected. Write down how you perceive it as being "better" than the second one? What qualities or attributes make you believe it is superior in some way? Write down your thoughts without judgment or overthinking. Next, shift your focus to the second object. How do you perceive it as being "better" than the first one? What qualities or attributes make you believe it is superior in some way? Again, write down your thoughts without judgment.

_____

_____

_____

_____

How Did One Cause the Other?

Reflect on how you believe the first object may have caused the second one. Is there any connection, direct or indirect, that you can identify between them? Write down your thoughts and observations. Now, consider the reverse situation–how do you think the second object may have caused the first one? Are there any possible interactions or influences you can imagine between them? Write down your thoughts.

_____

_____

_____

_____

Reflect on Your Responses

Take a moment to review what you've written. Notice how your mind naturally creates relations and judgments between these two seemingly unrelated objects. Write down how you believe your perceptions and beliefs about them can be influenced by your thoughts and emotions.

_____

_____

_____

_____

Mindful Awareness

Practice being mindful of these thought patterns in your everyday life. Recognize that your mind often makes connections and judgments, even when there might not be any logical basis for them. Use this awareness to bring more mindfulness into your daily experiences.

The Object Relations Exploration exercise illustrates how our minds naturally create connections and judgments between various objects and concepts. In ACT, we learn to observe these thought patterns without attachment, allowing us to gain a deeper understanding of our thought processes and emotions. This awareness can help us make more conscious choices and find greater meaning and fulfillment in our lives.

The Six Tenets

Imagine you're in an escape room for fun. Part of the appeal of this experience lies in the fact that you know you'll be out of the room within an hour or so, whether you solve the puzzles or not. Now, consider applying this scenario to life itself. We spend our whole lives trying to "get out" of various challenges and difficulties. Our minds are often engaged in a constant problem-solving mode. This typically involves analyzing our current situation, reflecting on the past, and projecting into the future. Most traditional forms of therapy often encourage this problem-solving approach as the main way to come to terms with past experiences.

So, how do the ACT Tenets address this problem?

- **Being in the present moment:** ACT emphasizes the importance of being fully present in the current moment. Many of us, however, are fearful of being in the present moment, as it can bring up discomfort, anxiety, or pain. When we can accept that fear and acknowledge it without judgment, we become more empowered to see the possibilities that the present moment holds. Instead of being stuck in a never-ending puzzle room, constantly focused on "getting out" of our problems, we learn to stay put and explore what's happening right now.

- **Acceptance:** Acceptance, a fundamental tenet of ACT, encourages us to make room for all our experiences, including painful ones. Rather than resisting or avoiding difficult emotions, sensations, or thoughts, we embrace them as part of the human experience. By accepting the challenges that life presents, we free ourselves from the constant struggle to escape from discomfort. This shift in perspective allows us to find peace and clarity amid life's difficulties.

- **Pivotal shifts:** Each ACT tenet involves a pivotal shift in perspective or behavior, promoting greater psychological flexibility. These shifts are central to the practice of ACT.

Here are the six tenets:

1. **Defusion:** The first principle emphasizes the importance of perceiving thoughts, images, emotions, and memories as they truly are—mere psychological events. Instead of considering them as threats or undeniable truths, individuals who practice defusion establish a healthy distance from these thoughts. As someone who has experienced anxiety, defusion has proven to be a valuable technique for me. It enables me to recognize that the anxious thoughts that can arise are merely mental events and may not accurately represent reality. Through practicing defusion, I can change my relationship with these thoughts and reduce their impact on my well-being.

2. **Self as context (The observing self):** The second principle helps us realize that our thoughts and feelings do not define us. Instead, we are the stable backdrop or environment in which these experiences happen. Personally, as someone who has faced my mother's mental health struggles while trying to build my own life, Self as Context has given me a sense of consistency and stability in the midst of life's challenges. It enables me to detach myself from the passing stream of my thoughts and emotions, providing a more balanced viewpoint.

3. **Acceptance:** Acceptance means allowing yourself to experience painful feelings, sensations, urges, and emotions instead of trying to avoid or suppress them. It means accepting these experiences as a normal part of life rather than seeing them as obstacles to overcome. Personally, I have found acceptance to be very beneficial in managing my anxiety and stress. I now understand that it's normal to feel anxious at times, and that trying to avoid or get rid of these feelings can actually make things worse. By embracing my anxiety and accepting it as a

natural part of my experience, I am able to deal with it more effectively.

4. **Present moment awareness (Mindfulness):** The fourth tenet encourages us to be fully conscious and engaged in the present moment. This practice fosters awareness of current experiences with openness, interest, and receptiveness, without judgment. Being mindful has allowed me to fully engage with my daughter, enjoy my writing process, and strengthen my relationship with my husband. Instead of being lost in worries about the past or future, I have learned to be present and appreciate the beauty of each moment as often as possible.

5. **Values:** Identifying and clarifying personal values is crucial in ACT. Values are chosen qualities that guide and motivate intentional behavior. Personally, my values include self development and practicing self-care on more of a regular basis. It's important to note that these values are not fixed but rather continuously evolving. By committing to my values, I am able to make decisions and take actions that are aligned with what truly matters to me.

6. **Action:** The last principle of ACT focuses on developing habits that align with one's chosen values. I have discovered that by taking committed actions that are in line with my values, I have found a lot more purpose and satisfaction in my life. I actively engage in activities such as spending quality time with my family or working on my writing projects, as well as practicing these exercises, which reflect my values of creation, love, care, and participation.

Key Takeaways

1. **Relational Frame Theory (RFT):** A psychological framework that explores the connections between language, cognition, and behavior. It provides valuable insights into the power of language and the stories we tell ourselves, laying the foundation for Acceptance and Commitment Therapy (ACT).

2. **Understanding RFT:** It highlights the unique ability of humans to understand two-way relationships between words and their meanings, unlike animals that can only learn one-way associations. This understanding allows us to make complex connections and deductions.

3. **Language:** It goes beyond simple word associations- it involves learning to connect words in complex and dynamic ways. Our minds create intricate cognitive networks by linking one idea to another, even if they seem unrelated.

4. **The Object Relations Exploration exercise:** Demonstrates how our minds naturally create connections and judgments between seemingly unrelated objects and concepts. By observing these thought patterns without attachment, we gain a deeper understanding of our thought processes and emotions.

5. **The six tenets of ACT:** Promote psychological flexibility and mindful awareness. They include defusion, self as context, acceptance, present moment awareness (mindfulness), values, and action. By practicing these principles, we can find peace, clarity, and fulfillment in our lives.

In this chapter, we explored the fascinating science behind ACT. By exploring the intricate workings of the mind and the power of psychological flexibility, we have gained valuable insights into how ACT can help us navigate life's challenges. As we conclude this chapter, I invite you to embark on a journey of defusion in the next chapter. Get ready to discover the transformative practice of defusing from unhelpful thoughts and beliefs, as we continue to unlock the potential for growth and well-being.

Stop the habit of wishful thinking and start the habit of intentional, thoughtful wishes.

–MARY MARTIN

CHAPTER 3

Breaking Free: Embracing Defusion

Imagine being caught in a tangled web of thoughts, each one vying for your undivided attention, demanding that you follow their lead. It's as though these thoughts have a grip on your mind, steering your actions and emotions like a puppeteer pulling the strings. This experience is what psychologists call fusion—the state of becoming "hooked" by your thoughts.

In this chapter, we will delve into the concept of defusion and how it can liberate you from the shackles of your own thoughts. You'll learn to recognize when you've become hooked, believing that your thoughts are commands that must be obeyed, rules that dictate your actions, or absolute truths that you must unquestionably accept. While there are times when being immersed in your thoughts can be beneficial, such as daydreaming about a summer vacation or engaging in research for work, we don't want to be ensnared by thoughts that divert us from the life we truly desire.

Throughout these pages, we'll explore practical exercises and techniques to help you defuse from your thoughts, giving you the freedom to choose your responses and live a more meaningful and fulfilling life. So, let's embark on this journey of defusion together, allowing you to break free from the thought patterns that no longer serve you and step into the realm of greater self-awareness and contentment.

Why Ruminating Is Problematic

Ruminating can indeed be problematic, especially for those struggling with anxiety and other mental health issues. It's important to understand why rumination can be so harmful and how ACT provides a helpful perspective on dealing with it.

- **The endless loop:** Ruminating is the act of continuously and obsessively thinking about past events, problems, or anxieties. This repetitive cycle of negative thoughts can create an endless loop, making it challenging to find relief from emotions that make us feel unhappy.

- **Intense emotional turmoil:** When we ruminate, we tend to delve deeper into our negative emotions, making them feel even stronger. We ask ourselves questions such as "Why am I feeling like this?" or "Why am I like this?" These questions primarily revolve around self-judgment and criticism, which worsens our emotional distress.

- **Avoidance and suppression:** When we engage in constant analysis and overthinking, we may temporarily move our attention away from addressing the root causes or emotions. However, doing this can actually stall personal growth and emotional healing.

- **Impaired problem-solving:** Ruminating, which refers to overthinking or dwelling excessively on a problem or negative thoughts, can be counterproductive when it comes to effective problem-solving. Rather than helping us find solutions, it tends to keep us trapped in a cycle of worry and anxiety. By constantly replaying the same thoughts and concerns in our minds, we may struggle to break free from unproductive patterns of thinking and hinder our ability to come up with practical solutions to the challenges we face.

- ⊙ **Interference with life goals:** Constant rumination refers to the repetitive and intrusive thinking that often revolves around negative or distressing thoughts. When we engage in constant rumination, it can have a detrimental impact on various aspects of our lives. One significant consequence is that it interferes with our ability to focus on and pursue our goals. Instead of directing our attention and energy toward productive tasks, we become preoccupied with our thoughts, which can hinder our progress and productivity. This preoccupation can also have a negative impact on our relationships, as we may struggle to be fully present and engaged with others. Additionally, constant rumination can impede our personal development by preventing us from taking action and making positive changes in our lives. It can create a cycle of overthinking and inaction, preventing us from reaching our full potential. Therefore, it is important to find strategies to manage and reduce constant rumination in order to maintain focus, nurture healthy relationships, and foster personal growth.

ACT offers a valuable perspective on rumination, encouraging us to treat our thoughts and feelings differently:

- ⊙ **Mindfulness:** ACT teaches mindfulness techniques to help individuals observe their thoughts and emotions without judgment. Instead of trying to fight or suppress them, you learn to accept them as part of your experience.
- ⊙ **Acceptance:** One of the core principles of ACT is acceptance. It encourages you to accept your thoughts and feelings as they

are, without judgment or resistance. By doing so, you create space for more constructive actions and choices.

- ⊙ **Defusion:** ACT suggests that you defuse from your thoughts, treating them as mental events rather than facts. Imagine your thoughts and feelings as clouds passing through the sky of your mind. They come and go, but you are the constant, unchanging sky.

- ⊙ **Values and commitment:** ACT is a therapeutic approach that aims to help us clarify our values and align our actions with those values. Instead of getting stuck in overthinking or rumination, ACT encourages us to focus on what truly matters to us and take meaningful steps toward living a more fulfilling life. By identifying our core values, we can make conscious choices and commit to actions that are in line with those values. This process allows us to move away from being controlled by negative thoughts and emotions and instead move toward a life that is more aligned with our true desires and aspirations.

Am I Slipping Into Fusion?

I want to help you recognize when you may be slipping into fusion—that state where thoughts become overwhelming and dominate our consciousness. Consider the following important factors:

- ⊙ **Repetitive thoughts:** One of the signs of fusion is when your thoughts seem predictable and repetitive. These thoughts can create a mental loop that keeps you stuck. The first step is to make a conscious note of these repetitive thoughts. Write them down or simply acknowledge them when they arise. This awareness is crucial for defusing from them over time.

⊙ **Emerging from a daydream:** Fusion can often feel like you've disappeared into your thoughts for a while, and then suddenly you "wake up" to the present moment. When this happens, try to pinpoint the moment you drifted away. What triggered this fusion? Identifying the trigger can help you become more aware of the situations or thought patterns that lead to fusion.

⊙ **Evaluative and comparative thoughts:** Fusion tends to make your thoughts highly evaluative and comparative. You may find yourself constantly judging or comparing yourself to others. For example, you might catch yourself thinking, "Can I claim that new office chair as a tax deduction? I bet I can. I'm impressed I thought of it. So many would have missed it, but not me. My own bookkeeper even missed it." Recognizing these evaluative and comparative thoughts is a step toward defusing from them.

⊙ **My mind is in overdrive:** Fusion can often send your mind into overdrive, causing it to wrestle with itself. This internal struggle involves contradictions, rules, and self-criticisms. For example, you might find yourself thinking, "I shouldn't eat that chocolate bar. It'll make me obese. I'm already overweight, so it'll make me even unhealthier and heavier. That's probably why people don't want to be friends with me. But then again, it's just a chocolate bar." These conflicting thoughts can create a state of inner turmoil. Recognizing this overdrive mode is crucial for defusing the situation and finding clarity.

What Is Cognitive Defusion and How Can It Help?

Cognitive defusion is a core concept in ACT, and it revolves around the idea of detaching or defusing from your thoughts and beliefs. The goal is to stop being overly attached to your thoughts, allowing you to see them for what they are—just thoughts, not necessarily truths. This process helps us gain distance from our thoughts and enables us to observe them without being controlled or overwhelmed by them.

For me, cognitive defusion provided a valuable tool to address my anxiety and various other challenges. Here's how it can help:

- **Reducing anxiety**: Instead of constantly being trapped in a cycle of anxious thinking, you can learn to step back and view your anxious thoughts as passing mental events. This shift in perspective can help you reduce the intensity of your anxiety and panic attacks.

- **Busting patterns**: Cognitive defusion allows us to identify and challenge negative thought patterns that had been holding us back. Many of our thoughts are automatic and unhelpful, contributing to our anxiety and stress. By distancing ourself from these thoughts, we gain the ability to break free from their grip and choose more constructive ways of thinking.

- **Promoting self-reflection**: Learn to ask yourself a crucial question when faced with a distressing thought: *"If I use this thought for guidance, will it help me become the person I want to be, do the things I want to do, and build a better life in the long term?"* This inquiry encourages self-reflection and helps assess the usefulness of your thoughts in aligning with your values and goals.

⊙ **Quality of life**: As you engage in the practice of cognitive defusion, you will discover that it enables you to consciously slow down and fully embrace the beauty of the present moment. This newfound skill of managing your anxiety and releasing unhelpful thoughts has a profound impact on your overall well-being and significantly enhances the quality of your life.

In the ACT framework, cognitive defusion is a powerful tool that allows us to distance ourselves from our thoughts, view them as mere mental occurrences, and make choices that align with our values and goals. This practice is especially helpful for individuals dealing with anxiety and stress, as it enables them to break free from the hold of anxious thoughts and move towards a more meaningful and fulfilling life.

A Quick Note About Defusion Exercises

What's really cool about the defusion exercises, and many ACT exercises in general, is that you don't always have to write to do them. In fact, you can start by writing about them here or in your journal a few times, and then you'll find that a lot of them can be done mentally as you go about your day.

I personally love the ability to practice these exercises repeatedly throughout my day. It's incredibly helpful to have techniques readily available when my thoughts or feelings become overwhelming. Be mindful of fusing while doing the defusing exercises and then having thoughts like "I'm the best diffuser ever, I don't need to practice anymore."

EXERCISE: Dropping Anchor

In this exercise, we'll explore the powerful technique of defusion, which helps you create distance from your thoughts and feelings, allowing you to respond more skillfully to life's challenges. You can practice ACE (or Dropping Anchor) throughout the day, whenever you notice mild to intense feelings or find yourself on autopilot. This exercise was originally created by Russ Harris (Harris, 2019).

Step 1: Acknowledge Your Thoughts and Feelings (30 seconds)

Begin by acknowledging your thoughts and feelings. Some people find it easier to notice thoughts, while others are more attuned to their feelings. Start with the one that comes more naturally to you. If you can, try to notice both.

- Take 10-20 seconds to notice your thoughts. Use phrases like, "I'm noticing thoughts about ..." or "Here is a thought that ..." to describe them. For example, "I'm noticing thoughts about being worthless."
- Next, take 10-20 seconds to scan your body for feelings. Say to yourself, "Here is a feeling of ..." and name the emotion you're experiencing. For instance, "Here is a feeling of anger."

Remember, the goal is to acknowledge these thoughts and feelings without struggling with them or trying to make them go away. Simply notice and name them.

Step 2: Connect with Your Body (30 seconds)

While continuing to acknowledge your thoughts and feelings, connect with your body. The purpose of this step is not to eliminate your thoughts and feelings but to gain more control over your body.

Get creative with body movements. You can try any and all of these:

- Slowly and gently push your feet into the floor.
- Slowly and gently straighten your spine.
- Take slow, deep breaths.
- Raise your eyebrows up and down.
- Explore other gentle body movements that help you connect with your physical sensations.

This step helps you act effectively while your thoughts and feelings continue to arise.

Step 3: Engage in What You're Doing (30 seconds)

With your thoughts and feelings acknowledged and your body connected, bring your attention to the present moment. Engage fully in what you're doing. This step is about being mindful of your surroundings and your current activity.

- Take a moment to observe your surroundings in the room:
    - 5 things you can see.
    - 4 things you can hear.
    - Try to notice what you're doing at that very moment.

Stay present and focused on the activity you're engaged in.

Repeat the Exercise Three More Times

Now, run through the entire exercise three more times. Each repetition allows you to deepen your awareness and practice defusion.

The aim of this exercise is not distraction or the reduction of your thoughts and feelings. Instead, it's about cultivating mindfulness and acceptance. You're learning to notice your thoughts and feelings without becoming entangled in them. While this exercise may not completely alleviate intense emotions like crushing sadness or debilitating anxiety, it can provide a sense of calm during the storm. For less extreme emotions, you may find that the pain lessens or even disappears with practice.

EXERCISE: Leaves on a Stream

This exercise will help you detach from your thoughts and gain a better understanding of how they affect you.

Find a Quiet Space

Find a quiet and comfortable place where you can sit or lie down. Ensure that you won't be interrupted for the duration of this exercise.

Imagine the Stream

Visualize a serene and gently flowing stream in your mind. Imagine the water moving smoothly, carrying leaves downstream. This stream represents the flow of your thoughts.

Place Your Thoughts on Leaves

Whenever a thought arises, consciously place it on one of the leaves in your mind's eye. Picture the thought resting gently on the leaf.

Watch the Thoughts Drift Away

As you place your thoughts on leaves, watch them float away on the stream. Observe how they move downstream, becoming smaller and more distant.

Notice Cognitive Fusion

Pay attention to any thoughts that you become fused with, meaning you engage with them instead of allowing them to float away. When you catch yourself getting entangled with a thought, gently acknowledge it without judgment.

Return to the Stream

After noting how you became fused with a thought, return your focus to the stream. Watch it flow as it carries the leaves with your thoughts on them away.

Reflect

Write down any insights or observations that come up during this exercise. This can help you track patterns in your thought process.

_____

_____

_____

Continue Practicing

Repeat this exercise for at least 10-15 minutes or as long as you feel comfortable. Gradually, you'll develop a greater ability to detach from your thoughts and observe them without getting entangled.

EXERCISE: Mind Moniker

In this exercise, we will explore the concept of giving your mind a name to help you separate your identity from your thoughts.

- Choose a name:
    - Sit down in your happy place where you won't be bothered.
    - Close your eyes if you are comfortable doing so, take a few deep breaths, and center yourself.
    - Consider your mind as a distinct entity. Imagine it as a character at a dinner party, and it needs a name. It can be a fun or whimsical name like "Lady Labyrinth" or "Professor Ponder," or even a random name you like such as "Christopher", or "Elizabeth" or even something simple like "Mr. Mind," "Ms. Mind" or any other name that resonates with you. It is important that you don't use your own name or you could fuse with it. Take a moment to decide on a name. Write it down.

_____

_____

- Greet your mind:
    - Say hello to your mind, addressing it by the name you've selected. For example, if you chose "Ms. Mind," say, "Hello, Ms. Mind, welcome to the party!"
- Engage in a Conversation:
    - Imagine you are engaged in a polite conversation with your named mind. Ask it questions like you would with a guest at a dinner party.

- o You can start by asking, "Ms. Mind, how are you feeling today? What's on your mind?"
- o Allow yourself to listen attentively to the responses that come up in your thoughts.
- ⊙ Observe your thoughts:
    - o As you continue the conversation, notice any thoughts, worries, or concerns that Ms. Mind shares with you.
    - o Instead of identifying with these thoughts, observe them as if they belong to your named mind, separate from your true self.
- ⊙ Practice non-judgmental listening:
    - o As you engage in this exercise, try to maintain a non-judgmental and compassionate attitude toward your named mind. Remember, Ms. Mind (or your chosen name) is not you; it's just a part of your inner experience.
    - o Next, I want you to thank your mind in a non-judgmental way: "I appreciate it, Ms. Mind. Really, thank you." Or instead of thanking, you can say, "I see you there mind, trying to help. Relax, I've got this covered."
- ⊙ Reflect:
    - o After a few minutes of conversation, take a moment to reflect on how this exercise made you feel. Write down if it helped you gain a different perspective on your thoughts? Did it create some distance between you and your mind's chatter?

_____

_____

_____

_____

⊙ Revisit:

  o You can revisit this exercise whenever you find yourself overwhelmed by your thoughts. It's a helpful tool to remind yourself that your thoughts are not your identity.

EXERCISE: Sing It Out

Singing your sticky thoughts can be a fun and effective way to gain some distance from them and see them as just thoughts. Here's an example:

Original Sticky Thought

"I messed up at work today, and everyone is probably talking about it."

Turned Into a Sentence

"I made a mistake at work today, and it's on my mind."

Now, let's try singing it to the tune of "Twinkle Twinkle Little Star":

"I made a mistake at work today,
And it's on my mind, I must say.
Twinkle, twinkle, little star,
This thought won't get me very far."

The goal here is not to make the thought disappear but to observe it as a thought without getting too caught up in its emotional impact. You can experiment with different tunes, speeds, and variations to see what works best for you.

EXERCISE: Disobey on Purpose

In this exercise, you will intentionally disobey a simple command to experience the concept of ACT in a tangible way. This exercise is designed to help you understand the importance of accepting your internal experiences, even when they contradict your logical thoughts.

- ⊙ Find a quiet and comfortable space where you won't be disturbed. Take a few moments to center yourself by taking a few deep breaths.
- ⊙ Hold this book in your hands and say aloud, "I cannot walk around this room." Repeat this statement slowly and clearly, about five or six times.
- ⊙ After repeating the statement, set the book aside and stand up.
- ⊙ Begin to walk around the room intentionally, defying the statement you just made. Walk slowly and mindfully, paying attention to each step you take.
- ⊙ As you walk, notice any thoughts or feelings that arise. You may feel a sense of disobedience or conflict between what you said and what you are doing. Observe any judgments or self-criticism that may come up.
- ⊙ Continue walking around the room for a few minutes, all the while maintaining awareness of the internal experiences, thoughts, and emotions that arise as you deliberately disobey the initial statement.
- ⊙ After a few minutes, stop walking and return to your original position with the book.
- ⊙ Reflect on your experience. Consider the following questions:
    - o What thoughts and feelings did you experience while intentionally disobeying the statement?

o   Did you notice any physical sensations or discomfort?

_____

_____

_____

_____

How did it feel to go against the initial command, even though it was a simple one?

_____

_____

_____

_____

_____

Did you find yourself judging or criticizing yourself for not following the instruction?

_____

_____

_____

_____

_____

By intentionally disobeying the initial statement, you've learned that thoughts are not commands, and you have the power to choose how you respond to them. Consider how this exercise can be applied to your daily life. When you experience anxious or distressing thoughts, remember that they are not absolute truths, and you have the choice to respond to them with acceptance and mindfulness.

Key Takeaways

1. **Understand fusion:** Fusion is when your thoughts control your actions and emotions, like a puppet. Recognizing fusion is the first step to defusing from your thoughts.
2. **Ruminating problems:** Ruminating- obsessively thinking about the past- leads to emotional distress, avoidance, impaired problem-solving, and interference with life goals. ACT offers effective ways to deal with rumination.
3. **Recognize fusion signs:** Look out for repetitive thoughts, drifting away from the present, evaluative thinking, and an overactive mind engaged in inner turmoil.
4. **Cognitive defusion:** ACT's core concept, detaching from thoughts and beliefs, reduces anxiety, breaks negative thought patterns, promotes self-reflection, and enhances quality of life.
5. **ACT principles for handling rumination:** ACT emphasizes mindfulness, acceptance of thoughts and feelings, cognitive defusion, and aligning actions with values.

In this chapter, we've explored the transformative power of defusion, unlocking the potential to regain control over our responses, reduce anxiety, and foster self-awareness. As we move forward, we'll delve deeper into understanding our 'self' as context, embarking on a voyage of self-discovery to reshape our lives. The journey continues, and the best you is yet to come.

Know thyself.

–SOCRATES

CHAPTER 4

Discovering the Depths of Your True Self

In the grand tapestry of our lives, we often find ourselves entangled in the intricate threads of identity. We play various roles and wear numerous masks as we navigate the ever-changing landscapes of our existence. There are the selves we present to the world, the selves we reveal to our loved ones, and the secret selves we sometimes keep hidden even from ourselves. Within this complex mosaic, we encounter different versions of who we are, each carrying its own weight and significance.

This chapter invites you to embark on a journey of self-exploration. We'll explore the idea that you are not just the sum of your thoughts, feelings, and experiences. You are something greater, something more enduring, something beyond the changing tides of your inner world. We'll explore the various versions of your self, and through carefully crafted exercises, we'll learn how to step back and observe these selves with curiosity and compassion.

What Is the Transcendent Self?

In the journey of self-discovery and personal growth through ACT, we often encounter the concept of the Transcendent Self. This idea may initially sound abstract or elusive, but as we explore it further, it becomes a valuable tool in understanding and navigating our inner world.

To grasp the notion of the Transcendent Self, it's essential to first understand the concept of the Noticing or Observing Self. This aspect of our consciousness is like a silent observer, the one that steps back and watches our thoughts, emotions, and experiences without judgment or attachment. It is the observer behind the eyes, but it doesn't engage in thinking; it simply notices.

Think of it this way: Imagine your younger self, perhaps a child of four or five years old, and recall a memory from that time. Attempt to perceive the world from their perspective. Now, think about who is doing the looking in the present moment. That's the Noticing or Observing Self–the part of you that watches, witnesses, and perceives today.

The Transcendent Self is the aspect of our consciousness that transcends our thoughts, emotions, and experiences. It's the part of us that remains constant and unchanging, regardless of life's ups and downs. In essence, it's the core of our being, our true self.

The Transcendent Self doesn't get caught up in the whirlwind of thoughts or emotions. Instead, it rises above and observes them with a sense of detachment and curiosity. It's the part of you that can step back from the chaos of life and see things from a broader perspective. When you're overwhelmed by stress, anxiety, or any challenging emotion, the Transcendent Self can help you gain clarity.

By understanding and embracing the Transcendent Self, you can find a sense of peace, clarity, and purpose in your life. It allows you to navigate challenges with resilience and opens the door to a deeper understanding of yourself and the world around you.

What Is the Conceptualized Self?

This is a fundamental concept that plays a significant role in understanding how our minds work and how we relate to our thoughts and emotions. To grasp the idea of the conceptualized self, let's use an example you might find relatable.

The Story of Ourself

Imagine you're taking a leisurely walk in a beautiful park with your four-year-old daughter. The sun is shining, birds are chirping, and you're both enjoying the fresh air. In this moment, you are fully engaged with your daughter, observing the world around you, and experiencing the joy of being together. This state of pure awareness and presence is what we refer to as the "noticing self."

However, as you continue your walk, your mind starts to wander. You may find yourself thinking, *"I should be more attentive to my daughter,"* or *"What if something bad happens here?"* These thoughts, which often involve self-judgment or worry, represent the "thinking self."

In this example, the "noticing self" is the part of you that is fully engaged in the present moment, appreciating the beauty of the park and the time with your daughter. On the other hand, the "thinking self" is the part of your mind that generates thoughts, evaluations, and judgments about your actions or circumstances.

The Thinking Self

This is where many of us spend a significant portion of our mental energy. It's the part of our mind that produces thoughts about the past and future, often driven by fear, anxiety, or self-doubt. These thoughts can be helpful at times, providing us with planning and problem-solving abilities. However, they can also lead us down a rabbit hole of overthinking and distress if we become too attached to them.

In ACT, we recognize that the thinking self is just one aspect of who we are—it's the storyteller, the commentator, the analyzer. It's the part of us that constructs narratives about our past, makes predictions about the future, and judges our actions and experiences.

The Noticing Self

On the other hand, the noticing self is the part of us that can step back and observe these thoughts without getting entangled in them. It's the state of mindfulness and pure awareness—the ability to be fully present in the moment without judgment. When you're in the noticing self mode, you can appreciate the beauty of the park, the laughter of your daughter, and the warmth of the sun on your skin without being consumed by self-criticism or excessive worry.

The key to understanding the conceptualized self is recognizing that you are not just your thoughts. You are both the thinker (the thinking self) and the observer (the noticing self). ACT encourages us to cultivate a healthy relationship with our thoughts, allowing them to come and go without undue attachment or resistance. By doing so, you can learn to navigate your inner world more skillfully, reduce suffering, and open yourself up to a more meaningful and fulfilling life.

The Thinking Self and Self Pivot

It's essential to grasp the idea that our thinking self is like a never-ending negative news TV show. No matter how hard we try, there's no remote control to switch it off completely. Even Zen masters struggle with this constant broadcast. Sometimes, the show may pause on its own, but we can't force it to stop. What we can do, however, is learn to make it background noise as we focus on the more important things in our lives.

Think of your mind as the producer of this show. It's constantly broadcasting thoughts, emotions, memories, and often, they're not very helpful. It's like having a TV in the background, always blaring away. Sometimes, it's tempting to try and replace the negative broadcast with positive thinking, but this is akin to having a second TV in the same room, making it difficult to concentrate on anything else. Ignoring it is no different than trying to tune out a blaring fire truck siren.

Safety First: Staying in the Comfort Zone

Our mind operates under a "safety first" principle. It's programmed to give us warnings in the form of negative thoughts, uncomfortable emotions, and bad memories whenever we attempt something new or step outside our comfort zone. It's trying to keep us safe, but the irony is that life inside the comfort zone is often anything but comfortable. It's more like life in the stagnant zone, the misery zone, or the missing out on life zone.

So, how do we break free from this cycle and venture into the unknown, where real growth and fulfillment await? Two essential strategies come into play here:

1. **Expand unhooking skills:** We'll continue to explore this in later chapters, but expanding our skills in disentangling ourselves from unhelpful thoughts and emotions is crucial. It's like learning to change the channel or lower the volume of that negative news TV show.

2. **Find something worth leaving for:** To truly motivate ourselves to leave the comfort zone, we need to find something

that makes it all worthwhile. This could be a personal goal, a value you hold dear, or a life purpose that ignites your passion.

The Self Pivot: Becoming More Than Our Thoughts

This involves shifting from identifying solely with the content of our thoughts and feelings to a perspective of self-as-context. In this new perspective, we recognize ourselves as the observer of these experiences.

Imagine a pivot point where you move from thinking, *"I am my thoughts,"* to understanding that you are more than your thoughts, feelings, or experiences. This shift is profound because it separates you from the constant chatter of your thinking self.

The Formula for Connecting with a Deeper Sense of Self

To embrace the Self Pivot fully and connect with a deeper sense of self, we follow a formula:

1. **Challenging the bond with the conceptualized self:** Apply defusion methods, as described in the previous chapter, to the way you tell stories about yourself. Challenge the narratives that keep you stuck.

2. **Expand Your mental space:** Notice how defusion helps create mental space, enabling you to become aware of the perspective-taking that forms the basis of a sense of self. Understand that the transcendent sense of self is separate from thoughts—you are not defined by your thoughts, but you can observe them with awareness.

3. **Cultivate perspective taking:** Engage in exercises that shift your perspective along the dimensions of time, place, and

person. Understand how your sense of self relates to your past, your surroundings, and your connections with others.

4. **Build a sense of belonging:** Build a connection with others by using perspective taking. This expands your individual transcendent sense of self, transforming "me" into "we."

EXERCISE: Thought Safari

In this exercise, we will engage in a mindfulness activity inspired by wildlife photography to help you gain a better understanding of your thoughts and how they impact your experience.

- Imagine that you are a wildlife photographer embarking on a safari to observe and capture elusive thoughts. Picture yourself in a serene and exotic natural setting, such as a lush jungle, a tranquil savannah, or a serene forest.
- When you are comfortable, close your eyes. Start to scan your mind as if you are searching for unique and elusive creatures. Begin to notice your thoughts as they come and go, just as animals might appear and disappear in the wild.
- As you observe your thoughts, pay attention to their characteristics:

  - **Location:** Where do you notice the thought? Is it in the forefront of your mind or hiding in the background?
  - **Speed and Direction:** Is the thought racing through your mind like a cheetah, or is it moving slowly and steadily like a turtle? What direction is it heading in?
  - **Voice:** If you're someone who hears your thoughts, take note of where the voice seems to be coming from. Is it fast or slow? Loud or soft?

- Spend a few minutes in this mental safari, observing your thoughts without judgment. Remember that the thinking self has the thought, and the noticing self is the one observing and noting these distinctions.
- Whenever you catch a thought, acknowledge it without getting entangled in its storyline. Imagine capturing it in your mental camera, just like a wildlife photographer capturing a snapshot of an animal in its natural habitat.
- After a minute or two, open your eyes and return to the present moment. Take a moment to reflect on your experience during the Thought Safari.

Reflection Questions:

What did you discover about the nature of your thoughts during this exercise?

_____

_____

_____

_____

Were there any surprising insights about the location, speed, or voice of your thoughts?

_____

_____

_____

_____

_____

How did it feel to observe your thoughts without getting caught up in them?

_____

_____

_____

_____

_____

Did this exercise provide you with a sense of distance from your thoughts?

_____

_____

_____

_____

_____

EXERCISE: Catching Self Awareness on the Fly

This exercise is designed to help you develop self-awareness and mindfulness in your daily life. By asking yourself a simple question and defusing any judgmental thoughts that may arise you can become more present and less entangled in unhelpful thought patterns.

Begin by asking yourself the question, "And who is noticing that?"

As you ask this question, direct your attention to your thoughts, emotions, sensations, or any ongoing activity or experience in your surroundings. For example, if you're feeling anxious, you might ask,

"Who is noticing this anxiety?" If you're having a positive experience, such as spending time with your child, you can ask, "Who is noticing this joyful moment?"

Allow yourself to observe your inner experience without judgment or analysis. Simply notice what is happening without trying to change it or make sense of it.

If you notice that your mind starts to generate a mental essay about who you are or what your thoughts mean, use defusion techniques. Imagine hearing these thoughts in the voice of a playful character like Yoda or Elmo. This playful perspective can help you distance yourself from your thoughts and make them feel less serious or overwhelming.

Continue to practice this exercise throughout your day, especially during moments of stress, anxiety, or strong emotions. It can also be helpful during positive experiences to enhance your appreciation and presence.

Over time, you will develop greater self-awareness and mindfulness, allowing you to engage with your thoughts and emotions in a more flexible and accepting way.

EXERCISE: Exploring Your Self-Concept with ACT

The goal in this exercise is to help you better understand your self-perceptions, challenge them, and gain insight into who you truly are beneath the layers of your stories and defenses.

Part A: Identifying Self-Concept

Begin by completing three statements, starting with "I am." The first two statements should express positive one-word attributes about yourself, while the third should reflect a negative and feared attribute. For example:

a) I am confident.
b) I am empathetic.
c) I am anxious.

I am...
I am...
I am...

Part B: Questioning Your Self-Concept

For each statement above, ask yourself the following questions:

Is this true all the time, everywhere, toward everyone? Without exception?

_____

_____

_____

Do you feel this way in every situation and with every person?

_____

_____

_____

Apply these questions to the negative attribute (the last question) as well.

_____

_____

_____

Part C: Comparisons

Now, compare each attribute to others. For example:

- ⊘ Am I kinder than others?
- ⊘ Am I more confident than others?
- ⊘ Am I more anxious than others?
- ⊘ I am...
- ⊘ I am...
- ⊘ I am...

Part D: Adding "Or Not"

Add ", or not" at the end of each statement you created in Part A, turning them into open-ended questions. For example:

- ⊘ I am confident, or not.
- ⊘ I am empathetic, or not.
- ⊘ I am anxious, or not.

_____

_____

_____

_____

Part E: Letting Go of Self-Concept

Now, cross out all the text following "I am." What remains? Who would you be without those self-descriptions? Take a moment to contemplate what it would be like to let go of these stories and defenses.

Part F: Exploring Your Self in Different Contexts

Reflect and write down how your self-concept changes based on where you are and what you're doing. Notice the variations in how you perceive yourself in different contexts. For example:

- ⊙ At home, you might feel like you're caring and in control.
- ⊙ At work, you may feel inept.

_____

_____

_____

Part G: Transforming "I Am" into "I Think" or "I Feel"

Transform your "I am" statements into "I think" or "I feel" statements. For example:

- ⊙ "I am confident" becomes "I feel confident" or "I think I am confident."
- ⊙ "I am anxious" becomes "I feel anxious" or "I think I am anxious."

_____

_____

_____

Part H: Describing Situations, Actions, Thoughts, and Feelings

Create sentences that describe a situation, an action, and how you think or feel in that scenario. Use both positive and negative self-concepts. For example:

- ⊙ "When my friend needed support, and I offered my help, I felt empathetic."
- ⊙ "When I faced a challenging task at work, and I procrastinated, I did not feel confident."

_____

_____

_____

This exercise is designed to help you gain insight into your self-concept, challenge fixed beliefs about yourself, and promote self-awareness, all of which are fundamental elements of ACT.

Key Takeaways

1. **The complexity of identity**: Our identities are multifaceted, shaped by the roles we play and the masks we wear in different contexts. We often have public, private, and hidden versions of ourselves, each with its significance.

2. **The transcendent self**: Within the realm of self-exploration in ACT, the Transcendent Self represents the core of our being, untouched by the changing tides of thoughts and emotions. It is a constant observer that can provide clarity and detachment in challenging situations.

3. **The thinking and noticing Self**: ACT helps us recognize the distinction between the thinking self, which generates thoughts and judgments, and the noticing self, which observes without attachment. By cultivating a healthy relationship with our thoughts, we can reduce suffering and lead a more meaningful life.

In this chapter, we explored the many versions of self, influenced by the roles we assume in various life situations. We are now moving into acceptance and it is not at all what you may think. Turn the page to discover what acceptance truly is.

Accept—then act. Whatever the present moment contains, accept it as if you had chosen it. Always work with it, not against it.

–ECKHART TOLLE

CHAPTER 5

Embracing the Symphony of Emotions—The Art of Acceptance in ACT Therapy

Welcome to this chapter on acceptance, a fundamental part of ACT that can transform the way you relate to your thoughts and emotions. We'll explore what acceptance truly means and how it can help you navigate the challenges of life in a more meaningful and fulfilling way.

First, let's clarify a common misconception about acceptance: it is not about resigning yourself to a life of perpetual sadness, depression, or anxiety. Some people might mistakenly believe that acceptance means surrendering to negative emotions and simply enduring them forever. However, this notion couldn't be further from the truth, and it's important to debunk this myth.

So, let's embark on this journey of understanding and embracing acceptance, as it opens the door to greater self-awareness, inner peace, and the pursuit of a life filled with purpose and joy.

What Is Acceptance?

Acceptance is a powerful idea that is often misunderstood. It's not about giving up or embracing a life of pain or discomfort, and it's not about finding pleasure in negative emotions. Acceptance is simply about giving ourselves permission to feel the entire spectrum of human emotions, even the challenging ones, in a safe and compassionate manner.

We all yearn to feel, to connect with our emotions, because feeling is an integral part of being human. Think of it as the colors on an artist's palette; without the full spectrum, our lives would be dull and one-dimensional. But here's the catch—we want to feel within our comfort zones. When emotions push us beyond that zone, avoidance kicks in.

Avoidance is our mind's way of protecting us from what it perceives as dangerous or uncomfortable emotions. It's like a well-intentioned friend who suggests avoiding a scary movie because it might make us feel anxious. The mind often tricks us into believing that the solution to our discomfort is to suppress or get rid of these feelings, especially the "bad" ones.

This is where the acceptance pivot comes into play. It's the shift from fighting against or avoiding our internal experiences–whether they be difficult emotions, physical sensations, or intrusive thoughts–to accepting them as a natural and unavoidable part of life.

Please understand, acceptance doesn't mean you have to like or want these experiences. It's not about embracing pain or suffering. It's about acknowledging that these feelings exist, that they are a part of you, and that it's okay for them to be there without resistance or struggle.

Imagine being able to sit with your emotions, even the painful ones, without trying to change or escape them. That's the power of acceptance. It's about opening up to the full spectrum of human experience, allowing yourself to feel the depth and richness of life, and in doing so, finding a new level of freedom and peace.

Lean Into Defusion and Self Techniques

As we move further into the world of acceptance, it's important to recognize that when we allow ourselves to fully feel our pain and discomfort, our fight-or-flight instinct often kicks into high gear. Your mind may scream at you to suppress your anxiety or resort to old, unhelpful habits. Negative self-talk may rear its head, attempting to convince you to retreat from your emotions.

However, the true gift you receive with acceptance is the wisdom of being able to feel and remember in the present without getting trapped in a negative thought network. It's about acknowledging your feelings without judgment and allowing them to exist without trying to change or avoid them. This is where revisiting Defusion or Self techniques we discussed in earlier chapters comes into play, helping you detach from unhelpful thoughts and create space for acceptance.

Now, let's revisit RFT. Sometimes, even positive emotions can remind us of negative experiences. For example, love might trigger memories of abuse or past pain. This intricate web of associations can make it challenging to navigate our emotions and relationships, but ACT equips us with the tools, like RFT, to do so effectively.

We need to understand that all of ACT Acceptance Methods follow these three principles:

1. **Avoidance causes pain:** Imagine avoidance as quicksand. When a leg sinks into quicksand, the instinct is to immediately

yank it out forcefully but that would be the wrong move. If you did this, you would sink more. Instead you need to lie down and gradually pull yourself to solid ground. Similarly, in ACT, we gradually increase our contact with what we fear or avoid, rather than struggling to escape it.

2. **Acceptance is in the service of valued living:** Acceptance isn't solely about confronting your fears without purpose, but rather about aligning your actions with your values. For example, if you feel anxious about going to a crowded place, like a park, don't simply go there to expose yourself to anxiety. Instead, go with a specific purpose, such as getting some fresh air. Similarly, if you find yourself avoiding bodies of water due to a fear of drowning, consider visiting the beach not to conquer your fear, but to connect with nature or collect shells.

3. **Acceptance isn't about control:** It's important to know that you can't keep your emotions completely shut off when practicing exposure. If you set strict limits on how anxious you can feel during exposure, it won't be effective because your mind will always fear going beyond that limit. Instead, you can set limits based on time and the specific situations or emotions you choose to confront. Begin with less intense experiences, such as starting with a dip in a small pool rather than diving straight into the ocean.

EXERCISE: Say Yes

In this exercise, we'll explore the power of ACT by practicing the act of saying "Yes" to both external and internal experiences. This exercise will help you develop the skills to accept things as they are, fostering a greater sense of inner peace and flexibility.

Step 1: External Experiences

- Find a quiet and comfortable space where you won't be disturbed for a few minutes.
- Begin by looking around the room and identifying various objects and items. As you focus on each one, say "No" in your mind, as if you're judging or rejecting them. For example, you might think, "No, that chair shouldn't be there."
- After a few minutes of practicing this negativity, take a deep breath and reset your focus.
- Now, go through the room again, but this time, say "Yes" to each item. Embrace the notion that everything in the room is exactly as it should be, and it doesn't need to change. For example, you might think, "Yes, that chair is where it's meant to be."
- Pay attention to how it feels to shift from rejection to acceptance. Notice any changes in your body, emotions, or thoughts as you practice saying "Yes" to the external world.

Step 2: Internal Experiences

- It is time to turn your attention inward.
- Take a moment to write down your thoughts, memories, urges, and emotions. These may be related to your own worries, fears, or anxieties.

- Begin by mentally saying "No" to each of these internal experiences. For example, if you're thinking about a stressful situation, say "No" to that thought, resisting it.

- After a few minutes of practicing this resistance, take another deep breath and reset your focus.

- Now, repeat the process, but this time, say "Yes" to each internal experience. Accept that your thoughts, memories, urges, and emotions are all valid and don't need to change or be suppressed. For example, you might think, "Yes, I can allow myself to feel this fear."

- As you say "Yes" to your internal experiences, write down how it affects your relationship with these thoughts and emotions. Are you more at ease with them? Do they seem less overwhelming?

_____

_____

_____

_____

_____

Step 3: Combining with Physical Posture

- To deepen your practice, incorporate your body into the exercise.

- As you say "No" to external or internal experiences, adopt a closed or tense physical posture, like crossing your arms or clenching your fists.

- When you say "Yes," open up your physical posture, with your arms relaxed and palms open.

⊙ Experiment with this physical component as you alternate between saying "No" and "Yes" to experiences. Once you finish take some time to write down how it affects your overall sense of acceptance and willingness.

_____

_____

_____

_____

_____

EXERCISE: Embracing Your Inner Experience

In this exercise, we will practice embracing and accepting your inner experiences, particularly those that lead to unhelpful resistance.

⊙ **Choose a challenging feeling:** Begin by identifying a specific feeling or emotion that you often resist or struggle with. It could be anxiety, fear, sadness, anger, or any other emotion that comes to mind.

⊙ **Start small:** If the feeling you've chosen feels overwhelming, start with a milder or less intense version of it. The goal is to gradually build your capacity to embrace and accept your emotions.

⊙ **Create a quiet space:** Find a quiet and comfortable place where you won't be disturbed for a few minutes. Sit down or lie down in a relaxed position.

Visualization:

- ⊙ If you are comfortable doing so, close your eyes and take a few deep breaths.
- ⊙ Imagine that the challenging feeling you've chosen is a delicate flower. Visualize this flower in your mind, with all its unique colors and petals.

Embrace like a crying child:

- ⊙ Now, imagine that this feeling is like a crying child seeking comfort and understanding.
- ⊙ Picture yourself gently cradling this crying child in your arms. Hold it close, feeling its vulnerability and pain.

Practice mindful acceptance:

- ⊙ As you hold this feeling in your mind, observe it without judgment. Notice its presence and the physical sensations it brings with it.
- ⊙ Embrace the feeling with compassion, acknowledging that it is a part of you and that it's okay to feel this way.
- ⊙ If resistance or discomfort arises during this exercise, simply breathe and refocus on embracing the feeling like you would with a crying child.

Extend the practice:

- ⊙ Spend about one minute fully engaging with this visualization, embracing the feeling with care.
- ⊙ If you feel comfortable, you can try this exercise with other challenging emotions or feelings as well.

Reflect and journal:

After the exercise, take a few moments to reflect on your experience. What did you notice about your ability to embrace this feeling?

_____

_____

_____

_____

_____

Consider jotting down any additional thoughts, emotions, and insights.

_____

_____

_____

_____

_____

EXERCISE: Cultivating Compassion

This exercise is designed to help you develop greater compassion for yourself and others by exploring behaviors that bother you and recognizing similar behaviors in those around you.

⊙ **Self-reflection:** Start by identifying three behaviors or traits of your own that bother you or that you often criticize yourself for. These could be habits, personality traits, or ways you react to certain situations. Example:

  o Procrastination

- o Impatience
- o Self-doubt

◯ **Identify similarities:** Now, think about your friends, family members, colleagues, or acquaintances who exhibit similar behaviors or traits that you've identified in yourself. Write down their names next to each corresponding behavior. Example:

- o Procrastination: Friend

_____

_____

- o Impatience: Colleague

_____

_____

- o Self-doubt: Family Member

_____

_____

◯ **Reflection on your reactions:** For each behavior or trait you've listed, consider if you've ever commented on or criticized these individuals for their behavior. Reflect on how you reacted when they displayed the same behavior you have. Example:

- o Procrastination: I've criticized Friend A for missing deadlines.

_____

_____

- o Impatience: I've told Colleague B to be more patient during team meetings.

_____

_____

- o Self-doubt: I've encouraged Family Member C to have more confidence.

_____

_____

- **Support and empathy:** Now, think about whether you've ever supported or shown empathy to these individuals when they struggled with the same behavior. Have you offered help, understanding, or encouragement? Example:

  - o Procrastination: I've offered to help Friend A with time management.

_____

_____

  - o Impatience: I've shared tips with Colleague B on managing stress and impatience.

_____

_____

  - o Self-doubt: I've been a listening ear and provided reassurance to Family Member C.

_____

_____

⊙ **Self-compassion:** Finally, reflect on how you can extend the same compassion, understanding, and support to yourself for the behaviors or traits that bother you. Consider what practical steps or strategies you can take to be more compassionate towards yourself. Example:

- o Procrastination: I can acknowledge my challenges with procrastination without self-judgment and seek time management techniques.
- o Impatience: I can remind myself that impatience is a human trait, and practice mindfulness to be more patient with myself.
- o Self-doubt: I can practice self-affirmation and seek therapy or self-help resources to boost my self-confidence.

EXERCISE: Metaphor for Acceptance: Passengers on the Bus

In this exercise, we'll use a metaphor to help you understand and practice the concept of acceptance in ACT.

Step 1: Visualization

⊙ Find a quiet and comfortable space where you can sit or lie down. Close your eyes and take a few deep breaths to relax.
⊙ Imagine yourself as the bus driver, sitting in the driver's seat of a big, colorful bus. This bus represents your life journey.
⊙ Now, visualize the interior of the bus. See it filled with various passengers, each one representing a different thought or feeling. Some passengers may be positive and supportive, while others are critical, anxious, or negative.

⊙ Take a moment to observe these passengers. Notice their different appearances, voices, and attitudes. Some may be loud and demanding, while others are quiet and reserved.

Step 2: Acknowledging the Passengers

⊙ As you continue to visualize the scene, listen to what the passengers are saying. Pay attention to the critical or negative passengers who are shouting directions or trying to take control.

⊙ Without judgment or resistance, acknowledge the presence of these passengers and their voices. Say to yourself, "I see you, negative thoughts" or "I hear you, self-doubt."

⊙ Remember that it's normal to have a variety of thoughts and feelings on your bus. They are all part of your human experience.

Step 3: Staying on Course

⊙ Now, focus on the steering wheel in front of you. This steering wheel represents your values and the direction you want your life to go in.

⊙ As you grasp the steering wheel, remind yourself of your values-based destination. Write down what are the things that truly matter to you in life? It could be your family, relationships, personal growth, creativity, or something else.

_____

_____

_____

_____

- With determination, start driving the bus in the direction of your values-based destination, even with the passengers still on board.

Step 4: Mindful Driving

- As you drive towards your values-based destination, notice how the passengers react. Some may become quieter or less demanding, while others may still shout directions.

- Keep your focus on the road ahead and your values. Whenever a passenger's voice becomes too distracting or negative, gently acknowledge them and return your attention to your values-based journey.

- Practice this visualization for a few minutes, allowing yourself to become more comfortable with the idea of acknowledging your thoughts and feelings without letting them control your direction.

Step 5: Reflection

- When you're ready, open your eyes and take a moment to reflect on this exercise. Write down any insights or feelings that arose during the visualization.

_____

_____

_____

_____

_____

_____

_____

Recognize that in life, we can't always control our thoughts and feelings, but we can choose how we respond to them. ACT teaches us to accept these thoughts and feelings while taking purposeful actions aligned with our values.

In your daily life, remember this metaphor of the bus driver and the passengers. Whenever you encounter challenging thoughts or emotions, practice acknowledging them and steering your life towards what truly matters to you.

Key Takeaways

- ⊙ Acceptance is about allowing the full range of human emotions without resistance.
- ⊙ Acceptance helps us detach from unhelpful thoughts without judgment.
- ⊙ Acceptance doesn't mean full emotional control; set limits and confront gradually.

In this chapter, we've explored acceptance in ACT, debunking the misconception of enduring perpetual sadness. Acceptance allows us to experience the full range of emotions without resistance, finding peace and freedom by sitting with them. Acceptance isn't about control; it's about coexisting with emotions on our journey. Let's turn the page and explore present moment awareness.

If you want to conquer the anxiety of life, live in the moment, live in the breath.

–ANONYMOUS.

CHAPTER 6

Being Present in the Moment

In the world of therapy and self-help, you may have come across the term "being present" or "living in the present moment." It's a concept that often gets thrown around, but what does it really mean? Is it about shutting off your thoughts and existing in some blissful, thoughtless state? Well, not quite.

Being in the present moment isn't merely about inhabiting the here and now in a mindless or automatic manner. For instance, you can play video games for hours, fully absorbed in the virtual world, yet still be far from practicing true present moment awareness. So, what is it then?

Present moment awareness, in the context of ACT, is a state of mindful attention to the present that is fluid, flexible, and voluntary. It's not about escaping into a bubble of the "now" and disconnecting from the rest of your life. Rather, it's about embracing the moment with an open and aware mind.

Picture a bustling city with its never-ending traffic. Your imagination may wander through different scenarios, just like pedestrians navigating the busy streets. That's perfectly natural and part of the human experience. But what we aim for in present moment awareness is the ability to gently and consciously guide our attention back to the current, to the "now."

This is where mindfulness comes into play. Mindfulness is often associated with meditation, and while meditation is indeed one way to cultivate mindfulness, it is far from being the only path. Mindfulness is, at its core, the practice of paying purposeful attention to the present moment without judgment. It's about observing your thoughts, feelings, and sensations with an open heart and a curious mind.

In this chapter, we will delve deeper into the art of present moment awareness and how it intertwines with mindfulness. You'll discover that mindfulness extends beyond meditation and can be seamlessly integrated into your daily life. Through practical exercises and insights, you'll learn how to develop a more flexible and voluntary relationship with the present moment. This newfound awareness will not only help you manage anxiety but also allow you to savor the beauty of being with your loved ones, find joy in your creative pursuits, and live a life that feels truly meaningful.

So, let's embark on this journey together, as we explore the transformative power of being present and how it can enrich your life in ways you never thought possible.

The Mind's Orientation: Past, Present, and Future

Our minds have an innate tendency to seek orientation in our life's journey. Instead of focusing on where we are in the present moment and the opportunities it holds, our minds often get entangled in ruminations about the past and worries about the future. This tendency to constantly problem-solve can prevent us from appreciating the kindness of others or the simple joys that today can bring.

Mindfulness: An Empowerment Tool

Traditional mindfulness isn't an escape from life's pressures, worries, and fears; it's a tool for achieving "right action." It empowers us to be present in a way that aligns with our chosen values. Even though thoughts and the mind will inevitably bring up worries and concerns, mindfulness allows us to be aware of these thoughts without being controlled by them.

As Jon Kabat-Zinn puts it, mindfulness is "paying attention in a particular way: on purpose, in the present moment, and non-judgmentally (Barker, 2014)." My own journey with ACT has shown me the power of this perspective.

While meditation is a well-known practice for cultivating presence, it's not the only way. Let's look at various ways to practice focusing and presence, allowing you to find the method that resonates most with you.

The Presence Pivot

One of the core aspects of being present in ACT is the concept of the "Presence Pivot." This involves shifting your focus from dwelling on past events or worrying about future possibilities to fully engaging with the here and now. Mindfulness plays a crucial role in this process, enabling you to center your attention on your current experiences.

Letting Thoughts Pass

During the exercises below, you may find that thoughts come and go like passing cars. This is perfectly normal. The key is not to suppress or fight these thoughts but to acknowledge them and gently return your focus to the present moment.

EXERCISE: Pleasant Focus

In this exercise, you will practice mindfulness and being fully present in a pleasant activity. This exercise will help you experience the joy and fulfillment that comes with living in the moment.

- **Choose a pleasant activity:** Select a simple, everyday activity that you enjoy doing but often do on autopilot. It could be something as mundane as sipping your morning coffee, taking a walk in the park, or reading a book. The key is that you genuinely find it pleasurable and not something you're doing just to distract yourself or avoid other tasks.

- **Set aside time:** Allocate a specific time each day for this activity. It could be a few minutes or longer, depending on your schedule. Make sure you have enough time to engage in the activity without rushing.

- **Create a mindful environment:** Find a quiet and comfortable space to perform this activity. Remove distractions and ensure you can fully immerse yourself in the experience.

- **Pretend it's the first time:** Approach the activity with a beginner's mindset. Imagine that this is the first time you've ever done it. Pretend you are experiencing it for the very first time in your life. Imagine that very moment you tasted your favorite beverage.

- **Engage your senses:** As you begin the activity, focus your attention on your five senses:

  - **Sight:** Pay attention to the colors, shapes, and details around you.
  - **Sound:** Listen to any sounds associated with the activity or the environment.

- o **Touch:** Feel the textures, temperatures, and sensations involved.
- o **Smell:** Notice any scents or fragrances present.
- o **Taste:** If applicable, savor the taste and textures in your mouth.

- **Notice bodily responses:** Pay attention to how your body responds during the activity. Are there any sensations, muscle relaxations, or tensions? Be curious about these bodily reactions.
- **Be open to pleasure:** Allow yourself to fully experience the feelings of pleasure that arise during the activity. Savor the enjoyment without judgment or the need to analyze it.
- **Observe thoughts and feelings:** As you engage in the activity, you may notice thoughts and feelings arising. This is perfectly normal. Acknowledge them without judgment. Imagine them as passing clouds in the sky, and gently let them be.
- **Unhook and refocus:** Whenever you notice your mind drifting to other thoughts or concerns, gently unhook from them. Redirect your attention back to the activity and your senses. Refocus on the here and now.
- **Practice daily:** Make a commitment to practice this exercise every day. Consistency is key to building mindfulness and presence in your life.

By regularly engaging in this exercise, you will develop greater mindfulness, enjoy the simple pleasures of life, and learn to handle anxiety and worry in a more constructive way.

EXERCISE: Flexible Attention Exploration

In this exercise, we'll explore the concept of flexible attention, a fundamental aspect of ACT. This exercise will help you develop your ability to focus your attention on different targets, whether single or multiple, as a way to increase mindfulness and awareness in your daily life.

- Take a few deep breaths to center yourself and bring your attention to the present moment.
- Start by directing your attention to one specific area of your body, for example, your left arm. Focus solely on that area for a few moments. Pay attention to any sensations you can perceive in that arm, such as warmth, coolness, tingling, or muscle tension. Allow your awareness to fully embrace this part of your body.
- After a minute or so, gradually shift your attention to your right arm. Notice the sensations in your right arm in the same way you did with your left. Be fully present in this moment and immerse yourself in the sensory experience of your right arm.
- Now, experiment with flexible attention. Start switching your focus back and forth between your left and right arms. Spend a few moments with each arm before switching to the other. Observe any differences or similarities in the sensations between the two arms. Notice how your attention can shift and adapt.
- As you become comfortable with this practice, expand your awareness to include both arms simultaneously. Feel the sensations in both arms at once, allowing your attention to flow effortlessly between them.
- After exploring your arms, you can extend your awareness to other parts of your body if you'd like. Move your attention to

your legs, your chest, your head, or any other area of your body that you choose.

⊙ Throughout this exercise, remind yourself that it's normal for your mind to wander. When it does, gently guide your focus back to the sensations in your chosen body parts.

⊙ Continue this practice for as long as you wish, gradually increasing your comfort with flexible attention and deepening your mindfulness.

⊙ When you're ready to conclude the exercise, take a few deep breaths and open your eyes if they were closed. Reflect on how this practice helped you develop your ability to focus your attention flexibly and mindfully.

EXERCISE: Musical Focus

In this exercise, we will use the power of music to practice mindfulness and enhance your ability to be present in the moment. You can choose any song you like, preferably one with a variety of musical instruments or sounds. Alternatively, you can opt to focus on the ambient sounds in the room around you. This exercise will help you connect with your senses and bring your attention to the here and now.

Step 1: Choose Your Song or Ambient Sounds

Select a song that you enjoy or find interesting. It could be a favorite song, an instrumental piece, or even a piece of nature sounds if you prefer to focus on ambient noises. Ensure you have a quiet and comfortable space to sit or lie down.

Step 2: Find a Comfortable Position

Find a cozy spot to sit or lie down. And if you're up for it, go ahead and close your eyes.

Step 3: Start the Music or Tune Into the Sounds

If you're using a song, start playing it at a moderate volume. If you're focusing on ambient sounds, simply tune into the noises around you.

Step 4: Musical Instrument Focus

As you listen to the music or ambient sounds, shift your attention to different musical instruments or individual sounds within the composition. Try to pick out each instrument or sound as it comes into the mix. Pay attention to the unique qualities of each one.

For example, if you're listening to a song with multiple instruments, notice the rhythm of the drums, the melody of the guitar, the soothing quality of the piano, and any other instruments that are present. If you don't know what a certain instrument is, you can label it something like 'Mystery Instrument 1' or whatever you like- don't get hung up on needing to know the name of every instrument. Try to isolate each sound in your mind and focus on it for a few seconds.

Step 5: Mindful Observation

As you identify and focus on each musical instrument or sound, observe your thoughts and feelings without judgment. If your mind begins to wander or you become distracted, gently bring your focus back to the music or sounds.

Step 6: Breathing Awareness

Take a moment to notice your breath. Is it calm or quickened? Use your breath as an anchor to stay grounded in the present moment.

Step 7: Reflect and Journal

After the exercise, take a few minutes to reflect on your experience. Write down how it felt to truly immerse yourself in the music or ambient sounds. Did you notice any changes in your thoughts or feelings?

_____

_____

_____

_____

_____

_____

_____

_____

_____

This exercise can be a valuable tool to practice mindfulness and strengthen your ability to be present in everyday life. You can use it whenever you feel overwhelmed, anxious, or simply want to connect with the world around you. Remember, ACT is about finding meaning and fulfillment in the present moment, and this exercise can help you take a step in that direction.

EXERCISE: Body Scan

The body scan exercise is a powerful tool for developing mindfulness by bringing your awareness to the physical sensations in your body. This exercise can help you become more in tune with your body, reduce stress, and ground yourself in the present moment.

- ⊙ **Find your space:** Let's find a nice, quiet space for this exercise. Find a cozy spot where you can relax without any distractions. You can either sit or lie down, whatever feels more comfortable for you.

- ⊙ **Get comfortable:** If you're lying down, use a yoga mat, blanket, or cushion to make yourself comfortable. Place your hands by your sides, palms facing up, or rest them gently on your lap if you're sitting.

- ⊙ **Close your eyes:** Why don't you try gently closing your eyes? It can help minimize distractions and encourage inner focus.

- ⊙ **Begin the scan:** Alright, let's begin by starting at the top of your head and gradually moving your attention down through your body, taking it one part at a time. While you're focusing on each area, pay attention to any physical sensations, tension, or discomfort you might feel. Just be curious and open-minded about what you observe.

- ⊙ **Pay attention:** Spend a few moments with each body part, observing it as if you're shining a gentle spotlight on it. Continue down through your body, including your face, neck, shoulders, arms, chest, back, abdomen, pelvis, thighs, knees, lower legs, and finally, your feet.

- ⊙ **Release tension:** If you encounter any areas of tension or discomfort, imagine sending your breath to that area. As you exhale, visualize the tension melting away, leaving that part of your body relaxed and at ease.

- ⊙ **Embrace all sensations:** Remember, the goal is not to change anything but to observe and accept the sensations as they are. Be compassionate and kind to yourself during this process.
- ⊙ **Stay present:** If your mind starts to wander or you become distracted by thoughts or worries, gently bring your attention back to the body part you're scanning.
- ⊙ **Complete the scan:** Once you've managed to stand up, just take a moment to really feel your whole body. Pay attention to the sensations and how your body connects with the surface beneath you.
- ⊙ **Slowly return:** When you're ready, slowly open your eyes and take a few deep breaths. Notice how you feel after completing the body scan.
- ⊙ Reflection: Take a few moments to write down any sensations you noticed throughout this exercise.

_____

_____

_____

_____

_____

_____

_____

_____

_____

_____

Presence helps prevent boredom by keeping familiar thoughts at bay and ensuring that the world around us doesn't fade into the background. Our observing self is always ready to engage and bring our attention back. By acknowledging our tendency to get distracted and redirecting our focus, we can find contentment in life's simple pleasures. The goal is to seamlessly incorporate these practices into our lives until they become second nature, enabling us to effortlessly embrace the present moment.

Key Takeaways

- Being present is mindfully attending to the here and now with an open and aware mind, embracing each moment with conscious attention, rather than escaping life's responsibilities.
- Mindfulness empowers us to be present in alignment with our values, observing thoughts and emotions without being controlled by them.
- The "Presence Pivot" in ACT involves shifting focus from the past or future to fully engage with the present moment, aided by mindfulness.

In this journey, we've explored the transformative power of being present, the essence of present moment awareness, and its interconnection with mindfulness. In the next chapter, we will be exploring values and how they play into the importance of ACT.

When your values are clear to you, making decisions becomes easier.

−ROY E. DISNEY

CHAPTER 7

Values

In our journey through ACT, we've explored powerful techniques to help you navigate the challenges of anxiety, stress, and the ups and downs of life. Now, we're going to delve into a fundamental aspect of ACT that can truly transform the way you approach life: values.

What Are Values?

Values are like the North Star guiding your ship through the vast ocean of life. They are the principles and qualities that you hold dear, which give your life direction, purpose, and meaning. Values are unique to each individual and serve as a compass that helps you navigate your choices, actions, and decisions.

Values Versus Goals

One common stumbling block people face when trying to understand values is differentiating them from goals. It's crucial to grasp this distinction because values-based living can make your goals more meaningful, rather than seeing goals as valuable in themselves.

Goals are future-oriented achievements that you strive to attain. They are specific, measurable, and typically have a clear endpoint. For example, achieving financial wealth, obtaining a promotion, or losing a certain amount of weight are all goals. Goals are essential, and they provide direction and motivation in life. However, they are rooted in the future and, once accomplished, quickly become part of the past.

Values, on the other hand, are always in the now. They represent the qualities and principles that you prioritize and wish to embody in your everyday actions. Unlike goals, values are not achieved or completed; they are ongoing and serve as a guide for your daily choices and behaviors.

Examples of values:

To illustrate this difference more clearly, let's consider some examples:

- **Riches/financial vs. persistence/commitment:** Achieving wealth is typically framed as a goal, whereas the qualities of persistence and commitment are seen as values. Values like these are about the journey rather than the destination; they shape your daily actions and choices. For example, if you value persistence, this might guide you to consistently save money, invest thoughtfully, work efficiently, and spend within your means. Financial security can also be seen as a goal. Yet, the underlying values might be a dedication to enhancing your financial literacy and being responsible with your money.
- **Career success vs. professional growth:** Climbing the corporate ladder is a goal many pursue, but professional growth can be a value. Embracing professional growth means you prioritize learning, adapting, and expanding your skills throughout your career. You can always be growing.

In ACT, it's essential to recognize that both values and goals play crucial roles in your life. Goals provide direction and motivation, helping you set targets and strive for accomplishments. However, values give those goals depth and significance, ensuring that the pursuit of your goals is aligned with your core principles and what truly matters to you.

ACT teaches us that if you're pursuing goals that aren't in line with your values, it's a recipe for burnout, exhaustion, and misery. In fact, not even knowing your values while pursuing your goals can lead to even greater unhappiness.

Let me illustrate this concept with an example:

Sarah works at a job she doesn't particularly love. Her ultimate goal is to find a more fulfilling job that aligns with her interests and passions. However, instead of simply focusing on the end goal of getting a better job, Sarah takes the time to identify her core values. She realizes that her values include creativity, work-life balance, and personal growth. With this newfound clarity about her values, Sarah decides to make a few changes:

- **Creativity**: Even in her current job, which may not be her dream job, Sarah finds ways to infuse creativity into her daily tasks. She suggests new ideas, takes on creative projects, and tries to make the most out of her current role.
- **Work-Life Balance**: Sarah also values spending quality time with her family. She sets boundaries at work, ensures she leaves on time to be with her family, and reserves her weekends for family activities.
- **Personal Growth**: Sarah knows that personal growth is important to her. So, while she's at her current job, she takes advantage of any training or skill development opportunities that come her way. She also dedicates time each week to work on her side projects and hobbies, which bring her a sense of growth and accomplishment.

By pursuing her values while working at a job she doesn't love, Sarah finds that she's much happier and less miserable than if she were solely focused on the goal of getting a better job. Pursuing her values has made her current job more bearable and has also helped her maintain a positive attitude as she actively searches for a new job that aligns better with her values.

This example demonstrates the concept of a "Values Pivot." Instead of living according to social norms or pursuing goals out of fear or avoidance, a Values Pivot involves clarifying and committing to personal values that are meaningful and fulfilling. It's about making choices based on what truly matters to you as an individual.

Remember, your values are unique to you, just like your preferences. For instance, while one person may value adventure and spontaneity, someone else may value stability and routine. There's no right or wrong when it comes to values; they are your own guiding principles for a fulfilling life. So, take the time to identify your values and use them as a compass to navigate your journey towards a more meaningful and satisfying life.

The Appearance of Conflicting Values

Sometimes, when it feels like our values are clashing, it's not really about our values at all. Let's take the example of balancing "family versus career." It might seem like we're torn between two different values, but it's more about time management and how we divide our time and energy between these parts of our lives. Our values in family and work don't change just because we spend more or less time on them.

When you understand this, you can make smart choices about how you spread your time and effort across different areas of your life. You might not find a perfect answer, but trying different approaches and adjusting your priorities can help you figure out a balance that suits you.

Another example is taking care of yourself versus taking care of others. The value here is about being caring, whether it's for yourself or for those around you. The real question is how you split your time and energy between self-care and caring for others, and often, you can do both. Let go of the guilt—living your values isn't about the quantity of time spent- You can honor your values through intentional acts, large or small, without the burden of allocating equal amounts of time to all values every day.

In short, when you think you're in a values conflict, first check if it's genuinely about conflicting values or just about juggling your time and energy between different parts of your life. If it's the second case, focus on setting goals and planning your time well. Be ready to try different approaches and be kind to yourself, as there may not always be a perfect solution.

Conflicting Values Exercise

In this exercise, we will explore how conflicting values can impact your life and how to resolve such conflicts. Remember, it's okay to prioritize one area of life when values clash, and self-compassion is key.

Step 1: Identify Areas of Conflicting Values

Take a moment to reflect on your life and write down areas where your values seem to clash. These can be situations where what you believe in or want to achieve appears to conflict with another important value. Here are some examples:

⊙ **Career vs. family time:** Balancing your career ambitions with spending quality time with your loved ones can be a significant challenge.

⊙ **Independence vs. dependence:** You may value your independence, but sometimes, seeking help or relying on others is necessary for your well-being.

_____

_____

_____

_____

_____

_____

Step 2: Reflect on Past Conflicts and Feelings

Think about specific instances in your life where these conflicting values have caused inner turmoil or emotional distress. Describe how you felt during those times. It's essential to acknowledge your emotions and their impact.

_____

_____

_____

_____

_____

_____

Step 3: Brainstorm Solutions

Now, brainstorm ways to resolve these conflicts. Consider compromises, alternative actions, or strategies that can help you honor both conflicting values. For example:

- ⊙ Balancing career and family time could involve setting boundaries and priorities in your career.
- ⊙ Independence vs. dependence might mean seeking support when needed while maintaining your autonomy.

_____

_____

_____

_____

_____

_____

Step 4: Embrace Self-Compassion

Sometimes, you may find that conflicts are challenging to resolve completely. This is where self-compassion comes in. Understand that it's okay not to have all the answers right away. You can choose to focus on one area of your life that's most important to you at the moment and work on values related to that area.

Be kind to yourself, practice self-compassion, and keep working toward a life aligned with your values, just as I did on my path to greater well-being and fulfillment.

Discover Your True Values Exercise

In this exercise, we will explore your core values- those principles and qualities that matter most to you in your life. Please take your time and reflect on the values that resonate with you. Remember that your values may change over time, so it's essential to check in with yourself regularly.

⊙ Review the list of values provided below, and if you don't find some of your own values on this list, feel free to write them down in the "Other" section at the bottom.

- acceptance/self-acceptance
- adventure
- assertiveness
- authenticity
- caring/self-care
- compassion/self-compassion
- connection
- contribution and generosity
- cooperation
- courage
- creativity
- curiosity
- encouragement
- excitement
- fairness and justice
- fitness
- flexibility
- freedom and independence
- friendliness
- forgiveness/self-forgiveness
- fun and humor
- gratitude
- honesty

- o industry
- o intimacy
- o kindness
- o love
- o mindfulness
- o order
- o persistence and commitment
- o respect/self-respect
- o responsibility
- o safety and protection
- o sensuality and pleasure
- o sexuality
- o skillfulness
- o supportiveness
- o trust
- o Other: _____

⊙ Carefully read through each value and consider how important it is to you at this point in your life. As you go through the above list, place a V for very important, and I for important or an N for not important beside each of them.

- o Very Important (V)
- o Important (I)
- o Not Important (N)

⊙ Once you do this, circle the five values that resonate the most with you.

Reflect on your top five values. Which do you feel are most important at this time in your life?

_____

_____

_____

_____

_____

_____

_____

_____

Congratulations on identifying your core values. These values represent what truly matters to you and can serve as a compass to guide your decisions and actions. Remember that it's normal for your values to evolve over time, so revisit this exercise periodically to ensure you're aligning your life with what's most meaningful to you. Your values can help you find more purpose, happiness, and fulfillment in your journey through life.

EXERCISE: Valued Living Questionnaire

This questionnaire is a tool designed to help you identify and prioritize the domains in your life that are most important to you. By rating these domains from 1 to 10, with 10 being the most important, you can gain clarity on what truly matters to you. This exercise will also guide you in exploring your values and how they align with your desired behaviors and personal strengths in each domain.

Rate the following domains in your life on a scale of 1 to 10, with 10 being the most important to you at this time:

- ⊘ family (other than marriage and parenting)
- ⊘ marriage/intimate relationships
- ⊘ parenting
- ⊘ friends/social life
- ⊘ work
- ⊘ education/training
- ⊘ recreation/fun
- ⊘ spirituality
- ⊘ citizenship/community
- ⊘ physical self-care (diet, exercise, sleep)
- ⊘ environmental issues
- ⊘ art, creative expression

Choose one of the domains you deeply care about, one that you rated as highly important, and set aside 20 minutes for a free-writing exercise. During this time, explore your values in this domain. You can ask yourself questions like:

What do I care about in this area of my life?

_____

_____

_____

When in my life has this value been important to me?

_____

_____

_____

How does this domain contribute to my overall well-being and happiness?

_____

_____

_____

_____

Now, for each of the domains you rated, reflect on the following aspects:

What sort of person do I want to be in this domain?

_____

_____

_____

_____

What personal strengths do I want to cultivate?

_____

_____

_____

_____

What do I want to stand for in this area of my life?

_____

_____

_____

_____

How do I ideally want to behave in relation to this domain?

_____

_____

_____

_____

Example:

Let's say you rated "Parenting" as a highly important domain. Here's how you can approach the reflection questions:

- ⊙ What sort of person do I want to be in my role as a parent?

    - o   I want to be a loving and supportive parent who nurtures my child's growth and development.

- ⊙ What personal strengths do I want to cultivate as a parent?

    - o   I want to cultivate patience, empathy, and effective communication skills.

- ⊙ What do I want to stand for as a parent?

    - o   I want to stand for creating a safe and loving environment where my child can thrive and learn.

- ⊙ How do I ideally want to behave as a parent?

    - o   I want to behave by actively listening to my child, being present in their life, and providing guidance while respecting their autonomy.

By completing this exercise for each domain, you will gain a deeper understanding of your values and how they relate to your behavior and personal growth in various areas of your life. This insight can be a valuable tool in practicing ACT and living a more fulfilling life aligned with your values.

EXERCISE: Embracing Values and Letting Go of Struggles

In this exercise, we will explore the concept of embracing your values and letting go of struggles that may be holding you back. I found that ACT helped me find meaning and fulfillment in my life by shifting my focus from struggles and challenges to what truly matters to me. By completing this exercise, you can start to identify areas in your life where you may be getting stuck and discover what truly matters to you.

Struggles and Challenges	Rich and Meaningful

Struggles and Challenges

On the "Struggles and Challenges" side, list any current struggles, challenges, obsessive thoughts, worries, or issues that you feel are keeping you stuck in your life. These can be related to various aspects such as work, relationships, health, or personal goals.

Next to each struggle or challenge, answer the following questions:

- What are you doing that's keeping you stuck in this particular area?
- How is this struggle affecting your time, energy, money, health, or overall well-being?

Rich and Meaningful

On the "Rich and Meaningful" side, reflect on what truly matters to you. Consider your values, what you stand for, what you want to stand for in life, and how you want to be remembered.

List the values and meaningful aspects of your life that you want to prioritize.

For each value or meaningful aspect, answer the following questions:

- ⊙ How can you incorporate this value or aspect into your daily life?
- ⊙ What actions or changes can you make to align your life more closely with these values and meaningful aspects?

Compare and Reflect

Take a moment to look at both charts side by side.

Reflect on the differences between your struggles and challenges on one chart and your rich and meaningful values on the other.

Consider how you might be investing your time, energy, and resources in areas that do not align with your values.

Write down ways you can start letting go of the struggles that are not serving you and focus more on what truly matters to you.

_____

_____

_____

_____

_____

Commitment and Action

Choose one value or meaningful aspect from the "Rich and Meaningful" chart that you are particularly drawn to or feel is most important to you. Write it down.

_____

_____

_____

_____

_____

Set a specific, achievable action or goal that you can work towards to incorporate this value into your daily life. Write it down.

_____

_____

_____

_____

_____

Remember that this exercise is about self-reflection and taking steps toward a more meaningful and fulfilling life. It can be helpful to revisit these charts periodically to track your progress and make adjustments as needed. Embracing your values and letting go of unnecessary struggles can be a transformative journey, just as it was for me.

EXERCISE: Reflecting on a Fulfilling Life

In this exercise, we will imagine ourselves at our 80th birthday party, surrounded by loved ones who are giving speeches about us. The goal is to help you identify and clarify your values by considering what you would want people to say about you at this milestone celebration. Let's explore what different people in your life might say and what values they associate with you.

- ⊙ **Set the scene:** Find a nice, cozy spot where you can have some peace and quiet. Take a moment to take a few deep breaths and let yourself unwind and clear your thoughts.
- ⊙ **Visualization:** Close your eyes and imagine the scene at your 80th birthday party. Picture the people who are there to celebrate with you. Imagine the atmosphere, the joy, and the warmth of the occasion.

The three perspectives: Now, consider the following perspectives:

a. **Your spouse or partner:** Imagine your spouse or life partner standing at the podium to give a speech about you. What would they say were your most cherished values? Write down their speech or a summary of it.

_____

_____

_____

_____

_____

_____

b. **Your best friend:** Envision your best friend giving a heartfelt speech about you. What qualities and values do they think define you? Jot down their words or a summary.

_____

_____

_____

_____

c. **Your former boss:** Imagine your former boss addressing the audience. What attributes and values would they highlight in your professional life? Record their speech or a summary.

_____

_____

_____

_____

_____

Reflect on values: Review the speeches or summaries you've written from these three perspectives. Take some time to think about the common themes and values mentioned by these people. What values seem to be recurring or consistent across the different speeches?

_____

_____

_____

_____

_____

Identify your core values: Based on the speeches and your reflections, create a list of your core values. These are the values that matter most to you and shape the way you want to live your life.

_____

_____

_____

_____

_____

Personal commitment: Finally, make a personal commitment to align your actions and decisions with these core values, starting today. Consider how you can incorporate these values into your daily life to find greater fulfillment and purpose.

_____

_____

_____

_____

_____

Key Takeaways

- **Values are your guiding principles:** Values represent meaningful principles, providing direction, purpose, and meaning in your life.
- **Values vs. goals:** It's crucial to differentiate between values and goals. Goals are specific, future-oriented achievements, while

values are ongoing qualities and principles that inform your daily decisions.

- **The power of a values pivot:** The concept of a "Values Pivot" involves clarifying and committing to personal values that are meaningful and fulfilling, even in situations that may not align with your ultimate goals.

In this chapter we discovered that values are guiding principles that provide direction, purpose, and meaning in life. They serve as a moral compass, keeping us true to ourselves. Distinguishing values from goals is important. Goals are future-focused destinations, while values are enduring qualities that bring life to those objectives. Next up, committed action. Why it is so important?

Commitment is an act, not a word.

–JEAN-PAUL SARTRE

CHAPTER 8

The Importance of Committed Action

In our journey through ACT, we have explored various facets of our inner world, learning to accept our thoughts and emotions, defuse from unhelpful stories, and cultivate mindfulness. These foundational skills have paved the way for the transformative power of committed action.

But what is action, and why is it so pivotal in the ACT framework? Allow me to explain.

Action, in the context of ACT, is not merely about keeping ourselves busy or achieving external goals. It's about moving from a mindset of perfectionism and fear of failure to a place of embracing values-based action. It's about recognizing that our true purpose in life goes beyond accomplishments and accolades, and it extends to living a life aligned with our deepest values and aspirations.

Committed action is like the missing piece of the puzzle that brings it all together. It builds upon the skills we've developed in earlier chapters, seamlessly integrating them into a holistic approach to living a meaningful and fulfilling life.

Why does committed action come last in the ACT journey? The answer lies in the fact that it's a culmination of everything we've learned thus far. By accepting our thoughts and feelings, defusing from unhelpful stories, and being present in the moment, we've laid the groundwork for meaningful action. Without these foundational skills, our actions may be driven by old patterns and fears, rather than by our true values and desires.

In the pages ahead, we'll look deep into committed action and explore how it can help you build habits that align with your core values. You'll discover the joy of living life as a whole and complete person, liberated from the shackles of perfectionism and external validation.

Imperfection and Competence

A core concept in ACT is the understanding that you won't be amazing and competent right away when you start. Perfectionism, often fueled by avoidance and fear, can hinder your progress. Embracing the imperfections and acknowledging that competence is a process can be incredibly liberating. It allows you to focus on the journey itself rather than just the destination.

SMART Goals: The Roadmap to Your Values

In setting your course toward living in accordance with your values, it's essential to establish SMART goals. This acronym was developed by George Doran in 1981, and it stands for Specific, Measurable, Attainable, Results-focused, and Time-Bound (*Everything You*, 2023). These goals act as a roadmap, helping you break down your values into actionable steps.

The Role of Flexibility Skills

Lets review the range of flexibility skills ACT provides that complement the pursuit of your goals:

- ⊙ **Defusion:** This skill allows you to distance yourself from negative thoughts and judgments about your progress. It helps you recognize that your thoughts are just thoughts, not facts.
- ⊙ **Connecting to your transcendent self:** Keeping your focus on taking action because you genuinely care, rather than complying with social expectations or avoiding guilt, is vital for staying true to your values.
- ⊙ **Acceptance:** Maintaining grit and resilience when faced with difficulties is made possible through acceptance. It acknowledges that pain and discomfort are part of life but doesn't let them deter you from your path.
- ⊙ **Presence:** Staying focused on the process rather than obsessing over the end goal is what presence is all about. It allows you to enjoy the journey, even if you're far from your destination.
- ⊙ **Connecting with your values:** Remind yourself that the difficult actions you're taking are in service of living a life that you find meaningful. Your values are your North Star, guiding you towards a fulfilling existence.

ACT is not a quick fix or a magic pill; it's a journey toward personal growth, authenticity, and the pursuit of what truly matters to you. By clearly defining your values, setting SMART goals, and utilizing flexibility skills, you'll be better equipped to navigate this journey with purpose and grace.

Remember, it's okay not to be perfect, and it's okay to take imperfect actions guided by your values. The key is to embrace imperfection and build confidence through meaningful actions.

EXERCISE: Small Adjustments

Goal setting can sometimes feel overwhelming, especially when dealing with anxiety and other mental health challenges. This exercise is designed to help you break down your goals into tiny, manageable steps.

Step 1: Identify Your Goal

Begin by identifying the specific goal you want to work on. It could be something related to your mental health, personal growth, or any area of your life that you'd like to improve. For example, you might want to read more, journal regularly, exercise, or practice mindfulness. Write your goal down.

_____

_____

_____

_____

_____

Step 2: Break It Down

Now, take a moment to break down your goal into smaller, more achievable steps. The key is to make these steps incredibly small, so they feel almost effortless. For instance:

- If your goal is to read more:
    - Start with reading for just 15 minutes a day.
    - Choose a specific time slot for this daily reading (e.g., during your lunch break, before bedtime).

- If your goal is to journal every day:
  - Commit to journaling for just 5 minutes a day.
  - Set an alarm or choose a specific moment in your routine for this quick journaling session.

Break your goal down:

_____

_____

_____

_____

_____

Step 3: Schedule It

Once you've determined your small adjustments, write them down in your schedule. Having a specific time and place for these mini-tasks will make them easier to integrate into your daily life.

Step 4: Celebrate Your Progress

As you begin implementing these small adjustments, celebrate your achievements, no matter how minor they may seem. Acknowledge the effort you're putting into making positive changes in your life.

Step 5: Reflect and Adjust

After a week or so, take a moment to reflect on your progress. Have you been able to consistently follow through with your small adjustments? If not, don't be too hard on yourself. Adjustments may need to be even smaller or better integrated into your routine. Tweak your approach as needed to ensure success.

Step 6: Gradually Expand

As you become more comfortable with your small adjustments, you can gradually increase the time or effort you put into your goal. The key is to do so at a pace that feels comfortable for you. For example, if you've been reading for 15 minutes a day, consider increasing it to 20 minutes when you're ready.

EXERCISE: Values-Driven Goal Setting With ACT

This exercise aims to help you set meaningful and values-driven goals using principles from ACT. By aligning your goals with your core values and preparing for potential obstacles, you can increase your motivation and improve your chances of success.

Step 1: Choose Your Domain

Choose a specific area of your life that you would like to focus on. It could be related to your work, health, personal growth, education, free time, spirituality, parenting, friends, family, intimate relationships, or any other aspect of your life. Write it down.

_____

_____

_____

Step 2: Identify Your Values

Identify one or two core values (maximum three) that resonate with you and that you want to emphasize in your chosen area. These values will serve as the foundation for your goal-setting process, motivating and inspiring your actions.

Values:

_____

_____

Step 3: Set a Mindful Goal (ACT SMART)

S - Specific: Create a specific goal that outlines the actions you will take within your chosen life domain. Be precise and detailed, avoiding vague or poorly-defined objectives.

_____

_____

M - Motivated by values: Is your goal is aligned with the values you identified in How is this goal specifically connected with your core values?

_____

_____

A - Adaptive: Will this goal lead to positive improvements in your life and enhance your overall well-being?

_____

_____

R - Realistic: Assess whether the goal is realistic given your available resources (time, skills, money, physical health, social support, knowledge). If necessary, adjust the goal or identify steps to obtain the required resources.

_____

_____

T - Time-framed: Set a specific time frame for achieving your goal. Specify the day, date, and time as accurately as possible.

_____

_____

Step 4: Identify Benefits

Clarify the potential positive outcomes of achieving your goal. Focus on the benefits without indulging in excessive fantasizing about the future. Write them down.

_____

_____

_____

Step 5: Prepare for Obstacles

Anticipate possible internal and external obstacles that might hinder your progress toward your goal.

a) List any negative thoughts or challenging emotions. These are considered internal difficulties.

- ⊙
- ⊙
- ⊙

b) Write down any lack of resources or conflicts with others. We would classify these as external difficulties.

- ⊙
- ⊙
- ⊙

For internal difficulties, plan to use mindfulness skills or ACT techniques to address them:

- ⊙
- ⊙
- ⊙

For external difficulties, outline the steps you will take to overcome them:

- ⊙
- ⊙
- ⊙

Step 6: Rate Goal Realism

On a scale of 0 to 10, assess the realism of your goal.

(10 = completely realistic, 0 = totally unrealistic)

Rate the realism of your goals here: ___ (Must be at least a 7)

If your goal does not meet a minimum score of 7, consider adjusting it to make it more achievable or breaking it into smaller, simpler steps.

Step 7: Share Your Commitment

Research shows that making a public commitment to your goal increases your chances of success (Elephant, 2020). Share your SMART goal and commitment with someone else, ideally a trusted friend or family member. If you're not comfortable sharing it with others, make a commitment to yourself.

Read your SMART goal one more time, and then make a commitment out loud:

"I am committed to following through on this goal, and I will take steps to make it a reality."

If possible, say this commitment aloud to someone else. Otherwise, say it aloud to yourself.

By aligning your goals with your values and preparing for potential challenges, you can apply ACT principles to set and achieve meaningful objectives that lead to greater fulfillment and well-being in your life.

EXERCISE: Reverse Compass Habits-Creating Mindful Alternatives

This exercise is designed to help you replace unwanted habits with more mindful and positive alternatives. Instead of succumbing to habits that may not serve you well, this exercise encourages you to be aware of your impulses and consciously choose healthier alternatives that align with your values and well-being.

Identify the Habit

Begin by identifying the specific habit you want to change. It could be anything from nail-biting to snacking before bed or any other behavior that you wish to modify.

Recognize Triggers

Pay close attention to the triggers or situations that typically lead to the unwanted habit. What emotions, thoughts, or environmental cues trigger this behavior? Understanding your triggers is a crucial step in changing the habit.

Choose a *Mindful Alternative*

Now, select a mindful alternative that aligns with your goals and values. Consider the following examples: Nail biting or eating ice cream before bed.

- When you feel the urge to bite your nails, reach for the nearest object like a stress ball, a smooth stone, or a fidget toy. Engage your senses by feeling the texture of the object in your hand.
- Alternatively, practice deep breathing exercises or progressive muscle relaxation to redirect your anxiety or stress in a healthier way.
- If late-night snacking is your habit, create a calming bedtime routine. Instead of ice cream, make a cup of herbal tea with honey or sip on warm milk with a pinch of cinnamon.
- Listen to calming music, meditate, or read a book before bed to relax your mind and body.

Set Intentions

Before you find yourself in a triggering situation, set a clear intention to choose the mindful alternative. Remind yourself of the benefits and values associated with the new habit.

Practice Mindfulness

As you engage in the mindful alternative, be fully present in the moment. Focus on the sensations, tastes, or experiences associated with the new habit. Mindfulness will help you break the cycle of the old habit.

Track Your Progress

Keep a journal to record your experiences and progress. Note any improvements in how you feel, both physically and emotionally, as you replace the old habit with the new one.

Be Patient and Compassionate

Changing habits can be challenging, and setbacks may occur. Be patient with yourself and practice self-compassion. Remember that each moment is an opportunity to make a mindful choice.

Key Takeaways

- ⊙ Imperfection and competence: Embrace the understanding that perfectionism is a hindrance to growth and competence in the journey of ACT.
- ⊙ SMART goals: These help break down your values into actionable steps, making them more achievable and manageable.
- ⊙ Flexibility skills: These skills are essential for maintaining focus on your values and goals while navigating the challenges of life, allowing you to lead a more meaningful and authentic existence.

In the journey through Acceptance and Commitment Therapy (ACT), we have explored the importance of embracing imperfection and recognizing competence as a process. SMART goals have been introduced as a powerful tool to help you navigate your values and aspirations. Remember that ACT is not a quick fix, but a path toward personal growth and authenticity.

Long term consistency beats short term intensity.

–BRUCE LEE

CHAPTER 9

Practice Makes Progress: The Key to ACT Mastery

Just as with CBT and DBT, the skills you learn through ACT require continuous practice. Like a skillful athlete refining their technique or a musician mastering their instrument, our minds need regular training to stay sharp.

Rigid thought patterns and habitual reactions have a way of sneaking back into our lives, and that's perfectly normal. What sets us apart is our ability to recognize these patterns and continue to apply the principles of ACT.

As we explore the importance of ongoing practice in this chapter, remember that you are not alone on this journey. If at any point you feel the need for guidance and support from a trained ACT therapist, know that they are readily available to help you navigate the challenges that may arise.

Building Your ACT Toolkit: A Guide to Applying ACT in Everyday Life

Remember, ACT is not a one-size-fits-all approach, and you may find certain exercises resonate with you more than others. That's perfectly normal; the key is to find what works best for you.

I highly recommend creating a toolkit that includes your favorite set of exercises from this workbook for each tenet. Start with one or two exercises for each one. Over the next three months, focus on practicing and experimenting with these exercises until they become second nature in your daily routine. Once you feel comfortable with them, you can gradually introduce one more exercise at a time. With numerous exercises to explore, this approach allows you to build a personalized toolkit of what works best for you. Don't forget to jot down your favorite exercises for each tenet.

Blending the Skills

As you become more comfortable with these exercises, you can begin blending the skills from tenets. For example, use mindfulness (Acceptance) to observe your thoughts, practice cognitive defusion to detach from unhelpful thoughts, and identify values (Values Clarification) to guide your committed actions. These combinations allow you to navigate life's challenges with greater ease and clarity.

Keep a journal to record your favorite exercises, experiences, and insights. Over time, you'll find yourself naturally applying these ACT principles to various areas of your life, just as I have.

HARD Barriers

In order to identify and address your internal barriers that might be holding you back, it's important to focus on what Russ Harris has termed "HARD barriers." These barriers can be broken down into four key components: Hooked, Avoiding Discomfort, Remoteness from Values, and Doubtful Goals. Let's go through each one and understand how they can impact your ability to make meaningful changes in your life.

H = Hooked

Your mind often comes up with reasons for why you can't take action, reasons you shouldn't take action, or even arguments that action isn't necessary. These thoughts can create fear and doubt, making it challenging to step out of your comfort zone or tackle big challenges. It's crucial to recognize these negative thoughts and acknowledge that they exist.

> **Antidote:** The antidote to being "hooked" by these thoughts is to use your unhooking skills. While you can't stop your mind from generating these negative thoughts, you can choose not to engage with them. Practice mindfulness and cognitive defusion techniques to distance yourself from these unhelpful thoughts.

A = Avoiding Discomfort

Personal growth and meaningful change often require stepping out of your comfort zone, which naturally brings discomfort. You may encounter difficult thoughts, feelings, sensations, emotions, memories, and urges that you're unwilling to face. Avoiding discomfort can prevent you from taking action on what truly matters to you.

> **Antidote:** To overcome the avoidance of discomfort, you need to develop your "expansion" skills. This involves practicing

acceptance and willingness to make room for the discomfort that arises when you pursue meaningful goals. Prepare yourself for the discomfort that may come and remind yourself of your commitment to your values.

R = Remoteness from Values

When you choose not to engage in important tasks or responsibilities, you may unintentionally neglect or disregard your core values. By opting out of these crucial activities, you risk losing sight of what truly matters to you. It is vital to take the time to reconnect with your core values as they serve as a compass, providing meaning and motivation for your actions. By aligning your choices and actions with your values, you can lead a more fulfilling and purpose-driven life.

- ⊙ **Antidote:** To address remoteness from values, take time to connect with what truly matters to you. Reflect on the values that should guide your decisions and actions. What values will you uphold as you take steps toward your goals? Reminding yourself of your values can help you stay committed to what's meaningful.

D = Doubtful Goals

Revisit the exercise where you assessed the realism of your goals on a scale of 0 to 10. If your goals scored less than 7, it's doubtful that you'll follow through with them. Unrealistic or overly ambitious goals can be demotivating and hinder your progress.

- ⊙ **Antidote:** To address doubtful goals, consider setting more realistic and achievable objectives. Break your goals into smaller, simpler steps that are matched to your available resources, including time, money, energy, health, social support, and necessary skills. Ensure that your goals are aligned with your capabilities and circumstances.

Identifying and addressing your HARD barriers can help you overcome internal obstacles that hold you back from making meaningful changes in your life. By recognizing these barriers and applying the antidotes, you can improve your ability to step out of your comfort zone, face your fears, and work towards your goals in a more effective and fulfilling way.

EXERCISE: Three Choices in Difficult Situations

In life, we often find ourselves facing challenging situations that test our resilience and ability to cope. In these moments, it can be helpful to remember that we have three choices available to us. By recognizing these choices, we can make more intentional decisions and lead a life aligned with our values and goals. This exercise is designed to help you explore and apply these three choices in various aspects of your life.

Reflect on the Situation

Take a moment to think about a challenging situation you are currently facing or have faced in the past. It could be related to your relationships, work, personal goals, or any other aspect of your life. Write it down.

_____

_____

_____

_____

_____

Identify the Three Choices

Now, explore three possible choices you can make in response to the difficult situation:

a) leave
b) stay and live by your value
c) stay and give up

Consider whether leaving the situation is a viable option. Leaving might be appropriate in situations where the harm outweighs the benefits, such as a toxic relationship, an unhealthy job, or a harmful environment.

Explore the possibility of staying in the situation while aligning your actions with your values and principles. This choice involves actively working to improve the situation or finding ways to make it more bearable.

Share some examples of how you could choose to stay and live by your values in challenging circumstances.

_____

_____

_____

_____

_____

_____

_____

_____

_____

Examine the option of staying in the situation without actively working toward change or improvement. This choice often leads to stagnation, unhappiness, and potentially making the situation worse.

Write down the consequences of choosing to stay and give up in various aspects of life.

_____

_____

_____

_____

_____

_____

_____

Make Room for Pain and Self-Compassion

Acknowledge that choosing to stay and live by your values (Choice 2) can be difficult and painful at times. It may involve facing discomfort, uncertainty, or even rejection.

Emphasize the importance of being gentle with yourself during challenging times and allowing yourself to feel the emotions that come with the situation.

By recognizing these three choices in difficult situations and considering which one aligns with your values and goals, you can navigate life's challenges more effectively. Remember that we are all unique and it's okay to choose differently in various situations. The key is to make intentional choices that lead to personal growth, well-being, and fulfillment.

What f I Forget?

We have covered an incredible amount of exercises in this workbook. I don't want you to worry about forgetting any of the tenets or exercises we have discussed. If you don't have time in the moment to flip back through the pages, just go back to the basics of ACT.

The fundamental principles of ACT can be summarized in the basic formula: "Be present. Open up. Do what matters." This formula encapsulates the essence of ACT. Let's briefly review those here:

Be present:

- This first part of the formula emphasizes the importance of being fully present in the moment. It encourages individuals to bring their attention to the here and now rather than dwelling on the past or worrying about the future.
- Being present involves practicing mindfulness and paying non-judgmental attention to your thoughts, emotions, sensations, and the environment around you.
- It allows you to observe your experiences without trying to change or avoid them, fostering self-awareness and self-compassion.

Open up:

- "Open up" refers to the willingness to embrace and accept your thoughts and emotions, even if they are uncomfortable or distressing. Instead of struggling against them or trying to suppress them, you acknowledge their presence.
- This step encourages you to drop the struggle with your internal experiences and practice acceptance. It's about recognizing that

thoughts are just thoughts, and emotions are just emotions, without necessarily reflecting reality or dictating your actions.

○ By opening up, you create space for your thoughts and emotions to exist without judgment, allowing you to respond to them more skillfully.

Do what matters:

○ The final part of the formula, "Do what matters," emphasizes taking purposeful and values-based actions. It encourages individuals to clarify their values and commit to actions that align with those values.

○ Instead of being driven solely by the avoidance of discomfort or the pursuit of short-term pleasure, ACT promotes a more meaningful and values-driven approach to life.

○ This step challenges you to identify what truly matters to you, set meaningful goals, and take steps towards those goals, even in the presence of discomfort or difficult emotions.

Psychological flexibility is the overarching concept that ties these three elements together. It refers to the ability to adapt and respond effectively to the ever-changing circumstances of life. Psychological flexibility allows you to:

○ Be open to your thoughts and emotions, even when they are uncomfortable.

○ Stay in the present moment, rather than getting caught up in rumination or worry.

○ Make choices and take actions that align with your values and long-term goals.

In essence, ACT helps individuals cultivate psychological flexibility as a means to enhance their overall well-being and lead a more fulfilling life.

By practicing the basic formula we can develop greater resilience, emotional intelligence, and a deeper connection with their values and life's purpose.

Key Takeaways

- ⊙ **Continuous practice:** The skills learned through ACT require ongoing practice. Regular mental training is necessary to maintain psychological flexibility and effectively navigate life's challenges.
- ⊙ **Psychological flexibility:** ACT is based on the concept of psychological flexibility, which involves being present in the moment, opening up to thoughts and emotions, and doing what matters in alignment with one's values. This flexibility empowers individuals to adapt and respond effectively to life's ever-changing circumstances.
- ⊙ **Building Your ACT toolkit:** Creating a personalized toolkit of favorite ACT exercises for each tenet is highly recommended. Start with a few exercises for each tenet and gradually add more over time. You can easily google even more ACT exercises online for each tenet...there are dozens!

Incorporating ACT into your daily life requires consistent effort and practice. Remember that ACT is adaptive and we are unique, and it's perfectly normal to resonate more with certain exercises. Building your ACT toolkit empowers you to navigate life's challenges with greater ease and clarity, ultimately helping you live a life aligned with your values and goals.

Very little is needed to make a happy life; it is all within yourself, in your way of thinking.

–MARCUS AURELIUS ANTONINUS

CONCLUSION

ACT is more than just a therapeutic approach. It's a transformative journey that empowers us to live a richer, more authentic life. As we've explored the principles and exercises of ACT, I hope you've realized its immense power to positively shape our lives. It has had a profound impact on my own life, as well as on countless others.

One important change we've talked about is how we define success. In our society, success is usually limited to achieving big goals and seeking external validation. This can make many of us feel inadequate or unsatisfied as we compare ourselves to those who appear to have achieved great things. However, ACT offers a different approach to success. It encourages us to measure success based on our ability to live according to our values, rather than relying on external standards.

In this context, success means making a conscious effort to consistently align our everyday actions with our core values. It's important to remember that the significance of these actions, no matter how small, should not be underestimated. Whether it's choosing kindness over anger, spending quality time with loved ones, or pursuing a career that aligns with our personal values, each of these choices plays a crucial role in shaping a more purposeful and satisfying life experience.

ACT's core message is about embracing optimism and the belief that we can learn, adapt, and grow from life's challenges, setbacks, and tragedies. This therapy encourages us to find fulfillment and purpose by living a life that reflects our deepest values, even in the face of adversity. It reminds us that no matter how many times we stumble or lose our way, we always have the opportunity to start fresh and create a path that aligns with what truly matters to us.

Importantly, ACT is not a rigid set of rules to follow. It's a flexible toolkit that you can adapt to your unique journey. You are under no obligation to do anything that doesn't resonate with you. The beauty of ACT lies in its adaptability to your personal needs and circumstances. It's your tool, your compass, guiding you toward a life that feels true and fulfilling.

As we aim to live a life guided by our values, it's important to remember that making mistakes and facing setbacks are natural aspects of being human. During these moments, it is important to be gentle with ourselves and show self-compassion. Being excessively critical and harsh towards ourselves only keeps us stuck in old, unproductive patterns. Release the narrative that convinces you that you are inadequate, and instead, embrace self-kindness and self-compassion as essential components of your path to a more purposeful and genuine life.

I want to express my heartfelt gratitude for placing your trust in me as your guide throughout the ACT journey. It has been an absolute privilege to accompany you on this transformative path, offering you invaluable tools and profound insights. I sincerely hope that these resources have not only aided your personal growth but have also empowered you to conquer any challenges that come your way. If you discovered any exercises or concepts within this workbook that resonated with you and proved beneficial, I kindly ask you to consider sharing your thoughts through a review. Your feedback can help get this workbook into the hands of those who can benefit from this resource as much as you did.

In closing, always remember that ACT is a path toward a more meaningful, fulfilling, and compassionate life. Embrace your values, learn from your experiences, and, most importantly, always be kind to yourself. Your journey is unique, and you have the power to make it a remarkable one. Thank you for embarking on this transformative journey with me, and may your life continue to be filled with authenticity, purpose, and joy.

Thank You

I really appreciate you buying and finishing this book. I'm SO THANKFUL for your support and hope this book has been beneficial to you.

There are numerous books on this subject, so I'm grateful and appreciative that you chose this one.

Before you go, I wanted to ask you for one last small favor. **It would be very helpful to me if you considered leaving a review on Amazon. One of the best and simplest ways to support books from independent authors like me is to leave a review.**

Your opinions are very valuable to me. I'll be able to support other readers by continuing to write books like this. To hear from you would mean so much. I read every single review submitted.

REFERENCES

Ackerman, C. E. (2018, April 12). *What is relational frame theory? A psychologist explains*. PositivePsychology.com. https://positivepsychology.com/relational-frame-theory/

A quote by Eckhart Tolle. (n.d.). Www.goodreads.com. Retrieved January 13, 2024, from https://www.goodreads.com/quotes/853487-accept---then-act-whatever-the-present-moment-contains-accept#:~:text=Whatever%20the%20present%20moment%20contains

Barker, K. K. (2014). *Mindfulness meditation: Do-it-yourself medicalization of every moment*. Social Science & Medicine, *106*, 168–176. https://doi.org/10.1016/j.socscimed.2014.01.024

Eddins, R. (2023, April 13). *Acceptance and commitment therapy tools for anxiety*. Eddins Counseling Group. https://eddinscounseling.com/webinar-acceptance-and-commitment-therapy-tools-for-anxiety/

Everything you need to know about SMART goals. (2023, November 28). AchieveIt. https://www.achieveit.com/resources/blog/everything-you-need-to-know-about-smart-goals/

Fletcher, J. (2022, May 25). *What is ACT therapy? Overview, uses, and benefits*. Medical News Today. https://www.medicalnewstoday.com/articles/act-therapy

Gladwell, M. (n.d.). *Quotes imaging pearls*. CTisus. https://www.ctisus.com/learning/pearls/quotes

Glasofer, D. (2015). *Acceptance and commitment therapy (ACT) for GAD*. Verywell Mind https://www.verywellmind.com/acceptance-commitment-therapy-gad-1393175

Harris, R. (2011). *Acceptance and commitment therapy (ACT): An overview*. Psychotherapy..

https://www.psychotherapy.net/article/Acceptance-and-Commitment-Therapy-ACT

Harris, R. (2019). *The happiness trap*. The Happiness Trap. https://thehappinesstrap.com/

Harris, R. (2021, June). *ACT made simple -the extra bits* . Google Docs. https://drive.google.com/file/d/11aub3XrqtRuDt4GkYWMZk5ul puCZmZi7/view

Harris, R. (2023, November 29). *Acceptance and commitment therapy* . Act Mindfully. https://www.actmindfully.com.au/

Hayes, S. (n.d.). *The six core processes of ACT*. Contextual Science. https://contextualscience.org/the_six_core_processes_of_act

Hayes, S. C. (2019). *A liberated mind : How to pivot toward what matters*. Avery.

Keng, S. L., Smoski, M. J., & Robins, C. J. (2011). Effects of mindfulness on psychological health: A review of empirical studies. *Clinical Psychology Review, 31*(6), 1041–1056. https://doi.org/10.1016/j.cpr.2011.04.006

Know yourself — Socrates and how to develop self-knowledge - the school of life. (n.d.). Www.theschooloflife.com. https://www.theschooloflife.com/article/know-yourself/#:~:text=In%20Ancient%20Greece%2C%20the%20philoso pher

Lao Tzu quotes. (2019). BrainyQuote. https://www.brainyquote.com/quotes/lao_tzu_151126

Martin, M. (2015, April 21). *Quotes of the day: Actress Mary Martin on thoughtfulness*. Investor's Business Daily. https://www.investors.com/news/management/wisdom-to-live-by/quotes-of-the-day-actress-mary-martin-on-thoughtfulness/#:~:text=Stop%20the%20habit%20of%20wishful

Roy E. Disney Quotes. (n.d.). BrainyQuote. https://www.brainyquote.com/quotes/roy_e_disney_183365

Sansone, R. A., & Sansone, L. A. (2012). Rumination. *Innovations in Clinical Neuroscience, 9*(2), 29–34.

https://www.ncbi.nlm.nih.gov/pmc/articles/PMC3312901/#:~:text
=Rumination%20is%20a%20form%20of

Stromme, D., & Rothstein, L. (2021). *Space between stimulus and response.*
Extension. https://extension.umn.edu/two-you-video-series/space-
between-stimulus-and-response

WebMD Editors. (2021, April 9). *What is acceptance and commitment
therapy?* WebMD. https://www.webmd.com/mental-health/what-
is-acceptance-and-commitment-therapy

World Health Organization. (2023, March 31). *Depressive disorder
(depression).* https://www.who.int/news-room/fact-
sheets/detail/depression

Made in United States
Troutdale, OR
08/09/2024